D0256456

CHRIST
BEHIND
BARS

INSPIRING STORIES
OF PRISON REVIVAL

CHRIST
BEHIND
BARS

GILLIAN POWE
foreword by Graham Kendrick

ZONDERVAN™

GRAND RAPIDS, MICHIGAN 49530 USA

ZONDERVAN™

Christ Behind Bars
ISBN 0-310-24795-0

Requests for information should be addressed to:

Zondervan, *Grand Rapids, Michigan 49530*

The Cross Between Thieves first published in Great Britain in 1996 by Marshall Pickering

Copyright © 1996 by Gillian Powe

The Final Verdict first published in Great Britain in 1997 by Marshall Pickering

Copyright © 1997 by Gillian Powe

Gillian Powe asserts the moral right to be identified as the author of this work

Printed and bound in the United Kingdom

02 03 04 05 06 /CLY/ 12 11 10 9 8 7 6 5 4 3 2

CONTENTS

FOREWORD

'So where is the rubber chicken this time?'
Although it had been about a month since our last
visit, the security staff checking our equipment
clearly remembered their puzzled amusement over
this item, which was featured as part of the percus-
sionist's equipment list. The rubber chicken, which
probably originated in a joke shop, had become a
kind of mascot for the musician concerned, who
saw no reason to remove it from his case. It seemed
to have entered the folklore of this particular group
of prison officers, providing some light relief in the
otherwise tedious task of minutely checking and x-
raying everything passing into the establishment.

Security checks had long ago become routine,
but I was taken aback when Gillian Powe told me
that over seven years had passed since my first visit
to one of David's chapel services. I first started
coming when they were based down in Lewes,
Sussex, though now they have moved to Belmarsh,
a high security prison in Southeast London. I had
first heard David speak about his work when he
visited my home church years ago, telling the

down-to-earth, amusing and sometimes hair-raising incidents that punctuated his ministry. Something akin to a revival was happening and hundreds of prisoners were responding to the simple and direct message of the gospel. It was hearing their stories that inspired me to offer my services. Even though I had ministered in prisons on a number of occasions previously, I was curious to see for myself what was going on. I was exercised in my own heart and mind about using my musical gifts more in evangelism, which was the context that I originally began to write and perform songs. That one visit led to another, and another, and soon became part of the pattern of my life.

Although those visits, along with accompanying musicians, get the occasional mention here, mine is only a walk-on part. The main characters are the prisoners who have heard and responded to the message of God's love as it has been presented simply and directly in chapel and cell. As a result, they have had their lives transformed by the power of God. Yet my visits have convinced me more than ever of two things: First, that the gospel message simply and directly presented with a call to follow Christ is indeed the means by which God's power to save is encountered. Second, that the ordinary people of this nation, especially those in extreme need, are far more ready than most churches realise to respond to that message.

Far from this unchurched audience paying only cursory attention to the meaning of the songs I sing, I find the listening surprisingly profound. I can't claim to be on the cutting edge of the music culture that many of the prisoners are used to, but time after time I see the rapt attention on their faces as they drink in words about the God who loves them. I look around and see faces that I recognise from previous visits and see the changes in demeanour– tough, tattooed men learning how to worship, an inner peace showing on uplifted faces that just wasn't there before.

An upside to the largely Godless and aggressively hedonistic society in which most of these men grow up is that they have not received the dose of nominal religion that might have inoculated them against the real thing! Most of them are hearing the message for the very first time and it comes to them fresh and new, as an encounter rather than an abstract proposition.

While it is true that many of these men have committed terrible crimes, most of them are much like the rest of us, and chatting to them is as ordinary as chatting to anybody in a pub or at a bus stop. Hearing of the backgrounds and circumstances that contributed to their present situation, one is never far from thinking 'There but for the grace of God go I'. Far from being irrelevant, which some people might imagine, the Bible is surprisingly, almost shockingly, relevant to prisoners. Many biblical heroes such as Moses and the apostle Paul had committed crimes, even murder, before the grace of God got hold of them, and a whole succession of them from Jeremiah to John the Baptist spent time in prison. Jesus himself experienced arrest, imprisonment, trial and punishment, though innocent of any crime. Despite a frequent lack of literacy skills, prisoners read the Bible more avidly and extensively than those in many regular free congregations, and the Word of God is proved to be living and active, not dry and academic.

I hope you will be as encouraged and challenged as I have been as you meet these individuals and their stories through the pages of this book. I also hope that it will inspire and motivate many to support this type of work, and that not a few will find their way into active participation, the potential for which is enormous and the need growing as prisons become more and more crowded and society more and more fragmented. For those readers who have not yet experienced the reality of Jesus Christ in a personal way, it will surely inspire a response because if God can meet with these folk then he can also meet with you in the midst of your life's experience.

Of the wide cross-section of those who will appreciate this book, not least are those faithful servants of God in front-line ministry situations who, like David Powe, generally take proportionally more knocks, disappointments and criticisms than they get encouragements and commendations. Nevertheless, they get on with the job and doggedly refuse to give up in the face of difficulty. There are no superheroes here, just ordinary people who have decided to believe that God means what he says and does what he promises.

GRAHAM KENDRICK
MARCH 2002

PREFACE

Reading about your own experiences in a book is almost unnerving because, in spite of all attempts to be genuine and totally honest, there is always a need when writing to turn life into a story so it makes sense to the reader. However, by doing just that, many aspects of a situation are obviously omitted and, looking back later on events, there is so much more to say, to explain and to discuss.

As this omnibus edition of two previous books is published, I am able to find many things I could add to the writing that would add new perspectives, but I believe it is more important to celebrate the effect these real-life stories have had on both our own and others' lives. Excitingly, many letters have found their way to us from readers not only in this country, but also from all over the world. These have contained moving accounts of people who have had contact with men in prison, and of how the events that were told have been a source of comfort, challenge or hope. For these results of ministry we are very grateful to God, for it is not given to everyone to hear the effects of their work.

xi

We are also sure that many as of yet unknown stories are out there somewhere, just as genuine, whether we ever hear them or not!

The transitory nature of Christian work

We all seek immortality, either consciously or unconsciously, and hope that our contribution to the world will not be forgotten the moment we have passed on. Surely we have made some impact on our environment or those around us. This drive to be important is not always helpful or appropriate even in the secular world, where it does seem that some modern 'office slaves' feel compelled to strive for countless hours at some task that seems hugely important at the time. All too soon, however, this task becomes irrelevant, even pointless, when compared to personal life and relationships. Comfortingly, there are some signs in contemporary life that this particular penny is at last beginning to drop more often, not least after 11 September 2001.

In Christian service it is even more important to keep one's life and ministry in perspective, since we believe we are servants of a much greater master, whose service is said to be perfect freedom. Service and self-importance do not sit well together. Nevertheless, we can quickly begin to think that we are central to an aspect of God's work and that our absence from it would be disaster for the Great Plan.

Once we begin to think this, it becomes difficult indeed to leave a work whilst it is going well.

Indeed, we may face strong criticism for doing so, since it is sometimes argued that anything that is of genuine value must have longevity. This view holds little water really when seen in the light of some of the biographies in the Gospels; if length of ministry were the only guide to effectiveness, then several major players would of necessity be very soon eliminated!

However, such considerations often elude our thinking and while sometimes we long to be out of a situation, and the days drag by until our longed-for release appears, to move on when success is apparent and life is beginning to ease, that can hardly be necessary, can it? Well certainly for us in Lewes it was necessary, and we had to deal with a growing feeling that the ministry, which is described in this book, was to face a new phase elsewhere.

The original tales of transformed lives

This account records an exciting beginning to prison evangelism, the work for which we seemed to have been prepared over a large number of years. We were seeing many prisoners responding to the gospel. What could possibly be better? The tale of how a new work evolved through a further move, this time to Belmarsh in London will have to wait awhile. Just suffice it to say at this point that we have many more tales of transformed lives to share.

These events were originally written down for two reasons: firstly to celebrate the effect of a simple gospel message on a disenfranchised sector of society, and secondly to be an encouragement to ordinary Christians, so that they could come to accept that they too could make a difference, if only they would take up this or a similar challenge. In reality the publication had a further effect: the inmates loved these stories of men like themselves, who were trapped in similar situations both of their own and other's making, and began to apply the responses found in the book to their own lives.

This has resulted in several amusing incidents at Belmarsh prison, where David now works.

'You should read this book, you know, vicar,' explained Mike.

'Why's that?' asked a mischievous chaplain.

'Well, you could learn from this bloke.... He's really done something!'

'What's that then?' came the reply.

'He helped these inmates,' continued the prisoner warming to his educative task. 'It's full of stories about God helping men. Have you been to Lewes?'

'Yes, I have,' replied David honestly.

'Well, have you met him or not?' demanded an irritated questioner.

With that David leant forward and pointed to his name on the badge and then indicated at the name on the book.

'That's me,' he declared, 'and that's my wife's name, because she wrote it!'

The man looked bemused, and then very slowly the truth dawned and he began to grin.

✳

On another occasion I was sitting with a couple of inmates after the service just as the officers were calling out house blocks numbers for their return to the cells.

A tall intense man called Steve spoke to me earnestly, 'That bloke there was singing the words out of this book I'm reading.'

He was pointing at Graham Kendrick who was beginning to collapse his music stand and coil up the wires of his portable sound system. The latter has long developed an ability to do this at remarkable speed, since the operations of a maximum-security prison wait for no man, not even a famous Christian singer, but concentration is still needed to be effective.

'Was that "How much do you think you are worth, boy?"' I asked innocently.

'Yes,' came the response. 'Who is that up there?'

'Well,' I answered quietly, 'that's Graham, whom you read about in your book, and I'm Gillian Powe, who wrote the book. Would you like to meet Graham?'

'That's amazing,' gasped Steve. 'Just amazing ... I can't believe it. It's amazing.'

Steve went on to chat with Graham and could not resist telling his tale to absolutely everyone around him as he went out of the chapel. For me it was of course a cause of great delight, and Graham was pleased to meet a genuine fan, made all the more meaningful of course, because this man had found faith inside and he had been able to support him.

Bringing purpose out of tragedy

I hope you enjoy these stories of people beginning the path to meaningful faith, and I hope they provide you with the comfort, challenge and hope they have brought to others before you. Not everyone will witness reaping with this intensity, and indeed some may only ever sow the seeds that others later claim, but you will almost undoubtedly meet someone who has been touched by the spreading tentacles of crime and prison within your lifetime. When that time comes, hopefully you will be able to offer reasons for hope, rather than for despair. As these testimonies reveal, God is able and willing to meet people at their point of deepest need—wherever they are—and to bring purpose out of tragedy. As one inmate recently put it, 'I have been found innocent of any charge, and I am going home, but I do not resent the time I have spent inside, because it was there that I met God for the very first time.'

GILLIAN POWE
MARCH 2002

THE CROSS BETWEEN THIEVES

REPAIRING BROKEN LIVES

DEDICATED TO
THOMAS AND EDWARD
TWO VERY SPECIAL SONS

＊

Contents

CHAPTER 1

✳

'What We Need is a Camcorder...'

Wishful thinking can be a dangerous occupation.

I sat lazily in the dappled sunlit garden listening to the trickling of the waterfall into the pond and watching our young son happily throwing sand out of his sandpit onto the grass. I reached down and picked up my cooling lemonade and sipped it, enjoying the bright sunlight of that beautiful summer's afternoon. David opened the patio door, stepped out into the garden and stood looking down the length of the lawn with a contented smile on his face. He stood motionless for a few moments, simply taking pleasure in the scene before him. 'What we need is a camcorder,' he said seriously. 'This is just so wonderful.'

It had taken us a great deal of striving to be able to enjoy that garden. All our efforts at work had been ploughed into moving up the property market until we reached a modest but truly delightful four-bedroomed detached house. To say we loved this particular residence was an understatement and when we'd moved in I'd remarked, 'This is it; this is really it. We need never move again.' The ludicrous

1

irony of this comment was quite unknown to me at the time.

I loved the wooden units in the kitchen set off by glorious red tiles, a personal favourite. There was plenty of room to eat in the room, which I thought a great luxury. The large lounge had an exceptional open fireplace designed by the talented previous owners, friends of ours from church. Next to that fireplace I could sit looking out over the long beautifully-planned garden in the winter, or step out through the patio doors into the sunny south-facing lawn in the summer. Wisteria filled the back wall with its trailing mauve blossoms, and the mellow red brick walls formed the perfect backdrop. Oh yes, it was a 'chocolate-box' beauty and we revelled in it.

I heard myself agreeing with David that afternoon that recording what was basically our good fortune would be a good idea. Camcorders were still a huge novelty at that time, in 1987, and very expensive. David was a sales manager – a highly successful one at that – and although our income was actually fairly modest he was poised for much greater future success. A camcorder could well have been on the shopping list in a little while. However, inside something else was happening. I felt very ill at ease at this latest suggestion and although it's hard to explain in today's context where camcorders are everywhere, at all social events large or small, I felt that possession of this item would represent a level of greed and materialism I could not justify.

Later that evening I couldn't ignore the nagging feeling inside. 'What are we doing?' I asked David.

'Half the world is starving and we want to buy a camcorder.'

David listened quietly, paused for a moment and replied, 'I quite agree. After I said it, it really upset me. I don't think it's a good idea at all.'

That simple realization between us was the beginning of a huge change in our lives and one day soon afterwards I heard myself saying, 'I don't want to get to sixty and feel we've done nothing. There must be something more, I'm sure.'

David had already believed God wanted him in the Anglican ministry. Some years before he had even been to ACCM, the Anglican selection board, and had been accepted. For various family and financial reasons we had not followed that up and as an acceptance only lasts three years, David would have to reapply. But that was the track he felt we should take and the conviction grew and grew in both of us that we were to commit ourselves to a life in the ministry. That unfulfilled wish for a camcorder was the simple but effective device that God used to move us on to brand new adventures.

David's second selection conference was easier than the first in one way because, of course, he knew what to expect, but it was more difficult in another for now everyone wished to ask him why he was on his second round. Both he and I were confident, however, that this was now the right time to proceed and so he was able to give a good account of his personal pilgrimage which seemed to satisfy the enquirers.

David was no great academic but his easy, relaxed and humorous style belied his very quick wit and ability to grasp the kernel of a situation and offer just the right comment at the right time. This skill was one which would serve him so very well in his future ministry, we were to discover. ACCM conferences can be quite demanding. A group of men and nowadays women, as they test their vocation for Church of England ministry, live together for two or or three days with a group of assessors, all of whom are there to look at an aspect of the candidates' suitability. Academic, social and psychological factors are considered along with spiritual ones. Each night the selectors discuss the day and at the end of the conference meet to decide just whom they feel they can recommend for full training. There is an emphasis on no one failing. You are either 'recommended', or 'not recommended'. (Some are told to wait a while.) Of course this amounts to pass or fail to most candidates and it would be hard for most people to take 'not recommended' as a positive result, at least in the short term. Thus everyone is a little apprehensive to say the least.

Each mealtime the candidates had to sit with a different assessor so that he or she could get to know them more thoroughly. On David's conference it was obvious that the Dean was the sharpest mind on site. He became known very quickly as the one who asked the most pointed questions. David used his skills to avoid him by approaching all the other assessors himself at mealtimes rather than waiting to be asked.

On the last morning he was too slow.

'Have I sat next to you yet, David?' asked the Dean as he approached David at the table.

David flashed a huge grin. 'Oh, I'm sure you have, Dean,' he replied, not very convincingly.

'I don't think I have,' responded the Dean sitting firmly down beside David with a very large twinkle in his eye.

As the two men began their breakfast the Dean turned to David and asked, 'Well, David, and how do you think you have done?'

The whole table fell silent.

If David replied 'Well' it would sound overconfident, for the interviews scattered throughout the days had been lengthy and very thought-provoking, but if he were to reply 'Not very well' it might sound rather weak or even falsely modest.

David's sense of humour, as it so often did, bailed him out of the situation. Recalling the system in Rome, where the enclosed cardinals burn their ballot papers to indicate a new pontiff has been selected, he quipped, 'I'll just wait for the white smoke to appear – and then I'll know I've got through.'

The silence was broken by the Dean's loud laughter. 'Very droll!' he replied. 'Let's just hope that the smoke really is white in the end.'

For David the smoke did prove to be white, and the Bishop of Horsham rang a few weeks later to tell him the good news. 'Well, David,' he said proudly, 'you've passed for the second time. Let's get things moving now.'

So it was that over the new few months we visited various Anglican theological colleges, and David was accepted at Wycliffe Hall, Oxford. Within the year we set off to college with our three-year-old son Thomas, Edward, just three months old, masses of luggage, a pushchair and nearly a month's supply of disposable nappies, all squashed into or onto the car. We were moving to Wycliffe Hall for David's training and it was all very exciting. As we drove north along the busy trunk road towards Oxford we sat talking about the future in between handing food, drink and entertainment to the small occupants of the back seat.

Suddenly a huge gust of wind caught the contents of our roof rack and the 96 disposable nappies shot off the luggage pile and bounced back down the road. The plastic bag burst open scattering nappies all over the lanes of the road and onto the verges at either side. 'Oh no!' I cried. 'That's a huge investment! We must stop and collect them!'

Of course, I knew at once that this was not a real possibility, but I still grumbled inside when David stated the obvious. 'I'm not stopping and collecting nappies with traffic running at close on seventy miles an hour for anyone!' We both started to laugh at the ridiculous situation we were in and learned our first lesson in the importance of retaining our sense of humour. Before we finished our training we'd meet far worse situations than 96 nappies flying off a car roof and we were to need all the courage and good humour we could muster to get us through.

During our time in Oxford, we were to move three times, lose all our capital through the collapse in property prices and face numerous family and college problems. It is easy now to see it all as part of our preparation for what was to come but it didn't feel like that at the time.

When we sold our house in Sussex we had donated some sums of money to various causes because we felt we should do so. One of these was a donation of £1,000 to Whatcombe House, a wonderful retreat house we had often visited in Dorset. It was there we had met the Rev. Bob Parker and Vera Parker who had encouraged and inspired our entry into the ministry. Their kind present of some William Barclay books on the New Testament had a far more meaningful impact than they could have imagined and we valued them greatly. David had first experienced the fullness of the Spirit there and we'd often prayed for our sons and our future within its protective walls. The ministry of Canon John Gunstone there was also highly significant for us and the whole experience had been a positive contribution to our Christian lives. From time to time we had needed to draw apart and see where our busy lives were leading. We found God always seemed to have a change of direction for us when we visited Whatcombe. Perhaps we had just become stationary long enough for us to feel his leading, and the atmosphere there was certainly conducive to sensing the presence of God and weighing up our lives. It represented to us a peace and power we have seldom experienced elsewhere and we felt a deep sense of gratitude for the dedication and devotion of the small community who kept Whatcombe's doors open.

Because of all this we wanted to contribute to Whatcombe's work once we had the chance, and sent off our donation cheerfully. A few months later we learned that Whatcombe House was closing down and we could hardly believe it. We were very sad because of the community's place in our lives but trusted our donation would be used wisely.

Later that year we started to feel the pinch. Our finances were soon strained to breaking point and we did not know what to do. For many students at theological colleges the concern over finance forces other concerns well into the distance, and we were no exception. Driving back from a supermarket one Thursday, having agonized over the few purchases, David lost his cool.

'When I get to heaven,' he said, 'I'm going to ask God what happened to that money we gave away. I'm going to ask Him why we had to give it away – and He won't have an answer – He just won't have an answer.' I didn't reply because he'd expressed what I'd felt and we finished our journey in a rather unhappy mood.

But we should have known better, and within hours we were taught an unforgettable lesson. We'd given that money nine months previously and as far as we were concerned it was gone, but later that same evening, the telephone rang. David answered it and was shocked to the core.

'This is Neville, the former warden of Whatcombe House,' the caller said. 'I've been trying to track you down for months, but I understand you keep moving.' David gulped and realized that tracking us down would have been a very difficult job just recently.

'Anyway,' continued Neville, 'we never cashed your kind donation and have wanted to return it to you, as I'm sure you need it. I'll put a cheque in the post tonight.'

'Thank you,' said David, humbled and choked up. 'Thank you so much.' The amazing significance of what had happened began to dawn on him as he replaced the receiver. Not only had we a vital boost to our finances but we had been presented with a staggering example of God's provision and discipline. We certainly felt very chastened that night as we talked over the events of the day and were very grateful for the whole learning experience.

Over the next two years it seemed as though we'd moved into the fast lane of life. We had ups and downs just like every Christian we knew, but it now seemed that the ups were higher and the downs lower than we'd ever previously experienced. We began to live through very exciting times and thrilling events but we also went through troughs we never knew existed.

Once our time at college was over we needed to move to a curacy. In our naivety we'd assumed it would all be prayed about and lots of loving concern would be shown to help us find God's right place for our lives. The reality was far from the ideal. The placement of students was almost a competitive race with plenty of scope for using 'who you know'. Very early in the process, finding a job at all took precedence over finding the 'right' place. Unnerved by the whole experience, David accepted the first curacy he was offered in a parish on the Isle of Wight. We knew before we went, if we were honest, that it was wrong for us, but we went anyway, assuming that even if it wasn't perfect it would be OK as a start. We were very wrong and it proved to be the biggest disaster of our lives and could well have finished our ministry altogether had not God rescued us spectacularly at the end.

With the priest-in-charge we experienced a personality clash of monumental proportions and almost from day one, life became one long frustration. We felt that we had no purpose. We had to learn to watch every word and action, live with the effects of bad relationships and we experienced loneliness that we never believed possible. We were forced into a life of total inaction, and as active extroverts it was hard to bear. David began to border on depression, and every attempt we made to redeem our situation failed.

'I think that the Bishop would want someone more pious and prayerful to be a priest,' David was told by his priest-in-charge, and his final priesting was only allowed at the very last minute.

As our curacy came into its last year we began to wonder what the future held. We explored a ministry with young people as by then David was working for the diocese one day a week as Youth Officer for the Isle of Wight and we enjoyed it immensely. For some reason we shall never understand, the opposition to us trying to open a youth centre was cataclysmic and resulted in us receiving a letter from the Bishop terminating David's employment within four months in order to maintain the stability of the parish.

We were totally aghast as we found ourselves with no job, no home and the worst reference anyone had ever seen. There was no lower to go. Why had we come into the ministry at all, we asked ourselves repeatedly.

We had not only had a disastrous time there, but others seemed determined that we should never minister elsewhere either. We were described as totally individualistic and unable to work with others, charges we could deny until we were blue in the face, but to no avail in an organization that seemed to rely totally on the reference system.

Apart from our friend Debbie, Dr Stephen Porter was the only Christian who was there for us. No one else seemed to understand what we were going through. He came round when David was at his lowest ebb, when all hope was gone and only despair was left, and he prayed a simple but powerful prayer of release for him. I don't know how God worked through him, I only know that He did and from that moment on, hope began to re-emerge and a path opened out before us.

We ended up serving four deliriously happy months at St James' Church in Ryde whilst their minister and our friend, Rev. Canon Bernard Baker, went to Dubai. To us it felt like a miracle that people seemed really to appreciate David and benefit from our very short-term ministry, but their ministry to us far outpassed any help we may have given them. Indeed, they will probably never understand how greatly God used them to restore us to vitality and purpose, but it was certainly their love and fellowship that prepared us for our next move.

Without Beryl, Gill, Lil, Peter and Karen and so many others we would not be involved in our work today. Their love and support both then and now is a very precious gift and although the business of the ministry prevents us from meeting up very often we never forget to give thanks for their contribution to our work and their real friendship: This was Christian love in action. During these months we knew we must leave the Island and David suggested we considered prison ministry. It wasn't an idea out of the blue as in our third month at Ventnor we had used our day off to visit the Chaplain General of Prisons in London to discuss the possibility of such a ministry. David felt drawn to work in this area and I was willing to look into it, but had quickly changed my mind. It meant a probation year in a huge prison somewhere followed by another move to an unknown destination. I felt it would mean too much upheaval for the boys and too much uncertainty for myself. On the train coming home I expressed my views clearly. David too was worried about these areas and decided it wasn't a ministry for us, but went on to visit Parkhurst and its chaplain, the Rev. Brian Anderson, just the same.

Being realists we knew we would never be accepted in a church at this stage as we had been well and truly labelled unsuitable. Nevertheless we believed that God had led us into the ministry and that there was work for us to do somewhere. In the event we saw God guide us so swiftly it almost took our breath away. Despite our earlier reservations, David felt more and more drawn to prison ministry and I was led to support him. He applied and was invited to an interview at the Home Office, which employs chaplains in the Prison Service. Here, of course, no word of mouth suffices, as the selection processes are rigorous and demanding and made selection for the ministry seem quite tame in comparison. David went away to his residential selection board and faced role-playing, psychological analysis and assessments of all kinds. Nevertheless one thing was on his side – no references were read until after the process was completed. Of course, David's reference was still there in all it unpleasantness but by the time it was read David had got on so well no one either believed it or was influenced by it. The person described and the reality that was David made no recognizable match and we were left realizing that God had gone before and provided in the most amazing way for our future.

David was accepted for prison ministry and we were summoned to London to meet the Assistant Chaplain General who would tell us where we had been posted. On the train we sat with a Home Office booklet detailing the locations of all the prisons in the country and wondering how we would cope if we were sent to this place or that. We caught a cab to Cleland House, the headquarters of the chaplaincy at that time, and went in to find out our destination.

Rev. Brian Dodsworth, the Assistant Chaplain General, sat at his desk and told us we were going to Belmarsh Prison and that there was a modest but new quarter with the post. Both of us tried not to look bemused. Should we admit now or later that we had not got a clue where Belmarsh Prison was? I tried to sound really interested. 'Oh, right – could you tell us where that is please?' I requested.

Brian got out a map of London and proceeded to show us where SE28 was – right over to the east and the south of the river near Woolwich. It was a relatively new area reclaimed from marshland; the prison was a new top-security edifice and held some 650 inmates. I had been scared witless when we heard about our placement. It seemed to work against everything we'd planned. Where was the pastoral work we'd felt called to? How could I live in London? How could I keep on disrupting the boys' routine? The uncertainties went on. I was sure we wouldn't be in such a ministry for long, although David had felt much more drawn to the work and had considered it before even his curacy began. On retreat in Oxford one day he'd felt God wanted him for an evangelistic role but he could not see how it could ever be fulfilled. Afterwards, David visited a well-known evangelist and asked his advice. He received very short shrift as he had never actually led anyone to Christ, so how could he be called to such a role? Feeling he must have been mistaken, David pushed the idea away, but as we now know he couldn't have been wrong – it was only the timing that was not in line. Well, now it seemed that the pieces were finally coming together and things starting to move.

It proved to be quite a difficult area and although David's description that even the Rottweilers went round in pairs was an exaggeration it was a far cry from the Isle of Wight. Nevertheless, to me it was heaven in comparison to the Island as the clouds of the past were lifted and quite unexpected and thrilling experiences began. In spite of my former reservations I grew to love London and its bustle. I felt alive once more, and opportunities began to emerge from every quarter.

Once in Belmarsh, David's gifts rose quickly to the fore. He was working for Rev. Graham Herrett, the Senior Chaplain, who was a larger-than-life character and a pleasure to work with because of his trust and belief in David. Men began turning to Christ steadily and David slotted in perfectly to this new ministry. I discovered that I had a new energy after the stagnation of our time on the Island and I slipped back into teaching with ease.

David's references started to blossom, in stark contrast to his previous experience. Terms like 'easy to get on with', 'cheerful' and 'works well in a team' were so refreshing and releasing. Could these two sets of references be referring to the same man?

Before long we were both totally involved and fulfilled and we anticipated with enthusiasm the compulsory move at the end of the first year.

As a deputy chaplain David knew the posting was only of a year's duration. After this he would be free to apply for suitable posts as they came up. There was a panel who decided where each chaplain should be sent and in theory, although you could express your wishes, you could be sent anywhere in the country. We had expected, for various reasons, to be sent to East Anglia, thinking that Lewes Prison, which had a vacancy for a chaplain, was too big for a second appointment. David expressed his interest in the Sussex post but we felt sure we would not be heading that way at all. We both originated from Sussex and were naturally drawn back 'home'. The actual posting to Lewes came as a huge surprise and with only four weeks notice we were on our way south. It all seemed so right and the usual moving problems fell into place, one by one helped by the awareness that having been through one complete black hole everything else seemed bright in comparison.

There was no house with the job this time and that could well have presented unsurmountable problems. However, with only four weeks' notice of a move before me, I managed to find a half-time teaching post in Worthing which would enable us to buy a house in Lewes, even if it meant a 50-mile daily journey for me.

We'd been through a lot together in Sussex, not least ten years of marriage before we left for Oxford, and our return brought back many memories. We began to see just how our past had prepared us for our present and how elements of our experience were all working together. We were grateful for God's provision of just the right person at the right time throughout our lives and saw it as working to God's ends. There were the Rev. Brian Andrew and Eileen Andrew, who had sacrificially nurtured me towards a Christian wholeness and maturity just before our marriage, Alan Longhurst who had been on our side through thick and thin, and our many friends, Alison and Chris, Alex and Alan, Janet and Peter, Julia and Peter, Judy and Derek, Lawson and Sylvia who had given us hospitality over the years when we needed to come home. John Gwen and Chris Symonds had helped us personally over many obstacles since we joined their home fellowship group in the early days of our marriage. All these God used as strengtheners and comforters, and along with them were those who prayed for us, keeping their care as a trust before God and about whom we learned only later or perhaps never at all. Our support, like that of many others, was like a web, partly visible, partly invisible, but strong and sufficient just the same. We were glad to be back home.

David set about the duties of Anglican Chaplain in Lewes Prison with gusto. Responsible for the chapel services and the provision of resources for people of all faiths to practise in safety, he also had to ensure that each new prisoner was offered any spiritual help he might need. Dealing with crises was also a daily event. The pressure became intolerable for some people once they were inside and it was not uncommon that David would have to break bad news to an inmate – trauma or death in the family, perhaps. Their grief, pain and anger were compounded by the fact that they were unable to be with their families, giving and receiving support.

David immediately took on the work of an evangelist too. He felt compelled to offer the inmates the change of life the Gospel brings. At Belmarsh he had grown to understand he had been given a gift not only to make a clear and simple presentation of the Good News but also to perceive those who would respond positively to Christ.

Day by day he would come home with news of another convert and we would wonder at the response we were seeing. We had no idea at first how this work was going to grow – we only knew that men kept responding to the Gospel. At first I would sit amazed at the stories which evolved, some of which are recorded in the pages of this book, but gradually I became used to the experience and began to expect new people to become Christians nearly every day. It began to feel like we were living in a book and our natural excitement began to flow out as we told others about the exciting events in Lewes Prison. Nothing had been planned by us but God was surely moving, convincing prisoners of their wrongdoings and drawing them to Himself. We began to try to find Bibles, literature and help from outsiders and gradually the news spread and spread. Every month new developments arose and the pace quickened. I spent as much time in the chapel as I could both meeting inmates and taking part in the services. We knew we were both in the right place and our commitment was total. People began to visit us, offering help and advice, and both Christian and secular media took up the stories of various men, some hardened criminals, who had become

Christians. As the numbers of converts began to run into the hundreds, it seemed remarkable by anyone's standards. Eventually David was invited to various places to speak and we worked together both to encourage Christians that God was really at work and to raise support and funds for buying Bibles, books, and tapes for those who could not read. We had never been so fulfilled or for that matter so challenged, but we were just thrilled to be part of it and wondered at the God who had brought us to this work and provided so marvellously for us in it. We yearned that others would catch the thrill of spreading the Gospel in this way and we wanted them to be thoroughly encouraged to be positive, not negative and frightened, witnesses to their faith.

The outside ministry grew rapidly and we were so privileged to visit churches and fellowships of every kind. We never knew what we'd find when we agreed to speak at a church but the experiences were unforgettable. One week we'd be at a small formal church complete with 1662 Prayer Book and tranquillity – the next at a huge Free congregation with band and noisy prayer ministry. One visit would take us to small prayer groups and the next to the privilege of preaching in Chichester Cathedral. We learned to be open and to gain inspiration from all kinds of Christian worship. Each group would be devoted to its own style and structure but we found God in all of them as His people strove to worship in spirit and in truth. The children, whom we tried hard to protect from excessive pressure, enjoyed the experiences too, occasionally asking such innocent questions, as 'Are you telling them the one about Nick Pook, Dad? I like that one!' or 'Why are all these people praying on their backs?'(when we had been at a meeting where people had fallen down during times of ministry).

Attending a Catholic school, being Anglican and witnessing so much diversity in between made them understand ecumenism in a concrete way because everyone was concerned with spreading the Good News of Jesus and denominational issues seemed of no real importance at all.

One day David was attending a meeting organized in a hotel. He had no idea how many people would attend and had been led to believe only a small number regularly came. As he parked the car he became aware that there was in fact a large queue leading up to the entrance. This line of people he duly joined, not wishing to push past the patient group.

'Is he any good?' asked a woman pushing up against him in the queue. 'Have you heard him before?'

The amusement of the situation struck David at once. 'Well, yes actually. I have heard him before. I believe he's OK.'

'Well, I hope so,' returned the woman, 'I've come a long way and brought my friend.' Here she indicated with her hand towards another lady standing nearby. The queue gradually moved on and presumably the two ladies took their places in the room. David did not see them again and could only imagine their surprise when they saw just who this visiting preacher turned out to be. He hoped they wouldn't be too disappointed!

David actually proved to be a popular speaker for he spoke in an animated and exciting style. He recalled tales of great import in an elegant simplicity and with enormous humour. He seemed to fit into all occasions and situations with ease, and invitations began to pour in to share the experiences at Lewes Prison. His skills as a speaker apart, he certainly had an exciting story to tell.

CHAPTER 2

✳

I Trace the Rainbow
Through the Rain

O Love that wilt not let me go,
I rest my weary soul in Thee:
I give thee back the life I owe,
That in Thine ocean depths its flow
May richer, fuller be.

O Light that followest all my way,
I yield my flickering torch to Thee:
My heart restores its borrowed ray,
That in Thy sunshine's blaze its day
May brighter, fairer be.

O Joy that seekest me through pain,
I cannot close my heart to Thee:
I trace the rainbow through the rain,
And feel the promise is not vain,
That morn shall tearless be.

O Cross that liftest up my head,
I dare not ask to fly from Thee:
I lay in dust life's glory dead,
And from the ground there blossoms red
Life that shall endless be.

George Matheson 1842–1906

Lewes Prison stands starkly guarding the entrance to the town. A prominent castle-like edifice, it dominates the approach road and is often mistaken for the far less spectacular and altogether more modest Lewes Castle itself.

The prison held 300 inmates but, when David took up office, was in the process of a comprehensive refit and expansion so that it would house a considerably larger number. In spite of its almost awesome dimensions and the apparent thickness of the stone walls Lewes is a remand prison containing mainly local offenders. It is hard for the uninitiated perhaps to understand that large numbers of technically innocent people can be subjected to prison conditions before their trials. The truth proves to be a harsh reality for many young men. Once arrested on suspicion of a crime an offender is brought before a magistrate who may or may not offer them bail. If this is refused then the suspect must pass his time until the trial under lock and key. Some will wait many many months on remand in this way and although most may later be properly convicted not a small number are found not guilty and are returned unceremoniously to their families. Unfortunately, conditions in remand prisons are seldom as settled or pleasant as those with more stable communities. The population is in a permanent state of flux, making long-term organization or relationships virtually impossible. Every day up to 25 prisoners will be moved in or out and the comings and goings to court or other establishments dominate the arrangements of the day.

For some the frustration of working as a chaplain with such a fast moving congregation would be a huge barrier to fulfilment, but for David it meant challenge, freshness and an impetus to spread the Good News of Jesus quickly. There was a small, more stable, wing of convicted prisoners which was to produce some of the keenest, strongest converts but the fast-moving inmates on the other wings meant hundreds were to come into contact with the Gospel, an opportunity a more stable community would never be able to offer.

Most of us know about prisons only from TV and films or hearsay. The former probably provide us with exaggerated views of violence and excitement, the latter with suggestions of a more holiday-camp image of lazy, easy living. Only suspected offenders and convicted criminals really know the truth but those who work within the walls gain at least an informed perspective.

Prison is a very stark place indeed. When inmates arrive – brought through the gates by police van – they face a strange and fearsome initiation. Not only is their freedom curtailed but their very personhood is stripped bare and their dignity reduced to the lowest level. Although many have caused others pain and suffering the shock is nonetheless severe for they are totally unprepared for this place of deprivation. Possessions are removed and stored away until a later, unknown, date. Routine finger-prints are required and each finger is roughly inked and rolled onto paper in turn. A prison photo is taken and followed by a full strip search. If a man is already convicted he will be given a simple prison track suit to wear, and if remanded his own clothes will be returned. Finally he will be taken through the huge sliding door that leads to the blocks of cells where he will probably meet the man with whom he will share his space, his time and his privacy for some time to come. All this takes place routinely, for the officers may be greeting 25 prisoners in this way every day. The procedure is a natural part of prison life but is very unnatural to the new and sometimes very young inmate. It takes as short a time as possible and is therefore very impersonal and frightening to those who are thrust into prison life in this manner.

One possible, incidentally positive, result of the process is that the individual man receives a great deal of attention. This is, however, a mere momentary illusion and is unrepresentative of a spell in prison as a whole. 'Doing time' really means not attention but rather isolation, social deprivation and having too many hours on one's hands. Once in that cell there will be little consideration any more. There will be a blurring of hours into days and weeks into months and an almost numbing boredom and sameness.

In a typical cell there is a claustrophobic atmosphere as a prisoner can see little through the small barred window situated high up on one wall. The solid door had no handle on the inside, of course, and the window barely opens. The lack of circulation hardly helps the unpleasantness of the 'en suite' facilities as one can imagine. The bunk beds dominate the space and the simple chairs and the tiny table have to serve many purposes. In this little place two men who know nothing about each other will spend many hours together. From 8.00 p.m. to 8.00 a.m. that heavy door will remain firmly shut until it is formally opened to allow the collection of breakfast, which like all meals is eaten in the cells.

The men are not normally of a contemplative nature, or people whose practice of the inner life is up and running, and so the restrictive deprivation of space strikes very hard, and the periods known as association when inmates may wander out of their cells certainly come as a great relief. There is a snooker table on the wing and cards are played regularly. Everyone covets the use of the card phone as a means of outside contact, although the queues are long and conversations are consequently brief and subject to harassment. Cards are purchased out of meagre allowances or payments for jobs and traded, prized and stolen as a real source of currency. Conversations are always monitored by Security, of course.

Some attend sessions in the education department where literacy may be addressed or more practical skills learned. Time in the gym can be granted and there are also games of football and other physical activities. On Sundays inmates who choose to attend chapel often have to sacrifice their valuable and restricted sports time in order to do so, which is quite a challenge for new Christians as you will imagine. Jobs meanwhile are scarce and greatly sought after, resulting in great disappointment for the unsuccessful.

It is hard for us to imagine the strain of the boredom for these men. Often the type to be out and about on the streets and often responsible to no one in particular, they find themselves restrained and unable to fill their time. It can hardly be surprising that thoughts turn either to plotting for the future or planning action on the wings. We found some people who were not only shocked that there were a few sports facilities but surprised that men were allowed out of cells to mix at all. The argument runs that nothing can be bad enough to punish them for whatever crime they have committed. Of course such a regime would be either unworkable or very cruel. Most of our prisoners were also on remand, which meant they had yet even to be proved guilty.

The truth is we cannot lock up hundreds of inmates for years and years with nothing to do and no facilities if we wish to maintain a controlled situation; and unless we can reduce conditions to those that are inhuman it will always be impossible. The punishment which society has selected for most crime is deprivation of liberty but we are not given the right to dehumanize in the process; these men will enter society again sooner or later and we would return embittered people at all our peril. Those who work in the Service are a little more realistic, knowing that a reduction of tension in very restricted conditions represents a major task.

Inmates have their own code or system of behaviour, of course. Punishments may take place for those who break the rules by owing money or phone cards, for example. A couple of batteries in a sock or a baton broken from a piece of furniture may be used to bring about conformity, and possessions deemed unsuitable or surplus to requirements may be unceremoniously removed.

Inmates who cause trouble are sent before a governor for adjudication. They may lose some entitlement for parole or if more serious they will be removed to the Segregation Unit, which consists of tiny cells with even fewer facilities and privileges. Occasionally an inmate is restrained for his own or others' protection and placed in a specially padded cell.

Into this world of unusual behaviour and code of conduct comes the new inmate and not surprisingly some find it difficult to cope. Often they have not fully foreseen or appreciated the consequences of their actions and they are often bewildered, alone and devastated by this turn of events. Sometimes David even had to deal with tragic cases where it was all too much and a suicide attempt had been made. Naturally, too, there were those who were hardened by frequent stretches spent inside and those who were of genuine evil intent, but they seemed to us to be in the minority in this mainly remand institution. We met many who did not know where to turn or how to live through the experience they now faced. As we chatted we found a large number for whom the whole of life had been a source of rejection, abuse and a general downward spiral. We often found they knew they had done wrong things and were not in any way trying to legitimize their activities by appealing to a bad past, but nevertheless they obviously were victims themselves in many ways and having been offered no alternative hope, life style or love had pursued petty crime until they were caught.

The words of George Matheson's marvellously moving hymn have always been an inspiration to me and many other Christians and as we settled in to working amongst these men its message seemed to me ever more apposite and relevant to the situation. Written in 1882 by a blind author, it addresses the problem, and the surprising fruit, of suffering. Feeling inadequate we find security in God alone and discover the paradox of the Christian life. In giving ourselves to Him we actually find our true selves. This whole book is a record of how many men found the reality of the first verse of this hymn. Finding no help in their own resources they surrendered to God and found themselves for the first time.

Some moved on from those first experiences and began to long for a deeper spirituality through Bible study and prayers. One group fasted and prayed for the salvation of others' souls and many witnessed openly and without fear to other inmates on their wings. For them the second verse of the hymn has special meaning.

Leaving verse three for a moment, verse four was equally appropriate, for the meaning of sacrifice becomes very real where living a true Christian life in prison is concerned. The cross was always the central point of our teaching ministry and the men realized, probably more than us, just what the cost of discipleship would be. They were always quick to affirm their beliefs, however, and showed little regard for either abuse or rebuffs.

However much I would affirm the connection between this whole hymn and our experience at

Lewes it must be verse three that stands out in its relevance. Into lives marked out by the rain of pain, sorrow, dissatisfaction and mistakes the hope of God had found an entrance. God himself visits any who turn to Him and transforms their lives so that the future may be 'tearless'. The image of the rainbow being traced through the rain is startlingly appropriate. Even in the depths of desolation or despair the rainbow of God's hope can be seen and His promise received. This was the experience of inmate after inmate who faced up to their past and dared to trust God for a new future. Similarly it is the experience of many Christians worldwide whether behind bars or free and is the simple offer to all men and women whatever their circumstances.

DARREN

Darren Vickers was just such an inmate. At 29 he was inside for a serious offence and was really at rock bottom. His life had been a catalogue of bad relationships and as the result of a final major dispute with a girl whom he still loved he found himself charged with crimes against her which he firmly denied. He had been sent to boarding school early in life which left him with deep-seated feelings of rejection and loss. He felt no one wanted or loved him and he carried the resulting insecurity with him through his life. He couldn't settle in jobs and was devastated when he failed to make a sound relationship with a woman. Each time he failed he despaired, re-enacting the rejection experienced in his early life. He had been sexually abused at that school and had always been scared to complain through fear of violence. He was fully adult before he told his mother and the effects had obviously never been dealt with. Four or five times he felt suicidal so he overdosed three times and cut his wrists on other occasions.

Then Darren met the girl he felt was to change his life, for she seemed to offer the stability and love he craved. He felt he had it all at last, but for reasons we don't really know or understand it all went sadly wrong. Perhaps Darren just didn't have the resources within himself that are necessary to build a true and lasting relationship, or maybe he made too many demands, awkwardly attempting to make up for past rejections and inadequacies. It matters not really, for the result was sure. The relationship broke up under a cloud of accusations and Darren found himself in Lewes Prison.

Darren was petrified because he knew nothing about a life of crime or criminals. The charges were being made by someone he still dearly loved and once more there was no one on his side, no one cared and he was deeply scared. He confessed, 'I can't put into words the fear I experienced. I was not used to mixing with inmates at all.'

However someone did see his desperation and although we don't know the identity of this particular Good Samaritan he suggested Darren go to chapel on Sunday.

'I met David the Chaplain there,' said Darren. 'David Powe – the man who changed my life that day in my cell.'

David had put Darren's name down in his diary to visit in the week after the service and had duly gone to see him. Darren still describes what happened in clear, direct terms for it represents the time his whole life took a new turn – the time when he finally did trace the rainbow through the rain of his life and discovered that not every morning needs to be full of tears. 'We talked for half an hour,' explained Darren seriously, 'and all my troubles disappeared. He laid his hands on my head and said a prayer. There was a feeling of adrenaline just passing through me. It was totally incredible.'

Darren was lost for comparisons at this point but has had time to discuss the meaning of his experience with others since that time and has felt happy to use some of their vocabulary.

'It was like being reborn, starting again,' he declared confidently.

'All my guilt, rejection just washed away,' he reported, lingering on the words guilt and rejection for they obviously held deep significance for him.

'David put something inside me. It was love. It was God. It was the Holy Spirit.'

Darren no longer sounds depressed or dispirited but rather exudes a quiet enthusiasm as he recalls his feelings and the changes in his life.

Darren knew that David cared for him enough to help him but he was in no doubt that his real saviour was deep inside him: 'Everything I've ever wanted is in there – inside me,' he stated. 'It's love.'

Describing this as the turning point in his life he expressed his thanks for being offered the Gospel. He'd known about God and had seen church services on TV and had heard people on the streets preaching in public places.

'It all went in one ear and out the other,' he said. 'It didn't interest me. They were Bible bashers, nutcases – mad.'

He couldn't understand religious people at all, not least because they didn't seem to mind any abuse that might come their way. Now he tells how it makes him angry when people snigger in chapel and that he wants to turn round and say, 'Listen and let them show you what God can do for you. He's done things for me. He loves me and has given me love and care. He's someone to cry to, to talk to, to be there when I wanted. He's given me all them things and doesn't ask for anything back. It's incredible. He fills all my empty spaces.' Darren's declaration of faith is itself incredible, for his previous 29 years are a catalogue of rejection and despair. Now he reads his Bible and comes to church. He looks forward to it as the main event of his week. He joins in the prayers and sees the new friends he's made.

Darren explained just how important these Christians who gave up their Sundays to meet with him were to him: 'They're incredible people. They've taken me without concern for their own worries. They've looked after me, helped me, prayed for me – been there for me.'

Darren was heavily supported by the prayer chain and those Sunday visitors and the results were obvious. 'I want to be known as a Christian,' he declared. 'I'm proud to say I'm a Christian now.'

He found he wasn't worried by rejection in the prison and even detected a general change in the atmosphere as more and more men found that message of the rainbow through their own particular source of rain.

'There's a big difference now,' Darren explained. 'A friend of mine outside even saw David's photo in a magazine. Things are going on in Lewes church,' he exclaimed, apparently pleasingly unaware of any potential difference between a chapel in prison and a church outside. 'Everyone knows about us in here – it's amazing,' he continued.

Darren could have been released at any time and he'd been found a church. He guessed the same sort of thing would happen in a congregation outside and that he would meet the same sort of people. We all pray that will indeed be his experience on the outside. When asked whether he would stay with the faith when released Darren was totally convinced and convincing: 'Oh yes – oh yes!' he declared. 'This is my life now.'

Darren's story is an inspiration. For him coming to prison was a turning point, not the end of the line. He no longer wants to commit suicide and has a new hope for his life. Others found God's grace in this way too. Their sad and conflict-ridden lives met the transforming power of God and a new start was made possible. One such man was Tony, a prisoner who totally lacked self-esteem and who knew no purpose for the future whatsoever. However, God still called him and picked him up out of despair and into a new hope. Time after time we were witnessing His desire to deal with those whom society had rejected as worthless.

TONY

Tony was a very tall, fair-haired man who stooped slightly as if trying to be less conspicuous. He sat at the back of chapel each week unable to sit in the body of the church because of the nature of his offences. Any man on 'K' Wing was a vulnerable prisoner who had been placed in this special block for his own protection. Some were scared of reprisals for 'grassing' or telling the authorities about other inmates. Some were placed in protection because they owed money or were the victims of bullying or a vendetta. Still others were under suspicion of crimes involving women, children or sexual deviance. Under inmates' rules these people were the 'lepers' of the prison, to be excluded, abused and attacked whenever possible. Under the statute known as rule 43 such inmates were entitled to a place on the protected wing and seldom met with other prisoners. In the early days when numbers were still modest at services David invited these 'K' Wing prisoners to the ordinary service, although later they had to be granted their own time for worship as the numbers made things less predictable.

Tony was an early convert. He felt he'd little real hope in life and responded eagerly to the offer of the Gospel. His life was like Darren's, in that he had suffered rejection and abuse and he too was unable to make lasting meaningful relationships.

He eventually married and stayed so for a long time, but the relationship can certainly only be described as rocky. There were constant rows as they tried to live with each other and finally Tony's violent temper drove him to attempt to take his wife's life with a hammer. He bitterly regretted this outburst and wished with all his heart that he could control his inner rage. Normally he was exceptionally mild mannered and reserved and it was hard to perceive him as a man of such violence.

In Lewes Prison he found Christ and could hardly believe that he was being offered a new start. How could God accept such a man or grant him forgiveness? God would and did, however, and to Tony's astonishment gave him a further blessing. On a chapel visit organized by David his wife was not only reconciled to him but also became a Christian. This staggering story must surely illustrate that no one is beyond the love of God or His grace and certainly inspires me and challenges me to lift my faith out of the textbook and apply it to real-life situations. Finding faith in Jesus certainly transformed this man and one day he asked if he could read out his thoughts to the other inmates gathered together one Sunday morning.

He was very brave, of course, because as a resident of 'K' Wing he was opening himself to any kind of abuse, but he rose to the challenge and read out his simple but meaningful poem that he had written in the solitude of his cell. All eyes were on him that morning as he stood leaning over the microphone and without raising his eyes from the page read:

God's Grace

I look into the mirror
And what do I see?
A man full of hate
And badness.
I look into the mirror
And what do I see?
A man gone old and grey
With nothing worth living for.

I look into the mirror
And what do I see?
I see a changed man
And that changed man
is me.
© Tony Phillips

There was a moment's silence as the men took in what they'd heard. ''Ere – well done, Tony,' shouted a voice from the back, breaking the stillness.

'Ooooh yeah,' joined in another.

A short burst of applause broke out and a grinning Tony stepped down back to his place, glowing with pride at his achievement and his acknowledgement of the change God had brought about in his life. We were all deeply moved at Tony's courage and God's good grace.

Sometimes it was a long time before we knew just how God had worked in an individual's life. Because, as has been said, Lewes is a remand prison and the average length of stay is seven weeks, inmates were shipped out to all parts of the country with great regularity and we had to try hard to maintain contact as much as possible with new Christians. We now aim to write to every inmate who moves to another prison, to encourage their growing faith and hopefully to link them with a supportive local church nearby. Writing to a new Christian in prison might seem a little daunting but actually proves to be immensely satisfying. Even more gratifying is to hear that an ex-inmate has settled in a local church and has found Christian supporters and friends. We exploited every contact we made to try to establish receptive churches. We would ring or write to chaplains in other prisons, members of Prison Fellowship, church teachers, friends, indeed any acquaintance we had made, to try to ensure introductions for new Christians. As an incidental element of this process we received many letters telling us of how God had been working in lives and this was really exciting and rewarding.

DOUG

Doug wrote from Wandsworth Prison to tell us about his feelings which he described as 'a personal drama'. He hoped his tale would help others in some small way and that is our prayer too.

'I am fine and every day is a pleasure to live.' Doug opened his letter with these splendid words but followed with an immediate admission that his life had not always been so positive an experience. He had become involved in drink and drugs at 15 and was in the habit of taking both morphine and substantial quantities of liquor. He denied being an alcoholic for many years but his life took on what he describes as a vicious cycle which he could not break. He had to steal to maintain his habits and so was arrested on numerous occasions. As a juvenile he was often sent to a Borstal but no help to break his habits was offered and he was all too soon back on the streets, whereupon 'It was only a matter of days before I had the needle back in my arm and the bottle to my lips.' Doug's graphic description is a sad indictment of a system designed to protect society and redirect the young offender. 'My life was like this,' he wrote. 'Mood, drink, habit, steal, busted.'

At 18 Doug attended an AA meeting where he heard God mentioned. An American missionary was explaining how God had helped him but he had nothing but a negative response from Doug.

'I interrupted the meeting,' he said, 'by saying, "I know I'm addicted to booze, but I don't want to get addicted to your God instead." ' He was invited to come back to the meeting one day when he wasn't drunk, but Doug was scared. He explained that it wasn't the mentioning of God that frightened him but rather the people, whom he dismissed at the time as 'out of their tiny minds'.

The truth was deeper.

'The people were happy,' he exclaimed, 'and that scared the pants off me.'

Doug's life went on its circular path after that meeting, but it is obvious that a tiny seed had been sown. He seemed to know from this point that he had no idea how to recover alone and that something inside now drove him to take drink and drugs and that that 'something' was not under his control. One day he overdosed and found himself not in a treatment centre but rather in Lewes Prison. He doesn't know to this day how it happened but he perceives it as not only remarkable that he survived the OD, but as 'cunning, baffling and powerful' that he came to meet the Christian community in Lewes jail.

More than that, of course, he met with Jesus. He was filled with the Holy Spirit and at once introduced us to his sparkling use of expressions: 'I feel like a pressure cooker,' he exclaimed, 'and I need to open the valve!'

His description of God's interest in him is also novel but significant: 'I often say God is a sucker for addicts. He knows we were born with faults and tries to give us every chance to get fixed up.' This is how he views God's grace and how he analyses his own conversion, for it was while he was in prison that he met with Jesus, repented from his past sins and chose to take a new direction in his life. It was so exciting to see this man's life change through the power of God because humanly speaking there was little real hope at all.

'I have replaced drink and drugs with God,' declared Doug, and this simple explanation certainly appears to have paid dividends. He is maintaining his faith in his London prison and we can but wonder at the simplicity of it all. Naturally he has lots to work out and through, and life will by no means be easy for one with such a past, but

Doug is amazingly sure that he now has a purpose in life and someone to help him too. What more can anyone want of life, we must ask? Doug wanted to offer one of his sayings to help any other people we might meet like him. Let's hope his desire comes true:

You don't believe in God you say?
There's nothing above a man?
Then how can a finger say to a thumb,
'I don't believe in a hand'?

It is not only inmates themselves who have been through despair, loneliness and pain. For many families the involvement of their sons in crime is a devastating experience which leaves them wondering where to turn and if anyone cares. Time after time we were to find that prisoners who found faith would have some relative or close friend who included them regularly in their prayer lists. Many were indeed as isolated and forgotten as they felt, but there were a good number who did have caring relatives but who had nevertheless gone wildly astray.

Some mothers and fathers would ring David when their sons entered Lewes and ask him to visit their offspring, often because they'd heard that inmates were turning to Christ. There were few things more rewarding than helping these earnest and faithful people. They were to discover that sometimes prison was not the total disaster they had anticipated but rather a catalyst to bring their wayward sons back to God.

JEREMIAH

Jeremiah met David in prison and was quite honest when asked if he wanted God to help him. 'All my family are evangelists,' he stated, although we believe he meant evangelicals.

Jeremiah had been adopted by a Christian family at a very young age and there had been high hopes for his development. All the prayers and care seemed to misfire, however, and Jeremiah proved to be a boy bent on trouble. We can only guess at the anguish and guilt that close family experienced over the years but we know they prayed and prayed for Jeremiah. They must have doubted they could help their adopted son as the years went by for he became involved in more and more dubious activities and petty crime. Where had they gone wrong? Was it their fault? Why did God not answer their prayers? Eventually the family despaired. They had done all in their power, they had prayed, they had sacrificed, but they had failed. Jeremiah had landed up in prison – Lewes Prison – and they felt they could support him no longer. Jeremiah had made his decision and they were no longer responsible for him.

God, however, had heard their pleas. In the still small hours of prayer they had received a response and God had not let Jeremiah go – far from it. Shocked by his own situation and the horrible consequences of his life style that he'd always believed he could avoid, Jeremiah was ready to respond to God. His family weren't contacting him very much – he felt alone and frightened and the very first time he was asked if he'd like to have God's help, he responded, 'Yes, please, I need God.'

David, of course, was unaware of Jeremiah's full background and was thrilled when he turned to God, and rejoiced as Jeremiah was filled with the Holy Spirit and his life changed ownership. After sharing some Bible passages with him he asked the penitent inmate, 'If your family are "evangelists" would you like to ring them up and tell them you've become a Christian?'

'Yes I would,' replied Jeremiah, 'but I'm no good on the phone. Would you do it for me?'

David was pleased to help for he realized the reaction at home would be positive, although he had no idea just how positive!

Jeremiah sat on one side of David's desk and held his hands close together. His cheerful face was tinged with nervousness as David dialled the number.

'Hello, is that Sylvia?' David asked as the phone was lifted up at the other end.

'Yes,' was the response.

'This is Lewes Prison,' continued David.

'Yes,' said Sylvia anxiously.

'This is the Chaplain at Lewes Prison,' smiled David, warming to his task.

'Yes,' was the by now very nervous response.

'It's about Jeremiah,' said David.

'Yes?' was the answer – the high-pitched voice very keen by now to know just why she was receiving this unsolicited call.

'Well – he's sitting here with me and wants to tell you he's just become a Christian . . . '

David waited for a reply – the expected excitement, a question, even disbelief – but instead there was a crack as the phone dropped followed by a moment's silence and then the distant shouting of an excited woman's voice as she ran about the house declaring in a loud voice, 'Jeremiah's become a Christian! Jeremiah's become a Christian!'

David grinned from ear to ear and turning to Jeremiah explained, 'I think she's gone to tell the family!'

Later that week Sylvia visited her new-born adopted son and checked in with David.

'We gave up when Jeremiah became a prisoner,' she said sadly. 'We just couldn't see how God could save him then. He'd just gone too far. How wrong we were. How wrong we were.' The happy lady just shook her head and held David's hand.

The years of prayer had been answered. She could now see that rainbow through the rain and she was thrilled to bits.

David rejoiced deeply and resolved to tell that story wherever he could to encourage those who long and pray for help in seemingly hopeless situations. The message was clear: 'Go on praying, God does and will answer – although often in very unexpected ways!'

Time after time David met young men who were in dire and obvious need. He wasn't the only person who greeted new inmates, but he met large numbers in the course of his daily duties. Some he approached, some requested to see him and still others he 'bumped into'. Only a very few reacted negatively to meeting a minister, most appearing to reach out to the 'man in the collar' as a friendly face in an alien environment. David always told a man about God's offer of help on the very first meeting and was seldom totally rebuffed. The early days of prison life rendered inmates very open to assistance as barriers were lowered, peers were an unknown quantity and the 'confidence of the street' was missing. David wished to be seen not only as a friend but as a source of help and in this he found the wearing of a clerical collar a huge advantage. This simple 'uniform' marked him out as different from all other civilians in the prison and seemed both to earn respect and ensure a calm meeting.

Occasionally, of course, this reaction was missing.

'Can't stand vicars,' said John.

David interrupted.

'I understand that,' he replied, keeping remarkably cool in the circumstances, 'but I've come to give you some good news today.' John was distracted enough to actually listen and did in fact respond positively to the Good News he was offered.

For the most part, however, inmates were immediately grateful for David's friendship and time.

The whole atmosphere of prison appeared to be opening people to the work of the Holy Spirit. Men who perhaps had never given God a thought or at least very little attention now seemed to be ready to face up to the serious issues of life. It was as if God was drawing people to Himself by using the most unfortunate circumstances they now found themselves in. It was very rare to find anyone who blamed God for his troubles, rather they seemed to be ready to accept responsibility and to seek help.

Graham told us how God used the prison regime to challenge his faith.

DIARY OF AN INMATE

Graham was one of our orderlies, and highly efficient. He knew all about electronic equipment, mikes, keyboards and the like and was a computer whizz kid if he were honest. He had travelled the world in his youth, working in the USA and Spain before settling in Britain as a production engineer. He built up his own company and filled in spare time being a DJ in London and Brighton. He married and had three children and although he never wished to elaborate he was in prison for abducting his own children and taking them with him to the South of France.

Vague belief had always been part of Graham's life, but it took prison to stir his beliefs into action. Such a bright go-getter type found prison a tremendous shock. From travelling the world, his life was now restricted to a meaningless repetitive series of daily events. He recorded this diary for us not to elicit undue sympathy but to reveal the true nature of a prison sentence. He felt he could be doing something more productive during his sentence and was thrilled to become orderly, first in the library and then in the chapel, so that his talents could be used for the benefit of others. He records his daily routine prior to his selection as orderly and it makes fairly grim reading. Of course it represents just one man's personal experience.

Graham uses the term 'peter' in this piece in order to indicate his cell. This is in common usage and indicates a connection with the imprisonment of Peter in the Acts of the Apostles. It is unlikely that most inmates understand the true origin of this word but it is regularly used just the same.

A DAY IN THE LIFE OF A PRISONER

0530 Wake up – for what reason I don't know, but since I've been here I wake up early and lie in bed as the day is breaking and the light starts to come in.

0550 Oh hell! a noisy screw (prison officer). Keys jangling across the landing. Click-bang-click-bang. Outside my door – click, on goes the light – bang. The flap in the door is lifted, privacy destroyed. 'I'm here,' I call out. Bang. The flap goes back down. Click-bang as he carries on along the landing. Even though fully awake, I still roll over and try to get another 40 winks.

0650 More keys! Doors being opened; the people going off to court today are being let out. Still I hang on to the last remnants of sleep. It's too much, too noisy.

0730 Out of bed. Have a wash, a shave – a rare occurrence as the prison-issue razors are worse than Jack the Ripper's, slashing your face to pieces. We all have more than a few days' growth because of the razors. My skin feels dry because of the soap and I have a 'No. 2' haircut because the prison-issue shampoo turns your hair to straw. I avoid the showers first thing in the morning for two reasons: firstly, not enough time and secondly, they're filthy.

0800 Hear voices outside, expect to be unlocked, but no, ten or fifteen minutes pass before we get unlocked.

0815 Screw walks down the landing unlocking doors. He gets to mine, flap's lifted, key goes into the hole and the door opens slightly. Time to watch your back. Plastic plate and bowl in hand, like a trained rat, I follow everyone else to the hotplate. The 'hotplate' is a real contra-diction in terms – everything that comes off it is luke warm. A marvellous selection. I offer up my bowl for a scoop of cornflakes. Walking down the line I pass on the warm soggy bread (they call it toast, anaemic as it is). I take the milk, realizing they can't really muck that up, and pass on the mixed-fruit jam to go on the 'toast'. Back to my peter (cell), sit down at my table and eat my cornflakes; it's a real shame that I have to look at my toilet bowl when I'm eating though. Still it's more hygienic than the tables they designate for us.

0825 Take my washing downstairs and queue up for clothing exchange. Ten minutes later I put my old kit in the bins provided. The CE screw says, 'What d'yer want?' 'Socks, boxers, tee shirts, track suit top and bottoms please.' I get handed a pile. Familiarity has taught me to check whatever I'm given. 'Give us another pair of boxers will you, these are small, I'm extra large, can I have a pair of bottoms that haven't got a large hole in the crutch and cigarette burns in them, and to be a real pain can I have a large tee shirt without holes, please?' I hand back what he's given me knowing that the person behind me will get that little lot. After acquiring a clean kit change, like a squirrel back to my peter to store it.

0840 'Holland, you going to the workshop or not?' 'Coming, guv.' 'Here now or bang-up for the morning.' 'I'm coming, guv.'

0845 Into the frazzle shop (workshop). Really exciting work here, sitting around at tables (four to a table) putting the foam pads on headphones for Virgin Airways. Still watching your back in case the idiots start throwing things. This is probably the most boring part of the day.

1055 'Excuse me, guv, can I go to exercise please?' 'No.' 'Oh come on, guv, I'm entitled to go.' 'No.' I see one of the other screws – he lets me out.

1100 Exercise – the highlight of my day. Walking in circles around a five-a-side pitch; watched by three monkeys (screws).

1145 Herded in like animals for lunch. Once inside the wing, it's all I can do to find a screw who isn't serving on the hotplate to unlock my door. Once unlocked, I am back in the queue, plastic plate in hand, queuing for lunch.

1155 I make the warmplate – no choice now, however, beefburger (anaemic), chips and beans. Take this upstairs to my peter, dump it on my table, grab my flask to get some hot water to make tea.

1200 'All done Holland?' 'Yes thanks, guv.' Bang, the door slams, I'm locked in again. I start to eat my meal, the chips are OK, the beans and burger aren't. I eat the chips, the rest goes down the toilet, I avoid the middle man – me. On my table is a letter from my wife and daughter. I read it, it brings a lump to my throat. My daughter tells me she loves me, misses me and wants to know when I'm coming home. My wife says pretty much the same. I look at one of their photos and feel very morose. I snap out of it by making myself a cup of tea. I then realize it will be ten days till I see them again (visits once per fortnight). I read a little of my book.

1345 Door gets unlocked; I hear 'Workshops' called. Like a sheep I follow the crowd. Exactly the same in the afternoon. Foam pads on headphones.

1545 Returned to the wing; struggle to get door unlocked. Get flask of hot water for tea.

1600 Locked in again. Write a letter back to the wife. Make tea and listen to radio.

1610 Oh no. The door's being unlocked. Two screws standing there. 'Spin, Holland.' Off come my tee shirt, trousers and pants. 'Turn around – bend over.' They're checking for drugs. I get my clothes back on and strip my bedclothes off, they're checked. I then go outside with one screw while the other one tries his hardest to find drugs or illegal items. I know he won't but in my mind I'm worried. Forty minutes it takes to spin my peter, everything I've got is left in an unceremonious heap on my bed. It takes hours to put everything back how I had it before. 'You're lucky this time, Holland.' Lucky, I thought, I don't even smoke, I thought. The door locks again, so I set about clearing up.

1705 The door opens again. 'Tea,' I hear. I hunt for my plastics and again, like a trained animal, go in search of food. Ten minutes queuing at the hotplate, I'm faced with a dilemma: the main course, chicken, or breaded plaice, the healthy option is tuna and salad roll. Very nice I hear you say. I don't eat chicken or fish (it's on my medical records). I tell the screws that, but am told that I'm not a vegetarian so I can't have the veggy choice. So no dinner for me. Bread and butter pudding and custard for afters – oh well, I won't go hungry. Back to my peter to eat it. Eat it, slam my door behind me.

1730 The door to the TV lounge opens, got to rush in to get a good seat.

1745 The video starts.

1820 The video finishes, everyone piles out of the TV lounge. I hang around on the twos talking to people.

1840 'Last call for hot water,' I hear, usual palaver to get door unlocked to get flask.

1900 Queue for the phone – missed it – the phone barons Ray and Gobby have beaten me to it. I wait and wait and wait.

1915 Finally get on the phone, speak to my wife and daughter, tell them I love them and ask them what they've been doing. 'Oi, you gonna be long, mate?' I hear in the background.

2000 Twos, threes and fours all away. That's it for the evening, I go into my peter, the door slams behind me. I can finally relax. I do 40 minutes of exercise, finish off any letters I'm writing, make a cup of tea and drink it, read a little bit from my Bible and a little bit from my ordinary reading book. It's now 8.50 p.m. At 9 p.m. the night screw comes around and checks we're all here. That's it then till 6 a.m. By 10 p.m. I've had it for the day. While I'm lying on my bed I look at the photos of my wife and my kids and blow them a kiss each. I say a special goodnight to my little one, Leanne, and then get up, turn the light off, get undressed and into bed, mentally crossing another day off my sentence. Only another 116 days to go.

1230 I'm woken by some idiot on the wing playing jungle music, I roll over, pull my blanket over my head and go back off to sleep.

Graham found out what it was like to be an inmate in prison and finding a real faith, went on not only to serve God in prison but to determine that he would go on with Him on release. The shock of his imprisonment led to a new freedom he had never anticipated.

The walls of a prison may seem the end of all hope for some but they represent no real barrier to the power of God and in fact may actually prove to be part of the very means God uses to bring His wayward children to Himself. That awful initiation into the life of the prison that all the new inmates must pass through can yet be the gateway to a more significant initiation – that of entry to the Kingdom of God itself. We all need to pray that yet more prisoners will find true faith in prison, and that they will give to God the life they do indeed owe Him and discover for themselves the love that will not let them go.

CHAPTER 3

✳

Have you Heard the One About the Angel and the Priest?

As part of a Gospel presentation at the prison the speaker once used a simple visual aid. It consisted of a small piece of card with a large 'X' on it, which the speaker held up to the audience. 'What does this mean to you?' he asked. His interested audience sat largely silent, realizing, of course, that the question was actually rhetorical. They knew the man would supply further information and so he did. 'Does it mean: 1. a sign of love at the bottom of a letter or 2. I got something wrong or even 3. a way to cast my vote?'

Keith was warming to his theme as he saw all the inmates closely following his line of reasoning. It was only a moment until he could explain a far more important meaning for that cross – because of course his talk was planned to bring the message of the cross of Christ to those inmates. Keith was a regular speaker and was quietly confident that the message would be meaningful.

'Well,' he continued, 'I wonder what this cross means to you?'

He paused for effect; but even he was totally taken by surprise when a hand was raised and a clear, cheerful voice declared, 'That's how I sign my name.'

The speaker halted as he realized not only that his flow had been interrupted but that also the heckler had a valid point, for many of the inmates did find writing and reading a great problem and they did sign their name in just the way that had been suggested. The talk then returned to its prepared path and duly reached its close. The service had been meaningful, there can be no doubt, but it was important in another way since it introduced us to a prisoner called Peter David Angel.

DAVID

Peter Angel preferred to be known as David and was a splendid character. He spoke in a loud, cheerful voice and seemed full of vigour. He laughed often and openly, revealing a bright spirit undaunted by the catalogue of problems he no doubtedly had. This bright personality sometimes seemed out of place in a prison full of the miserable, depressed and guilty, but it was refreshing nonetheless and certainly did not mean that he could not face up to the seriousness of life itself. He was just an extrovert and we thoroughly warmed to him.

David Angel was a wonderful example to us of how God could reach people in spite of their lack of literacy skills. All our own church experience was word-oriented. You have to be able to read to both understand and move on in the Christian life. Hymns, services, Bible studies, even notice sheets all assume a high level of reading ability. Christian literature is aimed at either educated adults or children, those with poor literacy abilities being scarcely considered. But in spite of our struggle to find ways of helping the illiterate, and the churches' notion of the necessity of education, God chose to speak to common uneducated men and bring them to Himself. I seem to remember that an accusation of a lack of education was aimed at the first followers of Jesus but God called and used them just the same.

Perhaps some ordinary people are failing to fill our pews for similar reasons, and it's no use pointing the finger at one denomination or another for we are all guilty of failing to make the Gospel accessible to all. Some of us use a complicated and diverse literacy and some use a vast array of ever-changing worship songs thrown carelessly onto a hard-to-see projector screen, but whatever our personal style we can easily confuse and embarrass any visitor who crosses our church door. I wonder just how at home David Peter Angel would be in either your church or mine?

David's home had been in Horsham in West Sussex where his father had been a farmer. He lived a varied life but was drawn to crime inexorably as he was introduced to the temptation and pull of drugs. He mixed with those who shared this risky habit but had just managed to steer clear of the law until one fateful day.

With the benefit of hindsight he was to learn to see his arrest as a beneficial event, as he believed he would have killed himself with his ever deepening drug-taking, but at the time he was frustrated with his own stupidity. He'd had an acrimonious break-up with his wife and in a blaze of fury he'd resolved to break into her house.

Because he was so high on drugs and was unaware of reality in any meaningful sense he had failed to use the normal levels of what he called his 'professionalism.'

He recalled, 'I just picked up a paving slab, put it through the front window and climbed in.' 'Drugs,' he continued, 'make you do stupid things like that.'

His capture and inevitable incarceration turned his life upside down, for he could not believe he had ended up behind those forbidding bars with his very valuable freedom so sharply curtailed.

David Angel had dabbled in religion previously. He had journeyed to Thailand using money he'd 'come across'. 'Thieving money,' he confessed, 'dodgy money.' Once there he'd been attracted to the mysterious and spiritual elements of the life style. There he'd met a Zen monk begging in the street who convinced him not to worry about materialism but to follow the six paths of Buddha. David, however, was not really so interested in the aesthetic life offered by the religion, but rather in the hope it brought for continuation after death.

'What interested me was this reincarnation business,' he cheerfully related. 'One doesn't like to think of oneself as mortal – you know – at the end of this life – dying.' He then laughed nervously.

This great question, over which all the famous philosophers have struggled down the ages, had touched this man, too, and he was drawn to a religion that offered him the chance of a new life. He was assured that reincarnation occurred within the same chain of DNA so that he would not return as a bird or butterfly but rather as a further member of his own family line – his own great grandson for example.

'I thought I'd give it a go,' he stated with his usual grin. Obviously this system of beliefs held out a hope for David, although it appears to have been a slender one.

His tenuous faith, however, had failed to have any practical effect on his everyday life. Materialism still had a sound grasp of him and he was granted no power to fight against his desires for drugs. His inner resources were not sufficient to take on such a challenge. David Angel met David the Chaplain when he was at a very low ebb. He wanted to take a different course and had wandered up to the chapel one Sunday to see what was going on there. My David had no idea that he'd had any interest in religious matters before and met him as he would any other inmate who entered that particular door. He was welcomed in and he sat with the other inmates patiently awaiting the start of the service. The talk about the meaning of the cross interested David and he made his vocal contributions loudly and clearly as he was thoroughly involved with the proceedings.

Later he chose to talk to David about God and went on to pray and receive the laying on of hands. 'I found out,' he declared positively, 'that you don't have to die to be born again.'

'It was very strange,' he went on. 'I was glowing rather than anything else. I was told later I was filled with the Holy Spirit and I would say that after that I did not want any more drugs again.'

David Angel was surprised at his new attitude to drugs because although he desperately wanted to give up taking them, and had done so for a long time, he knew the power that these substances held over those who took them.

'One who has taken drugs,' he said, 'knows what you would do to get drugs. I wouldn't kill or mug an old person but I felt enough pull to go out and rob to get them.' Here he laughed his nervous, vivacious laugh and continued his seemingly happy-go-lucky tale as if he were explaining to you just 'how it is' or as if he were having a chinwag with the lads down the pub on a Friday night.

David Angel's personality had not been removed by his conversion but rather transformed, redeemed and renewed. He had not become a sombre intellectual bewailing the evil pull of drug-taking, far from it – no – he just spoke as he'd always done in his chirpy style; but of course his actual message was now quite serious.

'I was on Class B drugs mainly,' he confided. 'Amphetamines. I only did a few Class A drugs – cocaine, heroin, diamorphine.' He went on to educate his listener with astonishing clarity, honesty and obvious innocence as to the effect his knowledge would have on a naive, long-standing, middle-class Christian.

'The difference is quite clear. Most B drugs are the sort you put up the nose – a daily powder. Class

A drugs are mainly liquid, you need a syringe for those.'

David Angel was not the only educator we met who would inform us about various aspects of drug-taking, but he was certainly one of the most blunt!

After David met with Jesus he requested a Bible for he knew that others who'd come to chapel had received one.

'How will you use it, David?' asked the chaplain; 'I know you can't read it properly.'

'Don't worry,' Angel assured him. 'I really want it. I'll manage.'

Sure enough David did manage, although not quite in the manner one might expect. He was visited a few days later and asked how he was getting on.

'Oh,' he said, 'I get my cellmate to read me a Bible story each night.'

'Well, that's remarkable,' said David the Chaplain. 'Just how do you do that? Is he interested in Christian things too?'

'Well, I just threaten to beat him up if he doesn't,' joked David Angel and burst into a loud guffaw, shaking his shoulders in a childlike reaction.

'Well, I guess you're still learning,' replied David. 'You can't change overnight.' And with that he grinned too, appreciating the amusing nature of the conversation.

In fact the tale turned out very well indeed because this apparent victim of enforced Bible reading was to become a Christian himself a few days later and not really out of fear. He noticed an immediate change in Angel's life and wanted whatever he had experienced for himself. And his name? Well, it was Mark Priest; and thus it was that a priest and an angel met God in Lewes Prison and began a new life style together.

When Angel recalled the story he hesitated and explained he was 'sort of involved in a friend of mine becoming a Christian.' For once his jocular style was curtailed as if he really did appreciate the importance of what he'd done for Mark.

He was also to bring a chap called Ivan to Christ and his explanation was quite simple. 'They saw a change in me. In fact it was phenomenal. So they wanted to have a go themselves and they became Christians as well.'

David was clearly thrilled by his ability to share his faith but he was also able to handle other people's different reactions well.

'Fifteen per cent say what a great change I've had, twenty-five per cent say I'm mad; and another lot say, "Here, what's that all about?"'

David's summary of the situation was just as matter-of-fact. 'But I don't mind, I want to be a missionary when I get out, I want to spread the word about Jesus Christ.' Then, growing more serious, he added, 'Whether they'll take me on or not I don't know, but I guess I'll still go around anyway and just tell the people I come across that if they don't turn their lives around, then they'll be very sorry about it later on.'

Although David's attitude to evangelism might seem simplistic, his desire was very real. He was quite determined to spread the news that had offered him hope where there had been none before. He did not wish to return to crime and after his marriage break-up felt he was now free to travel if he so wished.

'I won't have much money,' he confided, 'but by hook and *not* by crook I'm going to be a missionary I assure you.'

Because of previous problems David Angel spent much of his remaining time in prison in the Segregation Unit away from Sunday fellowship. He was visited by church members and other helpers. His problems with reading didn't help but he was always resourceful. He wrote to the judge dealing with his case – at least, he convinced some-one else to write for him. In it he confessed to his part in a burglary and declared he could no longer lie in front of God. I don't believe he thought this would help him out when the time came for sentencing, but it did help his own peace of mind considerably.

At the bottom of the letter appeared a cross, to signify his name, just as he'd mentioned at that chapel service before his conversion. At the top of the letter he drew a small childlike figure with a grinning face and an impish expression. 'That's to show the judge just how happy I am,' David declared in his straightforward manner, 'now I've become a Christian!'

David Angel was to find taped versions of the Bible very helpful over the following months and expressed his appreciation of this ministry in the terms of a former drug user. 'I get a fix,' he stated, 'like a Jesus fix. Yeah, it really is.' He laughed cheer-fully as he appreciated his own comparison.

'It gives me a daily rush, you know,' he continued in the same vein, for a 'rush' is the description a drug user employs to describe the first effect of an illegal substance on the body.

'I like hearing the Bible through the headphones,' he continued, and then, unable to contain his excitement, 'I've even worn my batteries out. But I got given some more today; I didn't even ask for them. God knew I needed them and I got them. It was a little miracle. Like he knew before I did – yeah.'

David's little miracle meant a lot to him although it may seem strange to hear God's provision being described in this way and the practice of a 'quiet time' being compared to a fix of drugs but we should not be surprised. Jesus has a way of lifting up the ordinary, our own experiences and the mundane, transforming them by his presence and redeeming them for his own purposes. All our expressions of faith are inadequate in explaining the reality of God in our lives and as long as they are used in genuine faith they must surely be equally valid.

David and I soon began to search every Christian bookshop we knew to track down materials for those with limited education. It proved a very difficult task indeed. We found books for adults, lots of them in fact, and many for brand-new Christians. We also found lots of children's books even for those children with only prereading skills. However we found nothing for adults with lower than average reading abilities. Similarly we found nothing even for those inmates who can read fluently, on subjects such as drink, drugs and pornography which, if one pauses to think for a moment, have often been the driving factors in their lives. Just what is the Christian view on these things and why?

One inmate was shocked to find he shouldn't have pornography in his cell – he didn't realize it wasn't the 'done thing' in Christian circles. Such was the moral vacuum in which we worked. David developed a policy of marginalizing such issues. It was no good going in too heavy-handed because there were just too many areas to cover. Once he entered a cell covered with unsuitable pictures. 'Which one is your wife?' he queried. The following day all the pictures had gone.

We began to plan around the fact that literature was scarce and that inmates often didn't find it useful anyway. We discovered the Bible Society's set of tapes which dramatize the text so that people can listen to rather than read the Bible. Called Faith by Hearing, we found them to be really inspirational, and were thrilled when we had a large quantity donated by the Bible Society, since each set was worth £25. We began to provide converts with tapes, a Walkman and a book called *Abundant Life* which leads new converts through the main themes of Scripture in a very basic 'fill-in-the-gaps' style of study. We realized, too, that tapes of all kinds were our greatest need, along with some books of course which were relevant to prisoner's needs. So began our visits to every church and group that would welcome us. David spoke about the work in the prison and we requested a donation to help cover the cost of the tapes, Walkmans and books together with some expenses to pay for a little secretarial help for David's ever-growing correspondence. Every penny we spent had to be raised in this way because as David always used to joke, 'We could have a collection, but it's doubtful we'd get any money back.'

The response was as varied as the places we visited but there is no doubt that those who helped us were giving enormous encouragement and benefit to those men who received a Walkman or tape or who where connected with a church on release because of the new secretary's time.

It might be thought that these problems of illiteracy and ignorance are unique to a prison environment but I doubt it. There are large parts of society where these, together with poverty, are dominant factors in people's lives. It was recently researched that one in three males under 25 have a criminal record so if our men were representative there are a lot of people in our country who have such difficulties. It could be good if Christian literature providers could fully grasp this nettle and if all of us could realize the true levels of need. Tracts for evangelism especially need to be extraordinarily simple and must assume almost no knowledge of the things of God. Of course the good news is that we found most of these men so ready to respond to the Good News. Indeed it was almost as if they were saying, 'Why ever didn't you come before? I've been waiting for you all along.'

David Angel was to be greatly helped, however, by someone else before he left for another prison.

That person had come a very long way to help David and also many others. He arrived as the result of much prayer and his own story is truly remarkable in many ways, but as far as Lewes was concerned he was a true 'Godsend' because he was able to help those who like David signed their name with a cross and who found the problems of illiteracy a barrier to spiritual growth. We will hear more about him later.

*

CHAPTER 4

Fishers of Men

New Christians were being added to the wings of the prison almost daily. Each night I would look forward to hearing David recall the day's adventures, much as you would anticipate the next episode of a favourite soap opera, although of course in our case the story lines were true. It was very exciting to hear how this inmate had been converted or that inmate had been challenged to change his life. The lives of hitherto dangerous men were being transformed into ones which were responsive and useful to God. We also found that it was these individual stories of changed men that so encouraged outside Christians. God was really working and people began to be inspired to be bolder themselves in preaching the Gospel. People are not all atheists or antagonistic to the things of God. Many were just waiting for someone to share the Good News with them. It was great to hear some good news about Christianity for a change.

Gradually it became quite obvious that David was by no means working alone. The inmates themselves, having experienced the presence of

God, showed themselves more than keen to pass on the Good News. Individuals brought their cell-mates to chapel groups and prayed in cells, so it became important to encourage these believers in their new-found roles as fishers of men. Of course they often wanted, and expected, instant results, and were quite hard on themselves about their poor 'conversion rates'. David eventually realized that some felt they should be able to bring everyone they met to Christ, and felt quite ashamed of the half-hearted efforts of his own early days of commitment. One of our first highly dedicated 'missioners' was Howard, and his story reveals how God is no respecter of certain life styles or of education. He will take just whom He chooses to fulfil His purposes, and use perhaps the most unusual men to bring others to Himself.

HOWARD

Howard, or Big Aitch as he liked to be known, was born in Rye, a beautiful coastal town on the eastern edge of East Sussex. His parents owned a pub and although they loved him dearly they were so busy that Howard found he had plenty of free time on his hands. He would wander down to the idyllic quayside and gaze at the boats bobbing on the water. To him that far distant shore of France was a tantalizing glimpse of adventure and opportunity, which he was sure lay on the other side of the water. As he sat and dreamed of faraway places he developed a love of sea, boats and the spirit of adventure.

He was only 14 when he and a friend first ran away. They stole a car and took it to France where they travelled the long journey via Paris and Lyon to the hot south coast. From there they journeyed to Italy in a stolen boat and checked out the tempting casinos they found there. For some reason they disliked the beaches which were full of boulders and, driven on by similar whims, they returned to France on a stolen motorcycle. At some point they were arrested but regained their freedom through fast talking and eventually stole a rubber dinghy in which they ended their round trip at the harbour in Rye.

'Not bad for fourteen,' Howard told me when he recalled the tale.

Howard was to grow to see that many of the things he had done in his life were wrong, but at the time he sought only to satiate his spirit of adventure, which he said drove his whole life. 'I wish the people who deal with young offenders would realize,' he told me thoughtfully, 'that crime offers young people many of the things they want – excitement, adventure, risk, danger and even money at the end of it for some. Recapturing their energies is the only way to satisfy their drives.' Perhaps we should consider his opinion carefully!

So Howard grew up into a strong, brave man, but always one with a gentle manner and spirit. He joined the fishing fleet and realized his boyhood ambition of sailing round the globe, although crime was always part of Howard's world. He smuggled illegal immigrants into Britain and when the trail got closer he ran away to sea. In 1970 he was in the

West Indies when a fearsome hurricane struck his inadequate vessel. By that time he was an experienced sailor and he knew the drill. He lightened his load, tied down everything he could and fought with all his strength against the elements. After a mammoth struggle it became obvious that Howard was fighting a losing battle. He could no longer wrestle with the storm and he knew the boat was breaking up. Downstairs in the tiny, wet cabin he knelt down and prayed to God. It was not the first occasion that he'd prayed, for he says that he had an awareness of the reality of God from his earliest days. 'Help me, God, because I don't know what to do. I know I'm dying.' Howard offered his simple prayer to God and sat back on his heels. Outside the storm raged and the towering waves crashed across the boat, which was tossed about like a child's paper craft in a swiftly running stream. He had written a last sad note to his mother for he felt he could not die without saying sorry. So certain was he that his end was approaching that he wrapped the letter in a plastic bag and pushed it securely into the top of his trousers. When his body was found, he thought, they would discover the note and at least he would have been able to make peace with his long-suffering mum. He then describes an amazing thing, for amidst that roaring storm and with little hope left he lay quietly down and fell asleep. When he woke it was morning. The storm had abated, the waves had calmed and Howard's little boat was drifting safely across the ocean. He didn't know what to feel. He just could not believe he was still alive. His hand slowly fingered the small plastic bag that held his last note to his mother and he whispered a quiet word of thanks that he would now be able to tell his own story to his mum back in Sussex.

Howard's adventurous life style did not end there, however. He tells how unfortunately he soon forgot God even though he believed it was He who had saved him. Now he sees this dramatic event as God's attempt at reaching him for Himself, but Howard was not ready to submit his life fully to God.

He then spent two years in Brazil where he lived with five others in the jungle in a spirit of comradeship and adventure. When he became involved in crime he and his friends were sent to a penal colony, but they escaped in a stolen plane and eventually returned to England's shores; his wanderlust at least temporarily satisfied.

Howard settled in the South and gained his skipper's ticket. He married, had a child and had the opportunity to live a stable life, but it was not to be. He became involved in smuggling again and both he and his wife started taking heroin.

'It was exactly what I wanted,' he confided. 'I was always in trouble and this offered an escape.'

His addiction resulted in him losing all he had and he was sent to prison for stealing to feed his habit. After two years he was desperate to break the addiction, for he realized 'I was no longer the same person.' His wife could not join him in this attempt to stop taking drugs and, although he said he never fell out of love with her, they went their separate ways.

Howard's eventful life now went through a long period when he was in and out of prison for dealing in stolen goods. He had set up in a small antiques business which he enjoyed and learned a great deal about. 'But being keen and greedy I dealt with stolen items,' he confessed.

Dealing in drugs was soon back on the agenda too, and eventually he was hounded by both the police and his own feelings. 'I hated what I had got and hated what I hadn't got,' he recalled. So it was that Howard Coster wound up in a Lewes Prison cell 'all on my own and still looking for love'.

He felt full of anger and a desire to seek revenge but God had His hand on Howard and he was selected to be the new chapel orderly. An orderly is in a position of responsibility in the prison. It means taking special care of a particular area, cleaning, organizing and tidying up. It usually brings a certain level of freedom to come and go to that area and because of that the jobs are sought after. However, 'no one,' reported Howard, 'is too keen to be chapel orderly. It's usually a job for wimps.'

Howard was different. He had been a chapel orderly before when he had been in Lewes and knew it was a job he liked. He soon realized, nevertheless, that the chapel had changed since his last stay in prison. It was so different.

'It was lively and exciting,' he explained. 'Real people from outside were coming in to talk to you. They had no ulterior motives either.' Howard saw Terry Tully there, a faithful helper from Prison Fellowship, who explained the Gospel message by means of paintings created during a service. He also saw other faces from Prison Fellowship,

YWAM, local churches and other visitors. All of these people, he realized, were coming in for the sake of the prisoners and he was greatly pleased. However, it was something in particular that moved Howard the most, and it illustrates how we can never pin God down in terms of just how He will speak to people or bring them to Himself. Several of the visitors were accustomed to worshipping in churches where they raise their hands in adoration during hymn singing. For Christians it is often the normal practice; no one is surprised, no one feels it's of special significance, but Howard was surprised and for him it had great significance. Whilst we might be a little concerned in case it put inmates off, he thought it was amazing. He told me, 'I saw visitors with their hands up, being counted for God, saying "I'm a Christian." Everyone could *see* them holding their hands up and I couldn't sing as my eyes filled with water.' Howard's voice slowed down as if he were right there remembering his feelings.

'I wanted to hold my hand up,' he continued. 'Oh God I wanted to hold my hand up and say I believed in God. I got so emotional when I realized I couldn't.'

So Howard swallowed hard instead and did not let people see the tears in his eyes. 'I'd go back to my cell,' he confessed, 'and I'd pray and pray for the courage to be a Christian – to be able to stand up and say I'm a Christian and to put my hand up too.'

So Howard was both delighted and confused at being chapel orderly again; he was pleased with the job and the excitement of the place but frustrated at his self-perceived inadequacy to be part of what was going on. 'It was,' he said, 'pretty tricky as chaplain's orderly, left alone – just me and God – wow!'

Howard began to realize over the weeks that followed that something significant was happening to him. He had no knowledge, of course, that he was surrounded by our prayers at this time or that Christians had spotted his tears during the services.

'Something's happening to Howard,' Liz, a young Christian friend, had explained. 'He's being moved by the services, I'm sure.'

Inside Howard there was a confrontation going on. 'I thought I'd always had a relationship with God,' said Howard. 'I guess ... well I did – but I'd asked God for credit really and he'd given it to me but I'd just never bothered to pay it back.'

Aitch offered an explanation of just how he'd obtained this startling and profound imagery. He had had a loan from a bank which somehow he'd never paid back many years previously and he felt his relationship with God was just like that unpaid loan. 'Except,' he said, 'this is different, because I want to pay this particular loan back to God.'

Howard played down what happened next, for his repentance was no Damascus road experience as far as he was concerned. His whole life had been leading to this point and he was adamant that his path to deep faith had been very long indeed. David prayed with big Aitch one day. They talked for a while and Howard said, 'I knew you'd come to get me.'

David grinned for they both knew it was time for Howard to take a positive change of direction. He confessed his past right there in the chapel and felt the power of God sweep through his body as he was filled with God's Holy Spirit. Months later he was to ask others if they too 'felt a rush' as they met with God through prayer. As has been said, it's a term used for the feeling that a drug user first experiences and eventually craves when he takes drugs. The inmates understand the term and agree the comparison, although, of course, they soon learn that the rush of God's Holy Spirit is in reality totally unlike any other drug for it brings with it no evil side effects, desperate addictions or cold turkey. 'Wow, that's better than crack!' exclaimed one inmate. 'That's better than any drug,' said another. 'Can you give my cellmate some of that? What am I on?' asked another. 'Can I have that twilight zone experience?' one even asked.

Howard's turning point was decisive. 'Now I know I like this,' he said definitely. 'I want to be a Christian. I want to learn something new every day. Whenever I mess up I can go to God now. I'm a Christian now.'

Howard then began to work out his new life in the prison context. He knew it meant helping people practically and helping them to come to Christ too.

'I want to be a good example,' he said. 'I want people to say, if he's not afraid to be called a Christian why should I be afraid either?' He was aware of what he called 'a dumb stigma' attached to Christianity. He didn't like using the word Christian really because of the misconceptions it conjured up.

'People don't know – they think Christians are Bible bashers – Jesus freaks or wimps,' Aitch explained to me one day. 'But it's not like that. Being a Christian is saying sorry to God – I messed up, but I want to change. It's turning around and changing – not being so selfish anymore.'

Howard enjoyed his new Christian confidence. He told me how he would sit in the chapel or in his cell and talk to God. 'I talk to Him – He listens to me and He answers – He talks to me back. I just like the way it makes me feel.'

I often listened to this tall powerful man who had come into our lives through our work in the prison. He had an amazing way of cutting through experience to pinpoint reality. His imagery was startling, his understanding enlightening. Just why did I find his thoughts so refreshing and why did they fill me with such hope? Was it because he was stripping back years of pointless discussions and frustrated feelings or self-justification that years in Church life can produce and revealing those simple Gospel truths that totally revolutionized the world in the first century? If God was not there for Howard then just who could He be there for?

Howard meantime was worried. 'I haven't had the courage to put my hand up yet and say I'm a Christian,' he confided.

He had no need to worry, however, for he explained how he was learning to say he was a Christian on the wing. 'I tell them I find it easy to believe when they laugh at me,' he said. 'God loves me, I tell them. He doesn't have to tell me, I know it. It's a fact that's all.'

He went on to explain how he tried to help the other prisoners on his section of the jail. 'I listen to them,' he said thoughtfully. 'I listen and then I tell them, "You need Christ in your life too," that's what I tell people.' His voice grew serious and definite. 'Because He's certainly made my life different, I assure you.'

KENNY

One day Howard told me about someone he knew well and introduced us. Kenny shook my hand at the chapel door. 'Hello, Kenny,' I said, 'I've been hearing all about you.' Kenny's face moved into a wide impish grin and I looked with close interest at the short, slight man who greeted me in return, for I knew that his appearance was very deceptive. This friendly, open-faced 34-year-old man that stood before me had a long history of violent crime behind him. At 34 he knew nothing but criminal behaviour and aggression. Kenny had been interviewed on tape by Howard in the chapel one afternoon and he was pleased to recount the story of his arrival at Lewes. The openness of his comments and the frankness of his expression were as refreshing as they were real and one may only wonder at the experiences that this man has been granted to go through.

'I went through my life blindly committing violence,' Kenny said. 'I was unaware of my victims.'

'Were you a hard man locally, Kenny?' questioned Howard on the tape.

'Well, yes – I had a reputation to maintain – so I used to maintain it, if you know what I mean,'

replied Kenny in a matter-of-fact way. He'd served
a series of sentences for his various offences and
this particular time was due to serve four years.

'I know this is only the beginning of the
sentence,' Kenny remarked, 'but things have
happened here and it doesn't seem so bad.'

Kenny had been moved from Lewes on remand
to Camp Hill on the Isle of Wight when convicted.
He had hated it there, not because of the conditions
or other inmates but because he could not receive
any visits from his wife and children. Being taken
from his local area was very threatening to Kenny
and he recalls how in desperation he began to pray
for the first time.

'I was so low down,' confessed Kenny, 'there was
nothing else I could do, but pray and hope something would happen.'

Kenny sees what happened next as the answer to
his prayer of despair. Like Howard before him it
was desperation that drove him to seek God and it
was at that point of reaching the end of himself that
God broke into his life.

A week and a half later he was back in Lewes and
was due to attend court once more. Many inmates
make different appearances over various offences
and they go to court several times. Kenny believed
his deep prayer had been answered and he saw the
events of the next night as a test of his new belief in
God. He was placed in a cell in Hastings where he
lay down to sleep the hours away before his court
appearance the following day. As he unwrapped
his blanket he made a startling discovery for out
fell a 5¼ inch carving knife. He was faced with an

opportunity for escape – an apparent way out of his sentence – a shiny silver tempting means of escape.

'Cor, I wanted to escape all right,' said Kenny seriously. He looked round the cramped miserable cell and was sorely tempted.

'You would have used the knife to escape then?' questioned Howard.

'As a rule, yeah!' responded Kenny briefly. 'A blade was my favourite weapon.'

'That gave you a chance then, Kenny?' continued Howard.

Kenny paused momentarily.

'I decided to hand the knife back,' he said. Kenny was true to his decision. He handed that knife and its opportunity to escape in to the officers on duty. As a result of the report on the affair, Kenny was given a commendation and it no doubt meant that his request to remain near his family in Lewes was looked on favourably, but Kenny sees another element to the story.

'God was testing my strength. I was given a chance. I know the screws would have let me go if I'd have used it, I turned the other cheek so to speak. I made the right decision,' he said proudly.

A few days after his arrival at Lewes, David met him properly in his cell.

'Do you want to be a Christian?' David asked.

'Yeah I do,' replied Kenny as he responded to the way he felt God had already been working in his life.

When David prayed with him Kenny reports, 'I started to cry – which I haven't done for over ten years. I didn't even cry at my son's funeral.' At this point Kenny gave a nervous cough as if he were finding that particular incident hard to recall. 'But,' he continued, 'I just felt I was being cleansed by my tears and the words Dave said strengthened me to believe.'

Kenny never filled us in about the death of his son, but it was obviously a huge tragedy in his life. In spite of his catalogue of offences, Kenny loved his family life and always expressed deep concern for all his relatives.

Kenny went on to explain how he believed his new Christian life would affect his life in prison. He now read the Bible every day and had a special regard for the Old Testament. 'I must also be a good prisoner – a model prisoner,' he said, 'and when I'm out I'll have a new aim and goal and someone to guide me.'

Howard dug deeper: 'What frightens people, Kenny, about Christianity do you think? It's one of the stand-off subjects, isn't it?'

Kenny's brief response has as valuable an insight as the content of some fairly substantial books on the subject of evangelism. 'Well, it's the reality that Christ and God may exist,' stated Kenny definitely. 'I suppose if they've lived a bad life they find it difficult to follow. Show me a miracle, they say, and then I'll believe it – but it's not really like that.'

I suspect he was beginning to look at his own former position and the truth that many people find it easier to avoid God or say he doesn't exist because if they did believe they'd have to do something about it.

'But it worked like that for you didn't it?' asked Howard.

'Well,' replied Kenny 'something did happen to me but you have to believe or nothing will happen. I believed God would answer my prayers.'

'Will you give up if something goes wrong?' continued Howard.

'I haven't given up yet. My wife finds it hard to believe. I guess my friends and the police will be cynical, but that's part of being a Christian isn't it?'

'Does your wife think you're going through a phase?'

'Well she'll have to believe it in the end,' answered an optimistic Kenny, 'as I'm going to keep it up!'

Kenny was relieved that he could see big Aitch ending the interview.

'I've been given a new life and a new chance,' Kenny offered enthusiastically.

'Through Christianity, Kenny?'

Kenny's answer was strong and sure, 'Yeah!' he replied.

KEITH

Kenny had known Aitch for many years and so Howard was pleased when he joined his new Christian family, but he was by no means alone for our Aitch was always at work helping men to find Christ and to live out their new Christian lives. Indeed we grew to trust Howard's judgement so much that he became part of our team, privy to prayer lists and discussions about the work. The men trusted him, too, and this big strong fisherman was captured for Jesus in such a way that he began to walk in the footsteps of those first fishers of men, the disciples. He reminded me of Andrew who, having found the master, brought his brother to Him straightaway so that he could change his life's direction.

Keith was nicknamed The Drain because he talked so much and he too was befriended by Aitch. Up to the age of eleven he had been a happy churchgoing young lad who liked to help out the old folk who came to services. In his twelfth year, however, he described how his normal life was taken away when he was sexually assaulted by a family friend. He said little about this event except that it changed his life for ever. He began to get into trouble and moved through stays in approved schools to sentences in prison. So the path of Keith's life was set and he found it impossible to break the cycle of crime and prison.

One day he woke up in a cell and he couldn't remember how he got there. Always prone to drinking too much, this situation had happened before so Keith felt confident to ask, 'Am I here for being drunk and disorderly?'

The officer whom he had asked looked grim. 'No,' he said simply. To Keith's horror he had been arrested for being in a fight and for killing someone. He was stunned because he had no recollection whatsoever of this tragic event. His drunkenness had led to this appalling situation and now he himself no longer wished to live. He would have to face a judge for taking away someone's precious life, not out of planned spite but out of sheer stupidity. It was only at this point, he told us, that he began to look at his own life. He too could go no further down for he was already at the bottom.

The judge gave him a life sentence for manslaughter and Keith began his punishment. However, he resolved not to spend his time inside in bitterness and regret but rather to make a new man of himself. It was a strong personal resolve and eleven years later he was sent out on parole from Ford Open Prison. Meeting the love of his life he moved into 'a nice home with a beautiful lady'. Everything was fine, he believed, because his personal resolve had worked. However, although he thought he was secure he was to find that he had seriously overestimated his own strength of will.

'I made a fatal mistake, for an alcoholic,' he admitted wistfully. 'I thought I could conquer drink. There was no way I was going back to the old ways. I was a new man and hey, I could hold one or two drinks – everyone can – it's all a matter of self-control ...' So Keith woke up back in prison, not knowing what had happened. He soon discovered he had lost his lady, his home and his chance of parole for a very long time. His self-villification knew no bounds and he was totally distraught. He was not as strong as he had believed and he had thrown away all his chances of a new start.

'It was then I knocked into a new friend,' Keith said. 'His name is Aitch. He took me in his arms and talked to me, but he did more than that. He took me to church and I met David. He did a meditation on me by putting his hands on me.' Keith told his tale with great sincerity, his craggy face earnestly searching for the right words. 'I cried,' he said. 'I've not cried since I was eleven. I was not allowed to because I had to be a man and a man never cries.'

Keith liked coming to church, describing it as the best thing that ever happened to him. The hate of the past was gone and God had worked His way into his heart. He couldn't explain his joy and inner calmness but he wanted to thank all those who had given him a new chance.

'I would like to thank everyone,' he said gratefully. 'Big Aitch – he's rock to rest on; David for his prayers and meditation; Nick Pook for talking to me to help me understand myself. And,' he continued, 'I'd like to thank the prayers – all those people outside who pray for us in here.'

We always told the men that people outside cared for them and that they prayed for them – the new Christians – and all their problems, and also that they gave us money to buy them tapes and Walkmans. The men were always impressed and were keen to meet all the outsiders who visited the prison. Keith was especially grateful because many of our supporters had taken time to encourage and be with him.

'There was something missing in my life,' he confessed. 'I didn't have the strength and I didn't have the knowledge before, but now I'm a new Christian and I'm elated.'

Howard smiled when I called him a fisher of men. He was used to having the respect of the inmates, for his strength of body and spirit marked him out as a force to be reckoned with, but this new role was a novelty to him. David had been very encouraged in his ministry by someone who suggested that when he got to heaven all the men whom he had led to Christ would be waiting there lining up to say, 'Thanks, mate.' I shared this with Aitch and suggested that he too would find this a reality one day. He turned his big friendly face to one side and looked at me. He laughed a short nervous laugh as if he were considering this surprising suggestion.

'Yeah,' he said, 'maybe.' For me there is no maybe. Howard is a real fisher of men and his pleasure in helping men now will be nothing to what he experiences when he fully grasps the importance of what he has done.

Whenever a new Christian joined our membership in the prison, David would soon link him up with Howard. 'Give him the works, Howard,' David would say, confident that Aitch would soon supply his new brother with tapes, Walkman, Bible notes and prayer partners.

'This one for the works, David?' Howard would say. 'Fine.' Then he would move over to the new Christian and offer him his large, hard-working hand, smile and say, 'Welcome to your new family. God's family.'

Oh yes; it's certainly been a privilege for us to know and work with the man they call Big Aitch.

Furthermore, time after time God used the most unlikely men to bring others to Himself. Just like Aitch they had never imagined themselves in any Christian role, or as a means by which their mates would develop a real faith.

TIM

Tim was inside for drugs offences and robbery. After a traumatic meeting with his solicitor over his court case, he was very worried. He asked David to help him, and after an intense discussion and an honest facing up to his situation, he decided to follow Christ. After he had prayed with David he stood up and asked, 'Have you got a pen at all?' David was a little taken aback, and wondered what this request was for. However, he could see by Tim's earnest face that it was important. David reached into his pocket, where he kept both a pen and his little black notebook. The two items were in constant use, but it was some time before he realized just how significant they were, not only to him but to many inmates. One day he had been promising to contact a relative for a distressed man when the man said, 'Will you write it in your little black notebook because then I'll know you'll do it. We all know you've got a little black notebook!'

So it was that David now drew out his famous notebook and pen, and offered them to Tim. 'Here you are,' he said, holding them out 'Oh just the pen, please,' replied Tim, and taking it from David's hand he walked to the already open door of his cell. On the panel outside was the usual small card giving the name and the professed religion of the inmate inside each cell. He carefully removed this card, and leaning up against the wall he crossed out the words 'Nil religion' and firmly wrote 'Christian' in their place. He then placed the card back in its slot, and returned the pen to David. 'I'm a Christian now,' stated Tim, 'so I'll have Christian on my card.'

Tim then decided to fetch some fresh water for his jug from the end of the corridor. As he passed a group of officers one asked, 'What did you want with the vicar, eh?' Tim looked him firmly in the eye. 'I've become a Christian. Are you one?' The officer looked quietly away, possibly startled by the inmate's courage. Tim walked on by, fetched his water and returned to his cell. His first act of witness had been made.

Tim went on to bring inmate after inmate to the chapel, praying them on to the same experience he had enjoyed. It was all a far cry from planning a robbery, and infinitely more satisfying.

ADAM

Adam was a very bright and perhaps unusually eloquent inmate who, having left school early, became involved in extensive crime. Burglary was a way of earning a living, and he became very professional and successful at it. Eventually caught and incarcerated in Lewes Prison the futility of his life hit him. Outside he'd developed a relationship with a Christian girl whose witness had no doubt affected him, and now inside he chose to change direction completely. He became a Christian and was so convicted by the Holy Spirit that he determined to sit in his cell and write to every one of his victims to apologize for the trauma and loss he had caused. His repentance was 'genuinely deep-rooted'. One by one he brought other inmates to Christ, having spent hours with each one painstakingly talking through problems and issues with them. He brought the deep-thinking, questioning types, and was a huge asset to the Christian community in the prison during his stay. Most might have written him off as a man too involved in crime to redeem, but God turned our understanding around and chose Adam to work for Him on his wing in the prison.

So David and his new converts worked steadily on, but all the time we knew much more help was needed. The lack of knowledge our new prison co-workers possessed would have been funny if it weren't so tragic. We prayed for a new helper, someone local who would be able to offer sustained and committed help to disciple the new Christians. He or she would have to be local, of course, we understood that, or regular help would not be forthcoming. God heard our prayers, there is no doubt, but it appeared that someone local was not available just now, so He sent us someone from further afield – just rather more further afield than we could ever have imagined in our wildest dreams. He sent us someone from Korea!

We had grown ever more concerned that because so many men were changing their lives and our primary task was to reach as many as possible, that we could not divert our attention to the vital area of discipleship. What could we do? Outside we met with some hostile reactions that seemed to imply it would be better to convert none if it meant we could not offer a full follow-up programme. We never felt happy with that scenario for to us it would be total hypocrisy to deny to others what we believed ourselves to be totally necessary for salvation. Instead we turned to God whom we believed must be more concerned than anyone for the wellbeing and growth of new believers. We already had people who would come in when work and family commitments permitted but, of course, David really needed much more assistance than that, grateful though we always are for any help that was or is offered.

We had had an article in the local paper and had grumbled a little because it had reported one or two details rather badly, but it must be said that in spite of this God used it in a remarkable way.

Yojoon Lee read that article and his interest was roused. He had been the pastor of a huge Korean church for some eleven years when he'd felt God's call to be a missionary to England. He'd left his 5,000 member congregation and been sent out to work with international students in Brighton.

Yojoon saw that newspaper article about Lewes Prison, which he realized was so nearby, and determined to visit for one day to discover the truth behind the news report.

David returned his phone call which he found on his answering machine one afternoon. By this time of course he was receiving many such requests and knew there was no real way of working out which calls would lead to exciting new avenues and which were on a par with asking for a tour round a local monument or place of interest. He invited Yojoon in to see him and the meeting duly took place one Thursday morning.

After a five minute introduction David whisked the surprised visitor straight off to the hospital wing. 'No point in hanging around,' David said. 'Let's see a few live ones!'

His grin and positive attitude obviously intrigued this serious, devoted man of God who had come so far to be shown round this English prison. Yojoon described the events that followed with amused satisfaction. 'I was hijacked,' he joked happily in a very strong accent. 'I came for one day and I was hijacked by David Powe and God.'

David's response was equally amusing: 'We need you, Yojoon, but we can't manage that Korean name. We'll call you Bruce after Bruce Lee and then we'll remember you.'

Yojoon looked bemused. 'Bruce? ... Bruce? ... Why Bruce?' he questioned in his strong Asian accent. 'OK – Bruce is OK.'

And so Yojoon became Bruce and all in Lewes Prison knew him as that to great effect, because this simple name change endeared him to everyone and greatly added to his recognition in the prison. We had prayed for someone local to come and help us, but God had sent us a Servant from Korea and His choice was to prove to be the very best both for us and for the new Christians at Lewes Prison.

YOJOON'S STORY

Bruce was born in South Korea into a Christian family. He traces the Christian influence back to his grandmother, who was converted to the faith through the ministry of British missionaries some 100 years ago. She had become a great woman of prayer who battled against her husband's persecution to win her whole family to Christ. She had dedicated her two sons to God and they had grown up to become famous ministers in South Korea. Prayer surrounded that household and Bruce was born into a caring extended Christian family. Nevertheless his own faith was to turn out to be merely nominal and he went on to study and concern himself with a career in architecture.

One day, when he was 24 years old, he attended an evangelistic meeting in Seoul and the seeds that had so obviously been sown by his family began at last to grow. He met with Christ in a real and personal way and his whole life took a dramatic change of direction. The job was abandoned in favour of ordained ministry in the Presbyterian Church where his father had ministered for so many years before him.

He found his service led him to become an educational director of two churches, one with a membership of 2,000 and one with 3,000 members. He spent all his time leading Bible studies for lay leaders and this role of discipleship training took precedence over any involvement in evangelistic work. At the time he had no idea why his experience was so concentrated in one area. Could it have been that he was being prepared for other things – perhaps in England?

After eleven years he resigned his post to become involved in missionary work. His uncle was the senior pastor in the Antioch Presbyterian Church in Jeon-ju city in the south of his country and the man responsible for the St Paul mission there. This man carried a huge burden for Britain because he

believed the Korean Church should fully appreciate the importance of the work of British missionaries in old Korea. He felt Britain had shown a deep
and real love for Korea which should be repaid. He
wanted to express his gratitude – and Bruce was
sent as a token of that esteem.

One Sunday much later we visited a church to
explain the work at Lewes and to request support.
We had invited Bruce to speak on this occasion and
as I watched this immaculately dressed Asian man
in his blue striped suit and smart red and blue tie
stand up, I felt a deep respect and emotion as he
declared himself to be one of the fruits of the great
missionary drive that marked out our churches all
those years ago. The church we were attending had
had a particular interest in missionary work and its
members were clearly moved. Here the wheel had
turned full circle and Korea was returning part of
its debt by sending us a missionary to help bring
men to Christ.

So Bruce had set out for Britain but it was some
time before he and David were to meet up. He had
attended a Bible school and lived in southwest
England and Scotland before he moved to the
Brighton area.

He tried to join various missionary societies but
met with rejection and doubt. Finally a society
specializing in his desired work turned him down
at final interview level with an unconvincing argument. Bruce nearly lost his track and he was greatly
troubled by these turns of events. His bold, long
and fruitful ministry had been for what – a period
of pain, rejection and a damaged spirit? Why had

God called him to this land where he could find no point of service? What was going on in his life?

Bruce had brought his dear wife, Sohyun, and his young son Hyunseung to Britain with him. The first year was a time of desperate homesickness for his son, and his wife found building relationships hard. She was used to loving, giving fellowship and our British reserve and suspicion left her lonely and afraid.

Finally, Bruce explains, there was 'a turn up for the books' for him and he read about and visited Lewes Prison. He had never expected to become involved in such work and in comparison to the long, slow introduction to our country his involvement in the prison came upon him almost unawares and extremely swiftly.

On his very first visit he was challenged by David's obvious eagerness for the lost and his openness to himself as a foreigner. He felt the alienation and rejection he had previously experienced just melt away. His judgement is quite straight: 'David was different from others. He is a man who can trust others in Christ and share his responsibility with others. It might be a reason God greatly uses him in prison.' Before long Bruce was visiting the prison regularly. He was drawn by the speed of the response to the Gospel and by the tremendous needs he could perceive in the inmates. David was thrilled to have a man of such experience and obvious depth of prayer to join in the ministry. The two men fitted together like pieces of a jigsaw puzzle – each supplying a balance to the other and yet working as one in many situations. Both men had had no original intention to work in a prison and neither had arrived via an easy road, but God invited them in His service and blessed their co-operation greatly. We can only wonder at God's purposes and provision in such situations.

Bruce's English was always a point of interest to us all. He was obviously aware that the British favour the use of idiom and expressions in colloquial speech and so he tried to follow suit wherever he could. The slight errors which resulted from his language endeared us to him all the more and actually lit up a problem on more than one occasion so that we could see it more clearly. Bruce thrived on David's sense of humour and word play and the general office banter and goodwill did much to lighten the heavy loads the work produced. Bruce felt his clumsy English was a huge bonus because it offered 'a kind of entertainment to the inmates'.

David would announce in meetings that 'Bruce's English is a little awkward but his Korean's terrific'; and it was quite true. However, Bruce's summing up of the situation is far more relevant: 'My shortage of English is the real blessing to me, because I cannot but concentrate only on Jesus and his Salvation. I cannot exaggerate or beautify the Gospel from our Lord with my eloquence. I cannot but simplify it. I think it is the real reason God has called a worker for his prison from the far east country. Anyhow I am doing my bit just as I am.'

Bruce found his arrival and his new ministry a huge surprise, there can be no doubt; but he grew to see it as all in God's plan for his life. Years previously someone had prophesied that he would go abroad and deliver many corrupted young people from their sin. He had sadly forgotten this word and had only recalled it as his work at Lewes began to develop. Was God now bringing this prophecy to pass? It would certainly seem like it. David and I were certainly thrilled to hear his story and gradually we grew more and more amazed as we began to learn the stories of how all our helpers were drawn to Lewes. Many of them had obviously been brought there for a special purpose and their stories were as diverse as their gifts. God was working in our midst and we had only to stand and praise Him for His glory.

Bruce was clearly part of the picture and a very important part at that. During the course of his Bible studies and prayer with inmates he was drawn to one Peter David Angel.

Separated from fellowship in the Segregation Unit Angel needed help and support in his new Christian life. This was provided in the form of steady help from Bruce. A great desire burdened this Asian Christian that men from Lewes would grow to such an extent that they would become evangelists and leaders of the future Church. Angel longed to become just that. Of course only time will tell if he fulfils his ambition although we do so hope he will, and if he does he will have had more than a little assistance along the way from 'Bruce Lee', God's obedient servant from Korea.

CHAPTER 5

✳

Does the Philippian Jailer Work Here?

Armed with several years' theological training, the Bishop's certificate in Christian Education, years of practice in leading Bible studies and a reasonable all-round Christian knowledge, David entered the cell of George Wilson. He was responding to a request to see a chaplain because George had filled in the required form and marked the purpose column with the words 'extremely personal'. Just why had this man summoned his assistance, wondered David? Was he concerned about problems in his family or traumatized by his crimes and questioning the meaning of life perhaps? George was standing impatiently in his cell when David arrived.

'Glad to see you,' he enthused. 'I've tried everyone with my problem. I've asked the governor, probation, the education people – everyone – you are my last resort.' David felt both honoured and concerned simultaneously. Would he be up to this obviously very demanding situation?

'Well, how can I help?' he asked hesitantly, eventually realizing that being someone's 'last resort' was not exactly a mark of flattery.

'Well,' said George, 'it's this light up here. It won't stop flickering. I've tried everything. It's driving me nuts. You do miracles – do one up there!'

David experienced several reactions at the same time; relief, surprise and amusement all hit him at once. Fortunately, the problem was soon solved and a man from the works department was requested to fix the irritation of the flickering light. In fact the whole opportunity proved far more fruitful than just lending a helpful hand would be, because the man found faith that day and a new light shone not only in his cell but also in his life.

Furthermore, the incident serves well to illustrate an important element in prison ministry. The Greek New Testaments of college, the theological debates and even the refined forms of worship experience are rarely the first tools to be taken out of the bag. Explaining the Christian faith in a prison context introduces a whole new concept of the word 'basic'. Nothing can be assumed and there is sometimes no basis of shared understanding on which to build. After an initial reaction of panic, Christian visitors often found the necessary simplicity of any message they might give to be a relief and an inspiration which eventually proved to be a real excitement in their lives. Anyone who took themselves and their particular persuasions too seriously was doomed to disappointment, but those willing to 'go with the flow' found endless humour and personal satisfaction.

Presuppositions are fairly ingrained after some thirty-odd years as a Christian. It is obvious that you sit quietly in a church service, that you don't interrupt or light up a cigarette. Similarly everyone can read and find a page number or follow a text. In prison this is not so; many men are totally unchurched and have little idea of 'the right way to conduct oneself in church'. School religion is often a complete non-event or at best of little consequence in the hard-pressed curriculum and we discovered some who barely knew who Jesus was at all, let alone had any concept of Christian habits or behaviour. After the initial bewilderment this became one of the great wonders and privileges of the work. It provided us with endless kindly laughter at the slips and faux pas we came across and also with the sheer joy of being able to tell people something new.

One morning I was telling the story of Daniel in the lions' den in chapel. I was taking the angle of a man who was stitched up by his jealous colleagues and it was ringing bells in the men's minds. As I told the story quite simply, as I probably would in a school assembly, I suddenly became aware not only of the engrossed features of the inmates' faces but that their bodies were leaning forward, anxiously awaiting the end. It dawned on me with great pleasure that here I was telling this ancient and much loved story to people who did not know how it ended! I warmed well to my task. I loved every minute of it and afterwards I long savoured both the privilege and satisfaction of it. Daniel escaped the lions' den because God saved him by blocking up the mouths of the lions. God is more powerful than our enemies and if we belong to Him we are on the winning side. That morning four people met with Jesus, inspired by that simple Bible story and the Holy Spirit's pinpricking and enlightening of their own situation.

Many Bible stories are so relevant to the men's lives just like that story of Daniel, and most Sundays a simple story was told of how Joseph, David, Noah, Zacchaeus, Peter, Paul or the anonymous crippled man met with God and the inmates were helped to see that God would meet with them too if they wanted it that way.

Ben is an example of someone who knew nothing about God at all really. At the age of eighteen he was out of his home territory of Liverpool and was caught in Sussex on a driving offence. For five weeks he came to chapel, so David and the team recognized his face. One day Roy came to David and said Ben was asking for help.

'Look,' said David, 'I've got all these new ones to deal with. Ben's OK.' But Ben wasn't OK and he persisted in requesting a visit. David went down to his cell after the service and asked him what he wanted. 'I'm sorry I've not seen you, Ben, but I have to concentrate on new Christians at the service.'

'But I want to become a Christian,' requested Ben.

'But, Ben, you are,' replied David. 'When I prayed with you, you became a real Christian. We just have to work it all out now.'

'I haven't become a Christian yet,' pleaded Ben. 'I've queued up every week but I never made it. I really do want to become a Christian, you know.'

David felt as if he'd just been flattened. He was deeply shocked and amazed. It reminded him of the time a man had called out and said, 'You've been past my cell three times and never asked me to become a Christian.' But this was far worse because Ben had come for five weeks and David thought he was already one of the fellowship and being followed up. 'I'm so sorry,' he said. 'I really thought you'd said the prayer and been filled with the Holy Spirit. Let's pray right now.'

Ben became the strongest Christian on 'B' Wing for some time and led many others to faith. However, he knew nothing about Jesus previously, as his testimony printed below reveals. God seems to have called him for service in spite of his ignorance, and the simplicity of his new faith is inspiring.

BEN'S TESTIMONY

Before I came to prison I had no beliefs, I was as you might say an atheist. When I came to prison I was approached by one of the chaplains who explained to me about the prison chapel and what services it offers to us, the prisoners. He also gave me a leaflet with all the details on, which I just threw to one side. A few days later I felt a strong urge to go to church, so on the Sunday off I went to church. With me being new in the prison I did not know anyone, so I sat at the back on my own. I just listened to what the chaplain said and I thought: 'Hey, this all means something, but what?' After the service, which I thought was very good, I got talking to a few outside people whom I thought were very friendly. I suddenly decided I want to learn more about Christ. Until this point, all I knew about Christ was that he was born on Christmas Day, fed five thousand people and died on a cross. On the Wednesday, a guy from the chapel came with some leaflets about becoming a Christian and I did not read through them properly. I just glanced at them. By this time I had already decided I wanted to become a Christian. Since becoming a Christian, I feel like a different person. I feel like I can tackle anything life has to offer me. One very important point that sticks out to me is that Christ forgives people who have sinned.

Ben's testimony illustrates the point well, many are not really anti-Christian or positively atheist, they just bungle along in life, ignorant of all that God has to offer. Time after time we saw people respond to the Good News of Jesus once they had heard it. Paul reminds us of this when he asks how people can respond if they have never heard the Gospel. So often we wonder why people won't come and join us in church, perhaps we should concentrate more on going out to meet people where they are so that then they might appreciate what they might be missing.

One morning David was preaching in the chapel and he felt one story was highly relevant. He told how Paul and Silas were in prison for being Christians and how they sang hymns in the night to keep their spirits up. Then he explained how an earthquake broke down the prison walls and all were free to escape. The men sat attentively identifying with these prisoners who could now so easily have stepped out of the jail. They listened with astonishment as David revealed that Paul and Silas stayed just where they were, because if they had fled the jailer would have been executed for failing in his duty. They were surprised but pleased when they discovered that the jailer's family all became Christians as a result of these events and although identification with prison officers was not usually high on their agenda, they liked the story and said so afterwards.

David was pleased as several men found God that morning and he was just about to wind up all the proceedings when a young inmate approached him.

'I liked that story this morning,' he said, clasping his cup of coffee and nibbling at his Wagon Wheel appreciatively. 'Can I ask you something?'

'Sure,' said David. 'Glad you liked it.'

'Well,' said the youngster, 'can I meet him? I mean does the Philippian jailer work here?'

David forced back the grin that was urging itself onto his features. 'Hmmm, no,' he said, looking to one side of the earnest inmate, 'I'm afraid that was a long time ago now, but there are lots of people who are Christians here this morning. Would you like to be one too?' 'Oh yes,' said the young man. 'Do you think I could get God at such short notice?'

'Yes, you certainly can,' replied David and invited him to one side to pray with him.

Another time an older man, probably in his sixties, and on remand for the non-payment of Council Tax, approached David with a serious question. 'What's a Deuteronomy?' he asked.

'It's a book in the Bible,' replied David confidently.

'It's not in my Bible,' asserted the man. David was flummoxed for a moment and resolved to discuss with me later whether there was any Bible I knew that failed to include the book of Deuteronomy.

'May I see your Bible?' David asked gently.

'Certainly,' returned the man. 'Here it is.'

He produced a tiny well-thumbed book and began to open it. 'I've read this every day for years,' he enthused; 'I find it a great comfort and now I'm in here, I read it all the time, but I can't work out why it mentions a Deuteronomy at the bottom here.' He pointed at the very edge of the page, where various books of the Bible were listed.

Light dawned for David as he gently took the precious book from the man's hands.

'This is a copy of *Daily Light*, Ron,' David said quietly. 'It's a selection of verses from the larger Bible that you can read if you're in a hurry.'

He led Ron over to the bookshelf and took down a large brown Good News Bible.

'This is the real thing, Ron. You can have it if you like.'

Ron stood in the corner of the chapel with his *Daily Light* in one hand and the new Bible in the other. He looked from one hand to the other hand and his jaw dropped noticeably. Then he gazed slowly up at David who saw moisture building up behind his eyes as he said, 'Do you mean I've been reading this book for all these years and there's more?' David nodded his head and held the man's arm.

'Can I really have this?' Ron asked.

'Oh yes,' said David, 'it's all yours. Oh and by the way ...' and he opened up the new Bible and pointed '... there's Deuteronomy – a whole book for you to read.'

Days later, David visited Ron, who had found the whole prison experience a living nightmare, and there he was in his cell reading and reading his new gift. As David looked in, Ron looked up and smiled.

'OK, Ron?' asked David.

'Fine,' replied Ron, 'just fine.' And with that he turned back to his Bible and read on.

Mick had a new Bible too, but he'd come to the prison in the very early days when the only Bibles David had to share were donated old ones. Mick hadn't minded at all. He was glad to have one. However the next Sunday he was up in chapel clutching his Bible and with an earnest request.

'Look, David – er – it's about this Bible. Could I have a different one?'

David looked at him and could sense a genuine concern in his voice.

'What's up Mick?' he asked. 'What's wrong with this one?'

'Well, I can't hack this one David. Eerm, God keeps speaking to me through it.'

David smiled. 'Well, yes,' he said, reassuringly, 'that's what He always does. We read the Bible and God tells us things,' David went to move on. Mick grabbed his arm.

'No, mate – you don't understand. He speaks to me – at night.' Here he paused and earnestly sought help with his eyes. 'I don't like it at all. I'd like an ordinary one.'

David took the slightly battered book out of Mick's hands and inspected it. Some Christian had obviously donated it having thumbed it rather well first.

As Bibles went, it wasn't too bad. We had had some Bibles given that were tied up with string because the spine had gone, ones with pages torn or falling out, some in gothic style script and hundreds, yes hundreds, of New English Bibles which no one wanted because the verse markings are so obscure, but this one was a lot better than any of those, David could see at a glance. However as he flicked through the pages he saw the real problem come to light. The former owner had been in the habit of highlighting the passages which struck him or her, by using a luminous pen. Obviously this glowed in the dark of the prison cell and had frightened the life out of the newly-converted Mick.

David smiled and gave Mick a brand new Bible he had brought in that week.

'There you are, Mick. Try this one.'

Mick's sense of relief was all too obvious.

'Thank's mate – you're a gem. God won't speak to me through this one then?'

'Well,' replied David, 'I think he'll tell you things as you read, but not quite in the same way.'

'Thank goodness for that,' sighed Mick and, clutching his new improved version, moved away to collect his tea and biscuits at the far end of the chapel. David stood there looking after him and thinking just what an unpredictable ministry this was all turning out to be!

When someone became a Christian, we tried to help them to learn to read and pray because they are Christian lifelines. Sometimes we would feel overwhelmed by the sheer numbers of people and our inadequacy at being able to explain sufficiently and quickly enough. How could we possibly establish Bible reading patterns in such short periods of time? Nevertheless, we had to learn that what God had started He would Himself bring to completion. We also had to learn to do all we could and leave the rest to others. Sometimes we would hear later what God had done; sometimes we didn't.

Bill was David's first new Christian in Lewes Prison and he had moved out after only a few weeks. David had given him what help he could but in those early days there was no Bruce, no Roy, no Jackie – in fact no team at all. Nearly two years later we heard about Bill once more. He had met Bob Smith, a sound Christian whom Terry Tully had followed right through to release and beyond. Bob had been talking about finding God in Lewes to all who would listen to him and he had known Bill years before. Bob told us what happened when they met up.

'I told him I was number seventy-four,' Bob said.

We had tried to avoid the numbers game after the first year but it was to no avail. Everyone else was hooked on it and we decided to let it happen if it was a source of encouragement to anyone. Bob liked his number although where he had got it from we did not know. There was a list of inmates who had come to faith for simple administrative and follow-up purposes and prisoners have ways and means of finding things out, we discovered.

Anyway Bob told Bill that he was number 74 with pride because he felt it was a very early number, but he received a surprise. Bill leaned forward, looked Bob straight in the face and said triumphantly 'But I'm number one!'

The two men laughed and Bob listened as Bill explained how he had been released from Lewes Prison with little money, all his possessions in a carrier bag and nowhere to go. As he wandered round Brighton he had sat for a rest on a wall obviously looking very low and despondent. Along the road came an older Christian woman who sensed this chap was in need. Very bravely she had asked if he required assistance and Bill had told her his story. She took him back to lodge in her spare room and had looked after him ever since. She introduced him to her church and built him up gradually and faithfully.

As we listened to Bob telling this story we were filled with amazement. God's provision was truly astonishing. We should not have been surprised but we were. God had his hand on these men and he was bringing them closer. Why then were we so surprised that God was providing for them in fabulous ways? Often we had to let people go into His care completely and were left with prayer. We guess one day we will hear some more tales of what could be called the unexpected but which we should probably rather call 'tales of the expected' because God so often provides in wonderful ways.

Joyce had to learn this lesson too. Her son Phil was always in trouble in spite of years and years of prayer, but she was distraught to discover that he was in prison, his drug-taking having caught up with him. She was told by a friend of the work of Prison Fellowship and was invited to a prayer meeting. Sophia sometimes came along on Sundays to chapel and was a strong Prison Fellowship member. She had told David about her friend's son Phil that Sunday and had advised Joyce to get in touch with David at the prison. The prayer meeting that night was well attended and Joyce sat down not knowing that David had made it himself that night. When it came to introductions, Joyce told her tale. With emotion she explained she had tried to contact the prison with no success, but she wanted to help anyone who was in jail, too, now that she realized how awful it was for the relatives of prisoners. David was sitting on the other side of the room. He listened to Joyce's story with concern and interest and as she finished he asked, 'What is your son's name, Joyce?'

'Phil,' replied Joyce looking across at David and, seeing his collar, realizing who he was.

'Well,' said David, 'I met Phil at 9.05 this morning and he became a Christian soon afterwards.'

There was a moment's silence and then Joyce burst into tears. 'I can't believe it,' she cried. 'Is it real? I can't believe it.'

David looked gently at her and replied, 'You have prayed for Phil for years and years and years. Now God has answered your prayers. Don't be surprised, I have only reaped where you have sown in many tears. Don't be a doubting Thomas. God has answered your prayers. Now concentrate on helping him grow.'

The rest of that meeting was a blur for Joyce and not surprisingly so. She was experiencing what many others had done before – the sense of almost disbelief at answered prayer mixed with the sheer exhilaration of realizing her son had finally become a Christian.

David and I chatted when he came home and just felt the excitement of it all. David retells incidents with remarkable clarity and I felt I'd been right there in that room with that happy woman. We prayed for all the other relatives who had longed for their sons, husbands or brothers to find faith – for those who now rejoiced like Joyce and for those who still pray on and on in faith, hope and love.

Day by day new people were responding to the Gospel and David learned that misunderstanding was no bar to faith. Inmates might be muddled, relatives doubtful, outsiders suspicious, but God still put His hand on people and brought them to Himself. Of course advice was offered from all directions and offers of help at every turn. David held fast to two pieces of advice he valued greatly and felt necessary to keep the aims and objectives of his ministry clear. In fact two experienced chaplains were responsible for giving David two most helpful tips for his work and they were to dominate his activity. Rev. Tom Johns, now an Assistant Chaplain General, was to offer a simple recommendation albeit a seemingly obvious one. Just as a social worker talks about personal problems or a probation officer talks about parole so it is that a chaplain should talk about God. As with any Christian, a chaplain is tempted to justify their position by talking about almost anything else except God. Now perhaps – although by no means certainly – in the outside world, there is plenty of time to converse at length, build friendships and move at a sedate pace towards witness, but in the cut and thrust of prison life, one may only meet someone once or twice, and needs are very polarized and intense. There is no time for inaction or sloth.

David found this good advice and resolved to let as few opportunities as possible slip by without a mention of God. To his delight the result was startling. Rejection and apathy were not common whilst a willingness to talk about God was commonplace.

The second piece of advice came from Rev. Brian Anderson, a chaplain who had spotted David's potential as a chaplain years before his entry to the profession and had faithfully prayed him in.

'Loiter with intent, David,' he had advised when David had visited him at Parkhurst. 'That's the best way.'

The theory was straightforward – he should be a presence, turn up where people are, walk through the wings and God would show him where to respond.

Now just as a chaplain or minister of any sort can be tempted to talk about anything but God so he can be tempted to do anything but mingle with the crowds. Writing sermons, reading circulars, attending support groups or planning evangelistic programmes, all serve well to prevent eye-to-eye contact with those in need of the Gospel message. David resolved to make personal work central in his mind and to sublimate all other activities. In practice this commitment was to prove very fruitful.

John was on the phone when David was wandering through the Health Care Centre one day – he waved at the chaplain and shouted, 'Have you got time for me?'

David crossed over to John, indicating a positive response, so the young inmate replaced the receiver and was ready to speak.

David had been loitering with intent and the opportunity as usual just cropped up.

An officer had witnessed the exchange and approached them. 'I'm moving this man in three minutes,' he declared, obviously assuming there was no time now for a personal chat with the chaplain for this inmate. David looked up and realizing that John must be in real need to summon him in this way he responded, 'Well then, I have three minutes to talk to him!'

The two men slipped into the holding room leaving the officer rather taken aback and pondering over the obvious logic of the argument. John sat down nervously on the simple wooden chair and looked intently at David. 'How do I get God?' he asked.

David was amazed at John's frankness and respected his obvious honesty. Together the two men prayed and John was led into a new life he would not have found if he had stayed on that telephone or been whisked away in a police van to a new prison.

He was finally moved a short while later, although the officer had granted him a few minutes' grace, which was greatly appreciated. We have to pray he found help in his new prison but he had proved he was willing to ask for help and we hoped he would do so again. In all our further conversations about this remarkable incident, John became known as 'the three-minute man'.

David often found that many men were not antagonistic towards the Gospel in the least but had rather never heard it or been offered it.

'Why did nobody tell me before?'

'I didn't know Jesus was still around.'

'Can God really help me?'

These and similar remarks are the everyday responses to David's policies of loitering with intent and always talking about God.

LUKE 9:57 FF

As they were walking along the road, a man said to him, 'I will follow you wherever you go.'
He said to another man, 'Follow me.'
Still another said, 'I will follow you, Lord.'

I refer to this passage in Luke at this point because I believe it illustrates what we have been thinking about. Jesus was a preacher of the itinerant kind. True, this text concerns the cost of discipleship, for Jesus stresses to each one that they may not follow lightly. His followers will have no true home just like their master, neither may they procrastinate, or look back, but they will certainly be offered a new start straight away, by Jesus Himself. The Lord appears to have missed no opportunity to offer peace with God to all whom He met. 'As they were walking down the road ...' is the only context we are given. We know no details of these people, their backgrounds are a mystery and we don't even know their final decision. Did the cost of true discipleship deter or did they see the Lord for whom He really was and forsaking all, follow Him? Our ignorance of these matters must not surprise us, for it is not for us to know what does not concern us. No, rather we must be meant to see other aspects of this story, one of which is the apparent straight talking of Jesus. Perhaps we have grown so accustomed to verbose and complex sermons that we have neglected the simplicity of Jesus' style. He spoke often and naturally about the things of God, picking up on the customs and culture of the day yes, but evading the point definitely no! Jesus came to talk about God and to lead people to Him, and this He did. Have we perhaps neglected this most basic element of our Christian walk, so in reality we are not faithfully following Him?

The second point from this story follows readily. Jesus not only spoke often about God, He did so with all those with whom He came into contact. He did not make special appointments, develop programmes of approach or target special audiences. In the pattern of His daily round, Jesus spoke to those God gave Him by bringing them across His path. Now, of course, Jesus had a definite mission, which He both understood and set about fulfilling; but even with this holy task before Him, He lived an ordinary existence of day-to-day activities. So it was that He met with folks along the road, talked in the synagogue, challenged fishermen and confronted people with their need of God, wherever He was. Maybe loitering with intent is an inappropriate term, but its inadequacies as a description of the activity of Jesus must not be allowed to obscure the fact that He did indeed walk about speaking with whomever God placed in His path. Furthermore, He commanded us to follow His example – to go about 'gossiping' the Gospel. Can we rise to these challenges, or will we continue in our views of evangelism as a task for the few, or a programme to be planned, or far worse as an optional extra? Perhaps you will read this passage for yourself and ask God to speak through it to you. Take time to consider your own presuppositions and prejudices, and consider how its message might apply in your particular circumstances.

One questioning response from some Christians concerned the reality of the conversion process for men such as these prisoners. There was the suspicion that inmates would gain some advantage or concession by declaring they had become Christians. Once initial benefits had been experienced they would naturally return to their former ways and give up their new-found faith.

I suppose that because the events that were happening around us were of such a spectacular and sustained nature, we were able to treat such arguments fairly lightly, but nonetheless it must be said that such readily-produced comments were a sad indictment of Christian expectations. Now, as a teacher I am aware of research that indicates that pupils rise to their teacher's expectations of them. Conversely, those who are expected to fail, do so. It is an awareness that strikes me as acutely relevant here. Many Christians seem to have adopted an air of failure. Expecting little, they achieve little, and this is nowhere more true than in the area of evangelism. This is well illustrated by the current use of the term 'low-key evangelism'. At first hearing this sounds comforting and, of course, nonconfrontational. Surely we may woo people into the Kingdom by gentle reasoning and a policy of no pressure? However, such an approach bears little resemblance in my mind to the vibrant activity of the early Church, which turned the world upside down and resulted ultimately in even our own hearing of the Gospel today.

We cannot recapture the experience of the early Church in every aspect. Our times are indeed different and we have to live in our own society and deal with our own contemporaries. However, we cannot believe that we may move so far from our origins that we may assume that the necessity for pioneering evangelism may be either neglected or watered down. How can we spend our time improving and enjoying our experience of the Christian faith whilst failing to ensure that as many people as possible will share our joy?

Similarly we have been encouraged to believe that society no longer believes in God and so we must tread carefully if we think of introducing people to Gospel issues. Thus we have a springing up of 'just looking' groups, and we encourage folk to come to events where we assure them there will be no pressure, or where they can sit at the back and no one will challenge them.

If we hold views such as this it will hardly be surprising if we are suspicious of any situation where a large number of people are coming to faith, for, if true, it would certainly challenge our thinking at the very least, and hopefully our behaviour. Nevertheless, large-scale conversions were far from rare in the early Church, a fact which is easily verified by the most cursory glance at the book of Acts.

On another tack, why should we doubt any person's conversion purely on the grounds that he has been in prison? The Bible contains many incidents where its main characters are confined in a cell – think of Joseph, Daniel, John the Baptist, Paul and Silas, or even Jonah, who responded to God from the belly of a whale. Indeed, one may just as easily question the motives or faith of any member of any church anywhere in the country. Of course some people drift from their new-found faith, and it is a tragedy when they do so, but we can never be audacious enough to pretend we can predict just who those backsliders may be. Surely we must decline excluding even our own names from the list of possibilities, or why did our Lord warn us to be sure to keep our lamps trimmed? Furthermore, the parable of the wheat and tares denies us the right to issue judgement on the validity of a person's faith. God is the only judge, and I guess we all know the anecdotes which imply that there will be more than a few surprises when we arrive in heaven as to just who has joined us there! In the meantime we must surely take people's confessions of faith as true if they make them freely, and look only to the fruit of the Spirit in their lives as the real evidence.

So discipling new converts became a driving and fascinating force and although we thoroughly enjoyed all the outside contacts the true excitement just had to be found inside those Lewes Prison walls. Speaking engagements were a great delight to us and we met so many wonderful Christians en route, but our main joy in the new work was undoubtedly the new Christians in prison. They were a source of constant inspiration and we treasured the stories of their lives. Watching some of them progress was an invaluable experience akin to watching young children develop and grow. Kenny was just one of our joys. After his initial conversion he had appeared on TV.

'I've been a Christian two days now,' he had broadcast, 'and no one can believe it, because I'm well known in the underworld out there ... as an ex-criminal.'

From that stage of extreme optimism Kenny had moved down into a great period of testing and trial. Just how could such a man of violence and crime change his whole way of life? Bruce Lee spent many hours metaphorically 'sweating' over Kenny's salvation – praying with him, sustaining him, teaching him his new life. Gradually Kenny emerged as an even stronger Christian, albeit a very humble one. 'I've only brought four converts to Christ,' he bewailed one day. 'It's not many in six months is it?'

After a prayer time one afternoon David felt led to tell Kenny that God would use him greatly to bring people to Himself and Kenny took it very seriously. 'OK David,' he said, 'you keep that net ready and I'll keep on fishing!'

So he started to care more and more and to find others. 'Just needs one of your blessings now, David,' he would say when he found someone ready to respond to Jesus.

Kenny also began to plan for his release. On appeal he had been given one year less sentence to serve and he was due out within the year. His reformed character had this time been taken into account and he was thrilled. He planned to work in Hastings with Bruce in a club for those wishing to both learn martial arts and experience God at the same time.

He was picked up by Rev. Stephen Nunn, who runs the Church in the Wood in Hastings, and we have no doubt he will continue to grow steadily on his release.

At the Christmas Service Kenny was asked to do a reading. There was a huge congregation of over 200 that night and over a hundred visitors from the town amongst them. Kenny read a modern Christmas poem by Steve Turner which he had practised a thousand times and he was excellent. This well-known criminal stood proudly in front of so very many and witnessed to all that he was a changed man.

We were so proud we could hardly contain it, because he was representing the whole aim and purpose of the prison ministry. Later there were refreshments in the chapel for all the visitors. We had had to move the service at very short notice into the gym because so many wished to attend but the after service celebration was held in the chapel. Our boys had been given special permission to attend and Kenny spoke to them.

'Your dad saved my life, boys,' he said kindly, stooping down. 'I owe him a lot and I'll never forget him.'

'Will you sign my autograph book?' asked my son Edward in innocence. He felt he knew Kenny and the others because he'd heard so much about them.

'Oh yes, and mine too,' said Thomas eagerly.

'It's a pleasure,' replied Kenny, duly writing in their books next to the mayor, the governor and the Bishop.

My two boys used to take their autograph books around with them to churches and enjoyed collecting the names of the people they'd met. They of course drew no distinction between the autograph of a very important person and Kenny Jones. They were all the same – famous people they knew.

They were innocently affirming a great truth – all these people were quite equal in the sight of God and deserved to be on the same page. In whatever station we find ourselves in life it is acceptance by Christ that counts and although our earthly paths may differ widely all who believe in Jesus will wind up at the same destination.

So we praise God for all the Kennys we've come to know and for the exciting work with which we have become involved. Perhaps I can share here a poem written by Kenny in his cell called 'Out of the Darkness and into the Light'. In it he attempts to come to terms with what God has done in his life and ends with his plea that others will have the same experience as him. It echoes our very own prayers in an honest and deeply meaningful way.

OUT OF THE DARKNESS
AND INTO THE LIGHT

I heard a bird singing, a wondrous delight in
   song!
Telling all spirits where their souls belong!
Praising the Heavens for all things we're
   needing!
Thankful for this garden of Eden!
He sang of the bitter fruits, its ways and its
   plight!
He sang of the sweet fruit, sweetness, delight!
Come out of the darkness, and into the light!
Lift up your souls to God's great delight!
Never feel lost, forgotten or forsaken!
You've been forgiven for the sins you keep
   making!
For the victims left behind in your haste!
For them too, God has a special place!
Come to God, don't let your life be a waste!

He sings how wondrous this would be!
A sinner entering heaven, for all to see!
He sings in praise for eternity!
Be thankful, He gave His only one!
Jesus Christ, our Saviour, His Son!
The great feast is eternal, a promise He gave
So you, you sinner can also be saved!
Put your faith into Jesus Christ.
He'll save your children, your mother, your
   wife;
That's why he sacrificed his own life.
In Paradise, the birds together sing

Glory to God, what a wondrous thing.
Believing is being given an inner sight –
Come out of the darkness and into the light!

CHAPTER 6

✳

Head-Hunted for a Dream Team

'You can't escape,' I exclaimed, 'it's definitely your turn, Bruce!' Gales of laughter filled the room and cries of 'Oh yes!', 'Great!' and 'Go for it!' were all heard at once.

There was a large group of people crammed into our small living room two nights before Christmas. Wrapping paper discarded from hastily unwrapped presents was strewn all over the floor and the remnants of crackers, odd jokes, plastic spiders and broken snappers were under our feet. I was sitting squashed at the end of the old sofa pushing buttons on the simple stereo system that was providing the pleasant strains of Art Garfunkel for a game of 'pass the hat' . The rather inane point of the proceedings was to pass the hat around the room so that each person should place it firmly on his or her head in turn. When the music stopped there was an immediate gasp of relief from those who had escaped, together with squeals of delight as the fate of the latest victim was contemplated. The poor person who had the hat still placed on their head was to pay a forfeit.

I scanned the forfeit list carefully. I had explained right from the start that the game and its penalties were totally 'fixed'. No sense of fair play or luck were involved in this game!

The alphabet backwards was a bit cruel for a Korean, I felt, and dancing a jig or being a news reader had already gone.

'Preach a three-point sermon in one minute,' I pointedly demanded and everyone drew their breath as Bruce looked slightly flustered – which of course was an expression seldom seen on his normally serene and calm face.

'I know,' he said, 'I know. You must all respect God.' He paused, thinking deeply. 'And you must respect your wife – and you must respect your children.'

He looked round the room with obvious concern that this was acceptable, but his face soon broke out into a huge grin. Everyone cheered and shouted, clapped and smiled.

'Great, Bruce!' said one.

'Well done!' responded another.

'Spot on!' cried yet another.

We were having a great time. Everyone was in the mood for a party and the cramped conditions made it all the more pleasurable as we struggled to find seats, place glasses of mulled wine, or fruit cup with small pieces of fruit floating about, onto each ledge and table corner, and ate great buffet delights with our elbows well tucked in.

Several hours later when the food so painstakingly displayed on the dining-room table no longer looked so appetizing, when there was a mountain of washing-up stacked helter-skelter all over the sparse kitchen worktops and when the last 'Happy Christmas' had been said to the final guests as they left the house, David and I sat down with a well-earned cup of tea.

'You know,' I mused, 'we just all got on so well tonight. It's just amazing. If we'd set out to create a team for this work with the prisoners we just wouldn't have this glorious mix of people at all.'

'What do you mean?' questioned David, sitting up and taking notice.

'Well if we'd been planning it all,' I went on, 'we'd have tried to find an administrator and perhaps a counsellor or someone with experience of prison work. Maybe we'd have looked for someone who'd worked in a probation office or the courts and perhaps a writer or a musician. I don't know – we'd have made plans – we'd have chosen people for some reason or another ...'

'But we wouldn't have chosen these people, you mean?' interrupted David.

'No, exactly,' I said excitedly warming to my own explanation. 'These people have been chosen – selected or sighted by God – just like they were for Gideon; we're in the front line – we needed the best – but only His best is good enough. We'd never have chosen right. I know that.'

We'd had lots of help over the months with the expanding work and the people had been marvellous. We'd had visits from Youth with a Mission, who had taken services, a local free church who'd spent hours supporting new prisoners with letters, attending services, praying for David's ministry, and numerous one-off supporting acts of kindness and generosity. We praised God for all of them, they'd all been necessary, fruitful, part of the building up of the work, but now the work was establishing itself. Things were no longer on an *ad hoc* basis but were growing – deepening – moving on. Without planning it that way at all a team spirit developed as the Holy Spirit appeared to draw people with long-term commitment and a sense of personal call into our path. It was not organized or manipulated but gradually distinct areas of responsibility had emerged and the much-needed personnel emerged with them.

We really were by any definition a motley crew – a group of people with only a very limited list of things in common who would never have met at all in normal circumstances. Yet we all loved God and felt drawn to serve Him by serving prisoners. We all had the 'bug' as I call it for working in a prison and seeing lives changed. None of us could imagine life without the present tasks to occupy ourselves although of course we knew we had to hold it all lightly and be ready for any change of plan that might be in store.

We had no real relevant qualifications apart from those gained from our Christian lives, yet we all had important tasks to perform. Gradually – very gradually – we all fell into place and began to find strength in each other's roles and developing ministry. We all belonged to different denominations and groups, and probably our theology varied widely, but our task-orientated group began to knit closer and we all benefited from it.

Maureen was there right from the beginning. She had been invited to a Prison Fellowship meeting several years previously and had joined the ranks of that organization. She had found Christ during a period of personal turmoil and linked up with a lively Free Church near Crawley in Sussex. She was pleased to be involved in new directions in her life and had met new friends and taken in new concerns. Lewes Prison was the nearest prison for many in the Crawley Prison Fellowship group and so the attention was focused there. Prison Fellowship is a marvellous organization that exists to support Christian work with prisoners all over this country and indeed abroad. Groups form in a town or area and begin to pray for local prisons and inmates. Every member has to belong to a group for six months to show real commitment before being trained for positive service inside a prison. This training is a vital aspect of Prison Fellowship's strength and makes their members such able volunteers inside a prison. They learn not only how to help offenders but how to work within the restrictions of the prison system, to respect the security needs of an establishment, and to give due regard to all governors and officers in every respect.

Prison Fellowship groups offer their services to the chaplains of prisons within their reach. They ask if they may come in to services or to visit and work with inmates and if they may help the chaplain in any other way. They are strictly educated to work under the restraint of the chaplain and not to resent any restrictions imposed on them. Sadly, their offers of help are sometimes refused or discounted, but in our experience they pray on, constantly working towards times when prisoners will find the power of God in their lives.

Some of the Crawley and Brighton group came into services once a month at Lewes prior to David arriving there. They had only a few minutes each time to chat to prisoners but they used them to the best of their ability. They covered that prison with prayer and yearned for 'something to happen there'! So concerned were they all that they organized a prayer walk around the walls. At each corner they stopped and claimed the prison and its population for God. They felt they were involved in a battle – a spiritual battle – and resolved to take a full part in it.

Maureen was fully involved in this vital battle – she too prayed and prayed for God's Spirit to blow through that prison. Then one day the chaplain suddenly left, leaving behind him not only a vacancy but also all the uncertainty of just who would be chosen to fill it. News eventually filtered out that a new appointee would be arriving from London. The group was nervous – would this mean a complete clampdown perhaps, or the arrival of someone to whom they couldn't relate at all? David's first Sunday was one where both Maureen and Terry Tully were present. They could see immediately that he took the service in a very commanding way. It would seem that a reasonable relationship with the inmates was on the cards. At the end of the service when the men had returned to their cells Maureen went to introduce herself properly to David.

'Hello, I'm Maureen – part of Prison Fellowship,' she ventured.

'Good to meet you,' replied David in his quick and smiling style. 'Coming in next week?'

Maureen took a step back, completely surprised by this suggestion.

'Well – well yes,' she spluttered, 'but we're not allowed in every week. We come in once a month.'

'My goodness,' said David, 'I'll need you more than that.'

David had worked very closely with the Prison Fellowship group at Belmarsh Prison.

Joyce Baines was the leader there and had been a tower of strength in supporting David. The group had prayed for David and with David, encouraged him in his evangelical activities and when he'd left, let him go with great reluctance and much continuing care. He knew the value of voluntary help and wanted to make good connections quickly.

Maureen struggled to take in this new approach and secretly couldn't wait to get out and 'spread the news' about the new freedom. She didn't know then, however, just how her involvement would escalate into an almost full-time free-time activity. She became our most faithful helper, turning up every week to sort out refreshments and to chat to prisoners. She also started and headed up the prayer line which was soon to grow to substantial proportions. Eventually she was contacted almost every working day with prayer needs and the names of new Christians. She thrived on it – took the task by the horns and went for it in splendid style. In the very early days she also personally bailed us out of a spot of personal trouble in a very self-sacrificing way and we will certainly never forget her generosity of spirit. Working as a cleaner in a Crawley firm she was to find her time well filled but she says she was thoroughly rewarded by God. She used her favourite expression to describe all this – a word so often on her lips that we regarded it as her catch phrase. 'It's wonderful,' she would say, 'just wonderful.'

Into the prison on a Sunday morning Maureen brought her small but spirited bunch of helpers. Encouraged by the new openness in the chapel she began to bring some young people with her both to help the prisoners and to encourage her young friends in their own Christian life. Years previously I had regularly attended Limpsfield – a young people's Christian houseparty run by the Rev. Kenneth Habeshon. This wonderful work is still running albeit in a new location – Mayfield in Sussex – and David and I went back one day to share with the young folk there the excitement of the Lewes experience. The aims of Limpsfield and latterly Mayfield were simple – to encourage teenagers to find Christ and to grow in Him towards commitment and dedication and to encourage young adults to develop their leadership skills and sense of responsibility for others' faith, in such a way that the fruits of this would spill out into their everyday adult lives. I learned much there and discovered the need to be fully dedicated to God's will in my life, and I will, amongst many others, be very grateful for the opportunities for learning and service I discovered there.

One thing stuck firmly in my mind – the need not only to help the young people but to train the leaders to support and continue the work. This secondary aim is fully in our minds at Lewes also. Each person who helps has the need to grow personally. Ministry means enabling others to use and appreciate their own gifts – discovering what is possible for them as they try out new things and take up opportunities. Our prayer is that we weren't just using the young visitors for services but that they might gain from the experience too. Many of us have grown up in churches where responsibility is the sole reserve of the 35-pluses and in some cases the over-60s. Young men and women need to be captured for God while they are still young enough to offer a lifetime's service. They rise to opportunity in a wonderful way, but who can blame them moving on from any place where they are patronized or expected always to be in secondary roles. Society may well worship the youth culture far too much with its emphasis on the vitality and strength of younger employees but perhaps some parts of the Church deny them the fulfilment and excitement of leadership they need to grow and prosper in their Christian lives.

So it was with great pleasure that we met Liz, Rachel, Mark, Bethan and Claire when Maureen brought them to join the service. Liz told me later how she felt about coming to the prison.

'Maureen came and spoke to our young people's group,' she said, 'and I was totally awestruck!'

Liz went on to explain how she'd listened with open ears and bated breath as some of the experiences at Lewes were related. She caught Maureen's

obvious enthusiasm for the task and when the talk
was finished, she rushed up and offered to come in
to help. One by one the other members of that little
band stepped forward and similarly volunteered
their services for prison duty and Maureen began to
organize their first trip down the winding country
lanes from Crawley to Lewes. Liz remembered that
first trip very well as she was really nervous and
had begun to have serious doubts about her rather
swift response. 'What have I let myself in for?' she
asked herself. 'Will I be able to handle this?'

So they parked round the back of the prison and
very daunted knocked on the door. 'It was a very
scary thing,' she confessed. Liz had expected to see
30 or 40 skinheads with tattoos if she was honest,
but although there were one or two who fitted her
presuppositions, she soon discovered that most of
them were just normal guys. Feeling pleased that it
was going all right, Liz soon forgot her previous
nerves. She felt she was going to make a contribution by showing that young people were Christians, that they weren't boring and that they were
ready to relate to prisoners. What she found was
that it was she who was being helped and strengthened and that the experience moved her greatly.
'They gave me huge satisfaction,' she explained. 'It
was so exciting to see them change. They'd come in
and look so down and miserable, and their eyes
were really sad, but they'd become Christians and
you could just see the difference.'

Liz learned, however, that such blessings were
received only through cost. Yes, it was to be a great
experience, a splendid privileged start to each week

but she had to forfeit her cosy bed each Sunday morning to travel to Lewes and give up her time and other commitments. Once there she and other visitors were expected to work hard – no hangers-on were valued there. She would have to make coffee and distribute biscuits to a huge queue of men and learn to chat openly with people with whom she had very little in common. She learned to cover the service with prayer, before, during and after, and to take her concern for people she met on Sunday with her throughout the week. 'You have to be dedicated to the work in Lewes,' Liz declared, 'but actually I enjoy it so much it doesn't feel much like dedication really!'

Unfortunately, helpers must be over 18 to come into the prison so of course the time quickly came for most of this particular group, apart from Liz, who was staying locally, to leave for college. They planned a service all by themselves, experienced both the excitement of progress and the desperation of seeming failure when half the contributors fell ill, and learned the sheer joy of having God carry them through a brand-new opportunity. They had just learned so much in less than a year and all because they'd taken up a new challenge and been expected to cope.

Of course we would expect to see such young people's commitment to be firm in the short term but transitory in the long term. For some it was a foretaste of things to come, for others an experience to carry into their later lives. Mark ended up in Ecuador for a while serving the Lord with a travelling speaker who came to the prison; while Liz developed further voluntary work in the hospital sector. She'd gone to a local photographer to have a shot taken for her prison security pass, a very important but usually very unflattering necessity of life in a prison! She was asked where she was going on holiday that required a passport photo.

'Oh no,' she'd said, 'I'm not going on holiday, I'm going to do voluntary work in the prison.'

'You're kidding!' was the surprised reply of the photographer. 'You are just the type I'm looking for,' he said, recognizing her obvious bravery and forthrightness. 'I need help in the hospital – in radio!'

So one voluntary act led to another for Liz and Mark, and the others will hopefully all have gained in similar ways. We just proved time and time again that all we needed in the prison was dedication and submission to God and that age, sex, experience, qualifications and ability were no barriers to His use of people who come in to help. David spoke one night to Maureen's church in Turners Hill. The subject was Gideon and his great task for God. He'd wanted so many warriors to face the battle ahead but God soon cut his army down to size. He commanded all the frightened ones to go home and selected only those who were the keenest and most ready. Poor Gideon was left with only 300 men and a great and mighty army ahead of him.

God, however, had sifted and selected those men as we can read in Judges 7:4: 'I will lift them out for you there. If I say, "This one shall go with you", he shall go; but if I say, "This one shall not go with you", he shall not go.'

This passage had just come into my mind and stayed put for several days. I knew David must speak about it. It was to be almost a statement of faith on our behalf because Gideon had won a mighty victory over the Midianites with just the 300 men God had chosen. We had a difficult task too, not in the physical sense but in the spiritual.

Men who are involved in crime and danger and violence do not easily change direction. We knew there were great powers at work in the prison, perhaps in a fairly concentrated form. We needed God's choice of personnel and we believed we were getting just that. David spoke that evening about the team and not only did it inspire the congregation as to the power of God, but it lifted us up and helped us to see just what God was doing in the overall pattern of events.

Incidentally, that evening Liz's boyfriend Mark found Christ for the first time and we all rejoiced. Liz had prayed and prayed for this boy seemingly to no avail, but she had not sacrificed her Christian work in the prison team or become involved so that she was dragged down. Instead, she was totally open with both him and all her fellow prison workers about his position, even requesting prayers for him from Howard and other inmates. Her patience and prayer were finally rewarded that night and he too is already looking for his place of service in the Christian community. Perhaps he will join us all in the prison one day too?

Just as Maureen had joined us Jackie came along from Crawley Prison Fellowship too, and there is no doubt that she had been sifted out for work in that prison. God had first taken hold of Jackie and her husband Peter when they were newly married, although they both had a modestly religious background. Both had been scared to be totally committed to God but circumstances, other Christians, and the tragedy of a lost child all worked together to make them pliable in God's hands at last. Jackie heard occasionally about Christian work in prisons and was always interested. Slowly her sense of involvement grew until she volunteered to join her local Prison Fellowship group. For five years she and a few friends ran a bus service for wives and relations of inmates to visit their loved ones in Lewes, and she also visited prisoners in Holloway, both in hospital and the drink and drug unit. She had even met Howard some six years before he became a Christian in Lewes so it was obvious that she was very committed to prison work.

One day the doors at Holloway closed, but God opened a new way for Jackie at Lewes. David had arrived and was looking for help. Not renowned for his office organizational skills he was in dire need of a secretary, and Jackie was on the spot and possessed the required talents, not least of which was an ability not to panic at an in-tray several inches high! For Jackie it was an answered prayer and for David and everyone else who ever needed to track him down it was a real Godsend. The pay was appalling, the workload punishing, but the satisfaction was tremendous.

Jackie was often out on the wings with messages, Bibles, words of support and letters. She found God gave her a sense of confidence and that her Prison Fellowship training was paying dividends. She loved watching the changes in the men and faced the challenge of keeping her own faith deep but simple. She felt she was experiencing events which were a taste of the excitement of the early Church. The Bible became real and vital to her afresh and she was faced with a deeper prayer ministry as the needs of the prisoners came before her every day.

Her overriding aim was to find the newly converted prisoners a spiritual home on release and this was no easy task. We started this quest with no denominational bias but rather sought to find congregations who would offer a welcome to a man with a previous conviction but with a desire for a new start. Constantly challenged about 'follow-up', we offered a surprising response. Our follow-up was only as good as the attitude of outside Christians. Yes, we had to educate and persuade, inspire and challenge groups of Christians whenever we met them, but at the end it was the churches who needed to offer the forgiveness and a new chance to play a better role in the community. Jackie worked long and hard in this area, meeting both joys and sorrows daily, but she always knew there was more to be done and strove to develop a network of supporting churches. We suspect this will be an ever-increasing priority and are always thrilled when we receive a positive reception for a new church member.

Terry Tully knew about welcoming new Christians outside for he had long canvassed for the Church to include the outsider and had a big heart for those on the edges of society. He'd been a member of Hebron Christian Trust and then Prison Fellowship for many years and had developed his particular artistic talent to speak to prisoners in chapel services. He used a sketchboard and pens to tell Biblical messages through slowly emerging diagrams and pictures. Everyone was always transfixed – wondering when the final meaning of the signs would become clear. Terry practised long and hard and it was well worth it.

Early in his career Terry had trained boxers and then moved into the building trade. These two areas forged great contacts for him which he has been able to use. Sometimes he meets prisoners whom he has known outside and he often continues to bump into new Christians once they are back in the community. He is basically a brave man with a caring heart and God has used him greatly.

Similarly Roy Kybett came into the prison and was used to real effect. Having been the pastor of his own community church for many years he found himself looking for a new avenue of service. Popping in for an occasional Bible study in the prison proved to be pivotal for him. Indeed Roy can recall his very first visit to Lewes.

As usual David had thrown the newcomer in at the deep end and asked him to run a Bible Study on, of all places, the Segregation Unit. Quite an initiation for a new helper! Six large inmates sat at a table in the common area as Roy began to explain a passage from the Bible. One inmate began to mumble 'Amen' at every opportunity. Roy endeavoured to ignore this response and ploughed on explaining the nature of Jesus.

The Amens grew louder and another very large inmate began to take offence. 'Here,' warned Stan, 'how can I hear what this vicar's saying with you making that racket all the time? Shut up will you?' He wouldn't shut up. In spite of Roy's instant promotion to Anglican Vicar as awarded by Stan he was beginning to feel out of his depth.

'You got a problem with me ... you come over here!' growled the inmate who liked to make a vocal contribution to his Bible Study. Before Roy knew what was happening the two men were in each other's grasp and delivering some nasty blows at each other before being pulled apart by officers and returned to their cells.

Roy summoned up all his courage and determination and returned his attention to the four remaining men, who'd not moved an inch since the encounter began. They obviously expected him to continue and thinking to himself that this was rather unlike any other Bible Study he'd either attended or run, Roy began to further explain the relevant passage.

Five minutes later a mature little lady appeared in the entrance and without a word to Roy all four men rose and went back to their cells. They emerged a minute later each holding a teddy bear which was minus a head. The lady was from education and had come to escort the men to the needlework class, where no doubt the missing heads were to be attached.

'There was no competition,' said Roy months later. 'Teddy bears win over Bible Study any time.'

When Roy returned to David's office he was asked if it had gone well.

'Well,' responded Roy, 'I'm not sure you would say that.'

If there was doubt in Roy's voice David failed to recognize or acknowledge it. 'So you will come again?' he asked earnestly.

'Oh yes,' replied Roy, 'how could I refuse? Yes. I certainly will.'

Like Bruce before him he was soon committed beyond his wildest imaginings. Indeed he was to become, with the assistance of his wife Barbara, a central, full-time co-worker, responsible with Bruce for aftercare. Everyone on our team was the subject of well-meaning teasing on many occasions and Roy was no exception. His early career had been in Smithfield Market and his open-air life style had given him a fairly rugged appearance.

'Meet Roy – he's an ex-inmate,' David would say to a new prisoner, who looking at the rough tattoos stretching up his muscular arms, found no reason to suspect otherwise and might innocently respond, 'Where did you serve your time then?' Roy grew to smile and use the situation to the bene-fit of God's work. There really was no place for the easily offended in this work, he suspected!

Roy's ministry was very meaningful on the wings of the prison and he would spend a lot of time both on his own and with Bruce explaining to inmates just what had happened to them when they'd accepted Jesus and how this new life would need to be worked on and lived out. Roy enjoyed seeing the inmates grow and was able to use years of experience to nurture and tend the new roots of faith in each individual. He also delighted in the moments of fun and humour the work granted.

'You never told me Jesus was a carpet fitter,' accused Liam one day, surprised by his new-found discovery.

'Well, no,' replied Roy, 'he wasn't. Jesus was a car-pen-ter,' he sounded each syllable clearly to emphasize the point.

'Well what's the difference?' questioned Liam, who was newly converted from an appalling life of crime and violence. 'They're the same thing aren't they?'

'No, Liam,' explained Roy with care, 'they're not. A carpet fitter fits carpets, a carpenter makes things out of wood like tables and chairs or fits doors or window frames.'

A puzzled look engulfed Liam's face as he assimilated this new information. 'That's a chippy!' he triumphed.

Roy shrugged his shoulders and tried not to grin as he realized the reaction he'd receive later as he retold this experience.

'Well,' continued Liam, determined to make his point, 'if Jesus was a chippy – why does it say he's a carpet fitter?'

Defeated, Roy could offer no convincing answer and, enjoying the moment, allowed Liam his moment of glory: 'I don't know, mate – I really don't know at all.'

Some new Christians were moved out very quickly, of course, sometimes within a few days of becoming a Christian, and even if not they were sometimes unavailable for individual follow-up. For this amongst other reasons the letter-writing ministry was developed. Various people worked long and hard on contacting new Christians by letter and supporting them with literature and words of comfort. Eventually Marjorie emerged as the mainstay of communications and her commitment to the role was monumental.

If Bruce was teased about his 'Korean connection' and Roy about his inmate appearance, Marjorie was in line for any Scottish banter that was going. She had a beautiful and well-entrenched accent that was all the more fascinating due to her highly animated facial expressions set off and framed by her splendid spectacles. Always cheerful and bright, her positive spirit was a great asset to our steadily expanding team.

Majorie had wended her way to Lewes from Edinburgh at the tender age of nineteen in pursuit of a boyfriend whom she planned to marry. Ian was working as an electrician in the Prison Service and had been posted to Lewes, but unfortunately the relationship foundered and Marjorie began to make plans to return home. While working her notice she met and fell in love with Peter and consequently stayed down south and eventually married – albeit to a different spouse than she first anticipated. The couple became Christians and after many years in one church moved to another which had just forged links with the chaplaincy at Lewes. Marjorie's life was to reconnect with the prison, and volunteering to write to one or two new Christians she little thought that within months she'd be heading up a whole team of writers and become so committed that she would sometimes write up to 39 letters in one day! She grew to believe that she'd been brought down so far from home for a purpose, even though that plan was not fully revealed for decades.

One night at church God touched her powerfully and she felt God told her that He had given her wings. Gently she felt her arms extend horizontally as she lay on the floor basking in the presence of God. Sensing God's protection, and believing she was given the image of a swan, Marjorie felt her experience was confirmed when two African acquaintances gave her the name Mokwaka. How shocked she was to find that this name meant bird! God seemed to use this experience to prepare and inspire Marjorie for her work in the prison. She felt she was being reassured that she would be able to take on a new role and that she would soar over any difficulties she might face. Sometimes unsure of her own capabilities, she felt inspired to take on a new and challenging role. Her strength and sustenance would be God Himself and she would find a freedom within the task that resembled a bird's freedom in flight. Her job requires a dedication beyond most people's capability and is combined with an outside occupation too. Her experience of the power of God was not a private boost to her own self-esteem or an excitement soon forgotten or laid aside, no, for Marjorie this was an impetus and a strengthening for the coming hard work. She said, 'I am so excited at the work God is doing in the prison and thrilled to be part of it.' But she also went on to confess, 'My opinions on people and attitudes towards things have surprised me. I didn't even realize I held some opinions or realize how narrow-minded I actually was. The men have written to me and I have learned much about life and changed my views.'

Marjorie had learned that some of our dearest beliefs prove to be based on prejudice and that close exposure to different members of society has the effect of breaking down barriers. This works two ways, of course, because the men began to forge useful relationships with the writers from an early stage.

'These people really care,' said one inmate.

'I've had a letter, I've had a letter!' shouted another waving the piece of paper triumphantly in the air.

Marjorie and her team were certainly involved in a very real ministry.

However Marjorie confessed: 'At the same time I became aware of the spiritual battle we are up against and it has caused me to pray more, realizing I can do nothing without God. I can't do anything in my own strength at all. Working in the prison reminded me afresh that I am in a privileged position. It's very exciting!'

So the little band of helpers has grown and is developing, all in ways we never planned or even foresaw. How good it was of God to send us Bruce from

Korea, Jackie and Maureén from Crawley, the young people from Turners Hill, Roy from Smithfield Market, Terry from the boxing ring and Marjorie from Scotland. All the jobs were interrelated yet independently organized, all the people were totally devoted to their tasks but all were united in purpose. Of course we had lots of extra help too. Many people gave generously of their time and talent and supported the work in many ways. Musicians, writers and prayers all added to the ministry and we trust gained from it too. Some stayed long-term, others short-term, but all were valuable, drawn by God and vital to the task on hand.

Naturally there were ups and downs but they were really minimal in comparison to the size of the work. Some moved out because the ministry was not for them or because our style didn't suit them or theirs didn't suit us. Perhaps disturbance was at a minimum, however, because of the task-orientated nature of the ministry. There was no time for the luxury of petty squabbles or doctrinal differences or for the wrangling that develops in highly democratic groups. It probably wouldn't be everyone's cup of tea but to us at the core of the work it was if some heavenly head-hunter of the highest calibre was at work. We didn't know the volunteers on a deep personal level before they joined us but God did. He knew who was going to serve and thrive on the ministry to prisoners and He brought them to us. We all deliberately avoided contention and submitted ourselves to the tasks ahead. In that sense it proved to be a dream team. We also knew that relationships prospered because of the ever deepening prayer cover offered by both our own prayer line and by those far and wide who supported the ministry.

Gradually we met more and more folk who having been drawn onto the edges of the work received great inspiration from it. 'I'm just so glad something's happening,' said one, 'it can be so demoralizing being a Christian sometimes.'

'It's wonderful to hear of a positive response,' said another, 'we all seem to be so negative.' Running down, finding fault with or generally debunking exciting works of God is so easy and rather common, it would seem, in British churches. We come across these attitudes of course but rejoice too that so many people were prepared to join in, in spirit at least, and rejoice with us all at the new spiritual lives being started. Our team were making it all possible and we were so grateful to them all, but even more grateful to the One who picked them, prepared them and sent them to us for His purposes.

It is exciting too to know that many other Christians, some even unknown to us, can share in our prison work because distance is no barrier to either prayer or letter-writing. Any wellwisher who feels drawn by God towards helping new Christian prisoners can join our prayer line, receive the prayer letters, offer themselves as a Christian correspondent or contribute by funding the supply of Walkmans, tapes and literature so vital to the ministry. In this way our team is ever expanding, involving more Christians in the task of welcoming new Christians to God's family. God's economies are never our own and time after time people have found that by giving in these ways they have received a great personal blessing. It is both challenging and immensely rewarding to write to someone who knows so very little about the Christian faith and to watch them slowly grow in understanding and love of God. People who would never normally meet with offenders have found them to be open and very grateful for their offered helping hand even if they find the conditions in prison rather unconducive to making replies.

'I've got a letter from a Christian outside,' shouted Craig waving the pages in front of David's face one day. 'Fancy bothering with me – would you like to read it too?'

David shared this man's special moment and just thanked God that there were Christian people who did care enough to 'bother with' Craig, for without them, the dream team would certainly not be complete at all. Finally, finding a supporting church or group of Christians for the new believers is arguably our most important follow-up task. It's not as easy as perhaps it should be. David returned one day from meeting a largish group of church leaders who'd expressed interest in the inmates' reaction to the Gospel.

David, however, was downcast. 'I asked them if anyone would be willing to take on an ex-inmate on their release,' he explained. 'I'm afraid not one approached me positively afterwards. It was very disappointing.'

'Not one?' I queried. 'Really?'

'Well one minister did come up,' David continued, 'but he said he'd only been in place eighteen months and was still finding his feet. He couldn't take on such a new member yet.'

We were so grateful for those who were brave enough to take on new Christians and quite often they discovered that, far from being a strain, the ex-inmate was keen and made a sound contribution to church life, albeit perhaps in an individual style. We always pray for more volunteers in this area and trust that God will bless those who are prepared to assist in this most valuable way. The expansion of this work is only restricted by the response of Christians outside. Hundreds of converts cannot be seriously followed up by one or two people however dedicated they may be. We realized this once it hit us that more men had become Christians than there are members in most local churches. Sowing, reaping and nurturing are all important roles and if one area is lacking it is to the detriment of the others. We would request that you, too, prayerfully consider any part you would play in this challenging but oh-so-exciting response to the Good News of Jesus Christ.

*

CHAPTER 7

The Proof of the Pudding
is in the Incident Book

Howard just couldn't prevent his excitement showing through. He was answering questions extremely well and thrust his fist into his hand, saying, 'Come on, give me a really hard one!'

We'd managed the almost impossible because Howard was on a pass-out from the prison to attend a meeting organized in a hotel in Lewes. Lewes itself is a rich but small country town, being the capital of East Sussex and full of historical connections. The castle and beautiful buildings are visited by many and the town's setting, nestling between rising downs, is an artist's dream. Delightfully safe, in spite of its prison connection, it fosters a privileged, parochial, way of life and a reluctance perhaps to take on new ideas.

A formal meeting had been arranged to let townsfolk know what was going on in Lewes Prison. The ministry had been going on for some time but we had the feeling that locally it was expected to be a flash in the pan that would soon die down. When it didn't, an interest began to grow, albeit in restrained style. David and I both felt a sense of unease about this meeting as it could well have been not a response to general interest but rather a means of forcing explanations and justifications. We felt no need to rise to such demands as although we were thrilled to tell the stories or happy to explain things to genuine enquirers, we did not believe it was not our place to persuade people to go along with us.

Sure enough we arrived at the meeting to find an audience arranged round a dais on which one chair was placed centrally. A microphone was strategically positioned and what looked like a spotlight focused where the occupant of that chair was to sit. It gave a whole new meaning to being 'on the spot', we observed. However, we had risen to the occasion and on arrival requested politely, 'May we have six chairs up there please?'

The question met with genuine surprise so David went on, 'I've brought my team with me too!'

Eventually the seats were provided and David, Bruce, Marjorie, Maureen, Howard and myself sat down. We had the distinct impression that this was not what had been expected, but it certainly made us feel more secure.

One by one we shared with the seventy-odd people what we did on the team and how we had experienced the happenings in the prison. Everyone listened. They couldn't help it, I believe, because it made for very interesting hearing. Maureen told about the prayer line, and Marjorie spoke about the letter-writing. She also pointed out our need for financial assistance for Bibles, Walkmans and secretarial help. I spoke about the services and Bruce about his follow-up tasks. Then David rose to introduce Howard. No one knew who Howard was, in fact no one had the least suspicion of his identity. Howard was in a leather jacket over jeans and as he rose he towered above the audience and looked around.

'This is Howard,' David said, 'and tonight we've made history. He has come out this evening to tell you what it's like to be a Christian inside, because he is an inmate at Lewes.'

The surprise could almost be felt and the rest of us enjoyed surveying the faces of the group from our privileged position on the dais. Now this would be interesting as they weren't expecting this, we were sure. Howard told them how he became a Christian and how others had started to believe too. He did well, and having been incredibly frightened, was now in full flow and loving it all. The questions flowed until one man asked, 'Has all this made any difference in the prison itself?'

Howard didn't hesitate. 'Well,' he responded thoughtfully, 'the proof of the pudding is in the incident book. Over the last few months hardly anyone has pushed the panic button. We sort things out ourselves. That's a real proof.'

In every corridor and room there stands an emergency button. Officers push it when they need assistance or when there is some trouble on the wings. Howard was suggesting that because so many people had become Christians on his wing the button was not in action very much at all. Of course the population of the prison is forever changing but at this point the balance of Christians was certainly strong enough to make a difference.

The questioner on this occasion was certainly satisfied, but he had made a genuine point. Prisons are dangerous places. Was Christianity able to tackle the real problems of violence that these men experienced?

Of course Christians who work in prisons believe God is their protection and strength and in many ways He is. However, assuming that one can walk into dangerous situations unprepared and casually is far too simplistic and lacking in common sense. Creating danger through ignorance or an uncaring attitude is highly irresponsible. Danger in a prison is everywhere. There is the danger of actual violence by inmates and this is the most spectacular sort, of course, but there are also the more subtle dangers of being trapped morally or through speech.

Anyone who works in a prison has to understand that the primary function of the establishment is security. If people make the work of that department more difficult, they are being unco-operative and unhelpful. Several people found working under restraint too difficult, but others learned that even with the utmost regard for security there was still plenty one could do. We always had to stress to visitors not to pass anything to inmates however generous they were feeling. Firstly, inmates were able to think up functions for ordinary objects that are well beyond the average person's imagination. Thus two batteries in a sock become a lethal weapon, a comb becomes a means of slitting a wrist, a piece of wire a means of wiring up a door to the light to render it a method of electrocution, or at the very least a nasty shock for an officer trying to enter.

Secondly, items could be sold on the 'prison market' for drugs or favours and thirdly any possessions have to be carefully recorded on a property card in case of movement by the prisoner or theft or 'taxing' on the wings.

People had to develop a whole new way of thinking, which for fairly innocent unstreetwise Christians was quite difficult. The seriousness of breaking any part of the code often took a long time to filter into the average brain but it was disregarded at everyone's peril. Even a word said out of turn could have far-reaching consequences. Prisoners are very cute and will hold you to what you've said; after all they have few relationships with outsiders and nothing to distract their memory from what they've heard in their limited conversational opportunities.

Sometimes people would promise to write to or visit a prisoner and then let that person down. Sometimes people were very casual about this, saying they were too busy or committed elsewhere or saying nothing at all, which was worse. Inmates had often been let down all their lives and here it was happening all over again. Christians were no different after all! Occasionally it was more serious because the inmate would fall into a depression. There is always the danger, of course, that one's words could cause someone to actually take their own life and although it has never yet happened in our experience that is not to say it never would or that we didn't pray constantly for a guard over our lips.

Similarly prisoners would look out for the slightest hypocrisy and one couldn't afford to be less than totally straight. They watch every move an individual makes and are ready to query any discrepancy. The officers too were on the look-out.

'You're not in my *News of the World* this week Rev,' proclaimed an officer at the gate with several others standing round.

'No,' David grinned, 'not this week.'

A touch of lightness disguised a serious point. The *News of the World* was well read within the walls and spotting the latest vicar scandal was almost a sport.

One day David received a personal call, or at least that is what it purported to be. Only when he was finally connected with David did the man reveal his true identity as a reporter from this aforementioned newspaper.

'Is it true a prisoner was shipped out because you passed him drugs?' was the stark question targeted at the totally unprepared and unsuspecting chaplain. Now here was an opportunity to ruin a reputation if ever there was one. A moment of fluster, a quick joke about how he did it all the time or a momentary lapse of concentration in another way could have resulted in a catastrophe. Headlines would have blazoned the 'news' across that famous paper with appalling consequences. The reporter had a job to do and he was after an angle.

David had learned to keep cool. His experience both with the prisoners recently and with his first priest-in-charge on the Isle of Wight had taught him to weigh every word and never say anything that could be taken down in evidence and used against you.

'All prisoners are moved. This is a remand prison,' said David calmly. 'I don't know where he's gone.'

'I understand the inmate's returned to drugs and you supplied them,' went on the journalist.

'I know of no such thing,' replied David, determined not to sound agitated or anxious in case it was misinterpreted as being caught out.

'We can tell you where he's gone,' said the man determined to grind something out of this situation. 'He's gone to Winchester.'

'I know nothing of that,' said David.

After several other attempts to either gain information or wear David down into saying something unwise the reporter gave it up as a bad job. He found no reaction – no denial – no anger – no refusal to speak – just words obviously given by God to calm the situation down – for there was no story the next day in the paper, although it took hours to inform security, the Home Office and others of the event.

In fact that reference to Winchester gave us a clue. It could have been a recent transfer of a prisoner to that particular prison that resulted in someone trying to gain payment from the paper for information. We shall never know, of course, but we're grateful that God helped David to be so calm in what was a very tricky situation. It had happened with a local paper before and could well occur in the future with less satisfactory results. The fact that there was no truth in the rumour at all mattered little to them as it would have sold a few papers and offered a small solace to those who choose to believe a leopard can never change his spots. The prayer line was very busy that night covering the situation with God's grace. Our dependency on them became ever more obvious.

However, not all the dangers are ones of reputation or security; there is of course real physical danger in the establishment. David tended to underplay this aspect because he didn't want it to become the main focus of people's attention. However, in reality he had to live with it on a day-to-day basis, as does everyone who works in a prison.

David went to meet Steve in all innocence but as he went to enter the cell an officer warned, 'He's quite violent, David, take care.'

David went in and began to make conversation. 'Do you want God to help you?' he soon asked.

'Go away,' was the swift response, 'I don't want God.'

Because he was on the wing anyway, David tried again the next day.

'Look,' said Steve, 'I hate vicars. Go away and if you ever mention God to me again, I'll kill you.' David looked at this huge man towering above him and, moving towards the door, realized that the man, who had 176 counts of violence against him, meant business.

For several days David avoided Steve's cell. Here was one man for whom he could do nothing, but of course he'd counted without God's intervention.

David was visiting someone in the hospital when he felt a tap on his shoulder. 'Hello, Vicar. I want a word with you.'

David turned slowly round and found himself face to face with Steve. His heart began to beat a little faster, his mouth dried up and he could hardly believe his ears. Later he joked that he'd told God he wasn't ready to go yet but I doubt he felt that chirpy at the time. Nervously he went with Steve into a small annexe and waited.

'I've decided I want your God,' Steve said grimly.

The wind was taken out of David's sails and it was a very timid chaplain who prayed with the man who not three days before had threatened to kill him.

Another incident happened in the hospital wing at Belmarsh Prison when David entered a tiny room to speak to Jason. He was suicidal and needed help.

'I want to kill myself,' he said, staring at the wall. 'There is no point in going on.'

'Are you really ready to meet God?' David gently asked and sat down on a simple chair backed up against the door, as there was little room anywhere else.

'What do you mean?' questioned Jason, slowly turning his head to include David in his gaze.

'Well, if you kill yourself, you'll meet God before you're ready,' said David, using a simple reasoning he'd used before.

'Are you ready to meet God then?' queried Jason.

'Yes, I am,' replied David quietly but confidently.

'Well then,' said Jason, reaching into his pocket, pulling out a short piece of rope and wrapping it round his fingers, 'I'll kill you instead.' He started to move his body steadily inch by inch closer to David, winding and twisting that rope all the time.

David had to think quickly and he realized straight away there was a problem. The first rules of visiting are leave the door free and check out the location of the panic button. Because of the hospital location there was no button and David's chair was up against the door. David knew there was no way to sweet-talk his way out of this one. This man was obviously unstable and help was needed. With sweaty palms he plucked the whistle from his key belt and putting it to his lips blew loudly. For one awful second there was silence and the two men eyed each other up almost in disbelief. Then down the corridor came the thundering sound of six duty officers running into the unit. With strong shoulders they set themselves against the door. David's chair lurched violently and he flew off across the tiny room, saving himself from injury by throwing his arms forward. Then the officers were in, Jason was restrained, the rope hastily removed and peace almost immediately restored. In a place of restrained violence such an event is almost commonplace. Three days later Jason surrendered to the lordship of Christ and became a Christian. David did not know how to help him, but God, since he had both made and loved Jason, certainly did.

James was so violent in Belmarsh Prison, London, he was restricted in the Segregation Unit and on what was known as a four-man unlock. This rule required four officers to be present whenever the door of the cell was unlocked or opened, in order to prevent a violent incident.

'You definitely can't go in there, Chaplain,' an officer told David in no uncertain manner. 'He's too dangerous.'

David looked at the cell door and thought for a moment. Here was a man who had requested help. He'd sent in an application form to see the priest. He wanted help, but how could David provide it through a cell door? 'You can speak to him through the hatch,' continued the officer, seeing that David was hesitating and wanted to speak.

'Oh, fine,' said David. 'Then that's what I'll do!' So pushing back the window hatch on the outside of the cell door David spoke to the man inside.

James looked up as the hatch door swung back. He was a lean, athletic chap who looked quite calm but who had piercing eyes. 'I need help,' he said, staring straight at David. 'What can I do with my life?' David looked with wonder at this man who was so violent in prison that four officers were needed to hand him his lunch, asking help of the chaplain.

David proceeded to talk quite normally to him about his need of God and God's love for him, albeit through a tiny space in the door. Eventually the time came to pray with him; and this too was conducted through the hatch. 'Move nearer, James,' said David, 'so I can reach you.'

James moved closer and leaned up against the door. This desperate man had got himself into trouble. His temper had rendered his life a misery. He needed a new power and strength in his life if ever anyone did. David reached both his hands through the door and placed them on James' head. He then prayed as he always did for God's powerful Holy Spirit to fill this man with love and strength. James rested against the door as David finished and fell silent. He did not think it strange that prayer had been conducted through a cell door, for he only knew his life was different. He'd been touched by the power of God in a real way.

David then passed a Bible through the same gap and began to explain how to use it. Although unusual in the retelling, it seemed quite natural at the time for obviously no cell bars can stop God's love reaching out to even the most violent of men.

David's work in Belmarsh included servicing a Category A unit where some very dangerous men were kept. Here stayed men in an altogether different league to those men on other wings. Members of terrorist gangs, murderers of the worst kind and other professional criminals all had to be kept quite separate from others.

One morning there had been a report in the *Guardian* that 40 of the most dangerous men in Britain were in that unit. As David entered a group formed round him. 'Do you know,' said one, 'you are surrounded by forty of the most dangerous men in Britain?'

David looked round him – what was he to say, for they were obviously proud of their new-found status and title and out to prove their toughness?

An arrow prayer shot up, because David needed the wisdom of Solomon, he was sure. Blessed with quick wit, he looked up at the inmate who had challenged him, glanced round at all the others and, turning to face the first man fully, replied, 'And which number are you then?'

There was a silence. Attention to David had now dissipated. The men had a new consideration to attend to. Just which one was the most dangerous? What would this man say? Would he claim a position higher than the others would accept? Of course the man actually said nothing. He could not think of a suitable answer that would not land him in trouble for too high a placing or embarrassment for too low a number. The men jeered a little and wandered off leaving David experiencing a very strong sense of relief and offering a heartfelt prayer of thanks.

Some violence David saw was of altogether another kind. If he was scared of overemphasizing the violence of inmates he was even more wary of mentioning strange practices or interest in genuine evil lest it detract from the basic evangelism and power of God to change lives. In his youth he had been to services of testimony sometimes based round baptisms where a huge emphasis had been placed on people's lives pre-conversion. He felt this had occasionally been an excuse for hearing about or creating interest in evil forces and was a contradiction of the biblical instruction to think on pure and holy things. He describes how people would switch off once the person got to the 'Christian bit', and how a minister might encourage attendance next week by indicating that at that service there might be someone even worse! Naturally things weren't quite as bad as that but there is always that tendency in us all to be drawn and fascinated by improper and wrong things so David felt he should never encourage such vicarious experience by dwelling on certain unusual events. Consequently references to occult or other powers were noticeably missing from sermons and talks and if mentioned at all were strictly relevant and short.

However, such things were present and whilst neither of us was prepared to see demons round every corner or accept strange interpretations for the merely unusual, many of the people in prison have dealt with elements of the occult and abnormal, even Satanic practices. Bob was under rule 43 because his offences involved children. He claimed involvement in appalling and unusual practices linked to devil worship and sacrifice. He was quite calm to speak to, but said he was bothered by his conscience.

David prayed with him as he always did with those who requested him to. He had no time to fetch outsiders, for Bob was due out next day. He knew Jesus was with him. What else could he do but follow through? As David prayed the man began to shake. Then forming his hand into a fist he let out an enormous scream and ran across the room slamming his fist into the metal basin at the side of the bed. He then fell silent, sat on the bed and said, 'It's gone.'

David sat on the chair wondering what had happened and offering up silent prayer constantly.

Later he tried to have Bob properly followed up, but this kind of situation was always difficult, as he would need professional help of all kinds after such a life style. Suffice to say that he now faced his rehabilitation with God and there was no reason why a full change in this man's life could not take place.

If the place was dangerous for David it was more so for prisoners. Time after time David's work would consist of helping the victims of violence within the prison. The inmates dish out their own discipline and retribution, some of it at second hand.

At night we might hear inmates chanting '1,000 Green Bottles' as a punishment, or someone would push a plate of food in another's face. Recompense for debts was often demanded and innocent cellmates were sometimes held responsible for another's 'crime'. One man convicted of arson had his hair set alight and another was so terrified of an attack that he could no longer retain control of his bowels.

As Christians we are used to the extraordinary coincidences the Church network opens us up to. We meet someone at a house party who knows someone with whom we used to sing in the choir. We hear of a minister in Durham who used to be in Hove or we meet people with a million and one other connections with us or our own acquaintances. 'It's a small world in Christian circles,' we proudly say.

As prisoners and members of the criminal community an inmate finds there is a similar network for him. This either works to his advantage for assistance or it works against him very badly. Messages about the nature of inmates' crimes move swiftly round the grapevines from prison to prison. Once on the debt list or picked out as the perpetrator of an unacceptable crime against women or children the tentacles reach out until there is no escape. Time and time again David found victims of this particular circuit. Bill was an American who had attacked his wife for some reason. This is an unacceptable crime *par excellence*. A group of self-appointed judges had heard on the grapevine that this man was now in Lewes, so they waited until he was in the shower and they poured a kettle of boiling water over him. David met him in the hospital unable even to wear his shirt for any length of time, but more than ready it must be said to meet with God.

Sometimes everything got on top of prisoners so that they were not victims of others' violence but rather victims of their own. The festive seasons brought their batches of attempted and, sadly, sometimes successful suicides. Bob was in prison and very unhappy. He regretted his crime and his only consolation was his weekly visit from his wife.

One afternoon he was walking through the wing when an officer waylaid him. 'Hey, Bob,' he said, 'you're off to Oxford tomorrow.' It was a cruel comment and harshly given. Bob was at breaking point for he knew his wife would seldom be able to make such a long trip and he would be deprived of his only golden moments in a very bleak calendar of events. That evening he made a strip from a sheet and twisted it round. Attaching it to the light socket he intended to end his misery by hanging himself

163

from the electric light. He quickly fell unconscious, but unbeknown to him the light gave way at the socket and he was slightly supported by the floor. Outside an officer on duty noticed a light had fused down the wing. It was quite annoying because his walk of duty after lights out was quite long and he could have been absent from that particular corridor for some time. He summoned a workman who fixed the bulb. For some reason he then decided to check all the cells in case their security lights had blown too. He went down the corridor opening all the hatches and looking briefly in. At Bob's cell he paused because his light was out. He got out his key and opening the door saw Bob hanging by the sheet from the light cable. Summoning help at once he cut Bob down and began to resuscitate him. That night that officer saved Bob's physical life but he actually did much more than that. David came to visit Bob, and Bob found Christ in the hospital wing. A near tragedy had been redeemed by the sheer grace of God.

Bob wrote, 'I never before felt like taking my life. I've always had what I thought was a strong character. I guess the build-up of certain problems caused me to be very anxious, so that I felt like taking my own life.'

Bob went on to say he was so glad he'd failed and that destiny had saved him from death. He spoke of his fear of being on his own in prison and how he loved his wife and family, but added, 'I feel safer. God seems to have shown me a different way of life. After your prayer, David, a heavy weight was taken off me. My wife can see a difference.

I'm not thinking of only myself any more. We're sorting our lives out now. Thank God for what he did for me.'

Such a testimony is bound to move us for we find God able to save the worst offenders and the most desperate men we have ever met. In comparison some of our problems pale into insignificance and we realize our doubts are irrational. Bob's witness will no doubt be a powerful means of helping others for many years to come.

As for Christians, were they exempt from attack? Far from it. As we found, becoming a Christian was no insurance policy at all. Simon became a Christian in Lewes and was quickly transferred to a London prison. He wrote monthly to both David and Marjorie and talked constantly about his new-found faith. Whilst in London, Simon was the unfortunate victim of a gang rape in a cell, a more appalling fate being hard to imagine. Transferred immediately to the Isle of Wight, Simon continued in his faith after an experience that would have thrown the best of us into a flurry of counselling, trauma and doubt. Having written regularly as ever, one month no letters arrived. David wondered why this faithful man had failed to send his usual contact. He needn't have worried, however, for Marjorie came panting up one Sunday morning and said, 'Simon's out – he's coming in to our church this morning.'

In spite of all these incidents, in one sense Howard was quite right. The evidence of lots of changed lives was the incident book. The Christians themselves learned to solve problems in other ways and would pray or talk things through. It didn't happen overnight, but it did happen. One day someone who owed a new Christian called Nick Pook arrived in the prison.

'I'll kill him!' announced Nick when he found out. Realizing already that this was no longer an available option he reduced the man's summary sentence to a thumping.

'Well, he took my car,' grumbled Nick. The team member involved took Nick slowly through the required response and eventually Nick accepted he could no longer take such revenge.

'This is hard,' grumbled Nick, reluctant but convinced.

Oh yes, it was hard but the evidence and fruit were beginning to show, and all the more real for not being an instant transformation. Like the rest of us these men had to learn that the Christian road is arduous and in some places difficult and full of self-discipline. With the joy comes the responsibility. Our pleasure was to see so many making huge moral strides, and our prayer was that they would continue. We also prayed that the Church outside would give due recognition to their achievements and offer their support so that they would grow even more. Christians are known by their fruit, yes, but I believe that moral progress is relative. It's no struggle for me to give up excessive drink or drugs because I don't want them anyway. My temptations will be something nearer to home, and personal for me. The ex-drug addict who resists taking drugs again, or the man who has made his way by violence who resists hitting someone, is making a huge step forward. God sees the secret efforts of our hearts, and His and not others', judgements are what really count after all!

Nick Pook's efforts to live out a new life style by turning from violence were heartening, but the story of his conversion and subsequent decisions were not only dramatic but also catalysts that would throw both Nick and the chaplaincy at Lewes into the national and international limelight.

CHAPTER 8

✳

The Truth, the Whole Truth, and Nothing but the Truth

The heavy wooden garden gate banged solidly and the front door clicked shut. Familiar sounds dragged me from that warm and cosy reverie halfway between sleeping and wakefulness. I sat up in bed, pulling the pillow up behind my back to support myself, and felt the stairs pound as my husband David raced upstairs and then burst into the room. 'We're in, we're in!' he exclaimed, rustling the *Observer* newspaper feverishly in his excitement. 'There's a big picture of Keith, Nick and myself,' he continued, barely pausing for breath. 'Hang on, I'll read it ...'

It was 7 o'clock on a Sunday morning and I was hardly on top form, but I was used to David's general excitement-level and had long ago decided to 'go with the flow' as opposed to attempting slowing tactics.

David and I had been in Lewes for some fifteen months since he became the Anglican Chaplain to the prison in the town. Many inmates had been making decisions to become Christians and this had caused great interest in local churches and even further afield. One particular inmate, Nick, because of his new-found faith, had chosen to tell the whole truth and plead guilty to certain offences and had consequently been 'sent down' for a longer term than expected. The *Observer* had picked up this story and had promised coverage this morning. So it was that we were full of anticipation as we scoured the prominent half-page story. We breathed a sigh of relief as we realized that every aspect of a 'nutty vicar' story was pleasingly absent.

We reread the article carefully and were thrilled at the clear presentation of our work and the well-told report of the dramatic series of events that had changed the life of the particularly notorious prisoner Nick Pook. The evidence was clear – the national media were eager to tell the story of this man who had been given a longer prison sentence for simply telling the truth!

Nick had been in Lewes some time before David met him. An obvious Londoner, he was a stocky, strong man who made use of his gym time to tone his muscles to perfection. He was what is called a 'baron' or 'head man' on the convicted wing, able to supply drugs to all who sought solace or meaning in them, and exerting power over the other prisoners on the wing. He was constantly in the Segregation Unit, a barren, bleak group of cells set apart for those who commit misdemeanours of various kinds. He was certainly an unlikely candidate for putting his name down for Sunday morning chapel. With his sturdy, muscular build and his controlling temperament, many of the younger inmates were terrified of him.

Nick was clever, however, because although he was a supplier of drugs, he was no addict himself. He could get hold of any amount of stuff, but was never tempted to use it himself. Every day, David meets prisoners whose lives revolve around finding and funding drugs and who are in prison because they have thieved and robbed to maintain their sad habit, but Nick was different, of course, because he only supplied them. However, one day he broke his own rule and whether he was driven by the boredom and frustrations of prison life or by anger and despair is hard to say, but his decision to take a huge dose of heroin was to prove critical in his life. He went on a very bad trip indeed and ended up alone, frightened and in total anguish in his cell. He was, in fact, at the point of taking his own life.

With prison riots and escapes so much in the news in recent years, no one imagines that the life of a prison officer is a bed of roses. The reaction of individuals to the stresses of the job is as varied as the men and women who pursue this particular career. Some are tough, some are nervous and some are both professional and kind. All the officers at Lewes found Nick a handful to put it mildly and many felt he was receiving his just desserts for his behaviour. Nick always acted tough on the wing and was constantly in trouble for being unco-operative and if he was now in a spot of bother, there may have been some who would have felt there was no harm in that. Officer Smith, however, had experience and wisdom enough to rise above any such thoughts. He called David to tell him that there was a man in the cells who really did need help. One thing the officers at

Lewes had learned about David was that he would respond to such requests with speed, and they were therefore willing to use him when the need arose.

Nick was sitting on the bed in his cell when David entered. He was wretched and miserable, and looking completely drained. David had seldom met a man more desperate.

In anguish after what had been a very bad experience, Nick could see only one way out of his troubles. He had acquired some bleach tablets from some unrevealed source and was threatening to take them. 'I want to kill myself,' he said starkly.

David knew this was no time to exercise counselling skills or to debate life-and-death philosophies. This was crisis ministry and it needed more than a cosy chat to solve Nick's overwhelming problems. 'Well God doesn't want you to kill yourself. He's got things for you to do.'

'Has he?' cried Nick. 'Can he do anything for someone like me?'

'He certainly can,' said David, and, miraculously, something stirred inside Nick. For perhaps the first time in his life Nick, used to being the tough guy, felt a need for someone greater than himself to help sort his life out. David began to pray and Nick responded with genuine remorse and repentance.

What did Nick pray? *Although he would not have known the meaning of the actual words remorse and repentance*, his cry to God was heartfelt. 'I'm sorry for everything I've done,' prayed Nick and then he continued as tears began to flow down his pained but concentrating face. 'I can't cope with my life any more. If You don't help me, then I'm going to kill myself. Please help me, I'm desperate.' Nick was shaking from head to toe and sobbing loudly. There could be no doubt that his cries for help were genuine.

So these two men, worlds apart perhaps in their experience of life, continued in prayer together. David encouraged and led Nick to ask Jesus to enter his life for the first time.

'I want you to come into my life, Jesus, and take over,' said Nick.

'Do you mean this?' David questioned him. 'This is no one-off fix, Nick, you know. This is for life.'

'I really mean it,' said Nick, 'I really do.'

As Nick knelt down by his bed in the cramped and rather dismal cell, David placed his hands on his head and asked God to fill Nick with the Holy Spirit. It was a simple prayer, partly in tongues, partly in plain speech, and as had happened so many times previously, David felt his fingers warm as God worked through him to fill this remorseful man with Himself.

As David finished praying Nick looked up and the change was remarkable. He looked relieved and calm. 'I feel so clean inside,' he explained.

Saying no more he walked across to the basin and splashed his face with running water. As he dabbed his features with the towel, he must have been aware that he had broken down for the first time in jail. The baron on the wing had in fact surrendered to God and the truth was he would never be the same again.

'My blood pressure's changed,' he announced incredulously. 'I feel wonderful. The trip's over, I'm OK.'

Whenever he spoke about those life-transforming moments, Nick insisted that his blood pressure changed. This was a crucial element of his dramatic conversion and for him ensured its reality. We all experience God's presence individually and express our encounters with him differently. Nick had no previous experiences to guide him, neither did he have the theological vocabulary to describe the moment that his life was turned around.

'My blood pressure's changed', was Nick's own testimony, his way of saying that God had powerfully met him and transformed his life.

This teaches us such an important lesson. We cannot expect the previously unchurched convert suddenly to adopt a language or mind set that happens to coincide with our own when it comes to expressing spirituality. Indeed, part of the joy of working among men like Nick is the refreshing and colourful turn of phrase which they so often use to describe spiritual experiences. If only we are prepared to listen to such simple yet profound expressions, our own understanding of the unexpected ways in which God works can be enlarged.

David gave Nick a Bible when he made his momentous choice, although initially it was an alien comfort. A complete Bible with its double columns of closely-printed text can be intimidating to someone who only ever reads the *Sun* newspaper or who cannot read at all. David suggested Nick started reading at Matthew 2 – a simple suggestion which he offers to all new Christians. Sometimes even that was misunderstood and some inmates asked David whether, having read that chapter for several days, they might now move on.

I had a chat with Nick a few days later about how to get the most out of the Bible. Very simply, I explained a bit about the Old and New Testaments and how it was a good idea to read the sections about Jesus first. Bible study guides are of limited value to people with no knowledge of religious language and even the most simple daily notes can seem daunting. I gave a booklet to Nick with the hope that its simple message would help to fill the gaps in his understanding of what had happened in him. He was so appreciative and drank in every word. His desire to learn was clearly apparent right from the start, even though he was beset by difficulties.

Part of his struggle involved his eyesight, which was not good. We sought out a large-print Bible for him and he was thrilled. We also gave him a Walkman and a set of dramatized Bible tapes from the Bible Society.

Armed with a Walkman paid for by our supporters, Nick was off. He read and reread all that was offered to him and listened to his tapes for hours on end. His thirst for the Word of God was exceptional and certainly inspirational. We felt ashamed that we had sometimes regarded our own daily Bible reading as a bit of a chore. Nick had a lot to learn but he was teaching us a great deal too.

Most of the music on the wings is loud and aggressive. Rap is a firm favourite, inflicted endlessly on all who are there to hear it. However, coming out of Nick's cell there was a new sound. At full volume the voice of the narrator reading the Bible proclaimed God's message to the world.

Cries of 'Turn that racket off!' and other less polite requests fell on deaf ears. Undaunted Nick continued, determined that everyone should share his new inspiration – all day long.

Of course reading the Bible is only one aspect of a life attuned to God, and Nick quickly began to make other changes. In order to go to Sunday chapel, men have to sign a list on Saturday. It is very easy to forget to do this because each day is much the same in prison and the markers we may use to progress through the week are missing. Nick never failed to sign up for chapel – this was an occasion he was not going to miss. His beaming face was always present at the chapel door as we stood there to greet the inmates as they came to worship each Sunday. Nick also began sharing his new-found faith and took his first steps in the life of prayer. These signs of new life are common to all new Christians but expressing them in the close, confined and aggressive atmosphere of a prison, with no Christian background to rely on, is far from easy. Any change in his life style was bound to be both dramatic and transparent. Nick was soon brought face to face with the real cost of living as Jesus' disciple in prison.

Life on the wing at Lewes Prison is claustrophobic. Some prisoners live with two others in a tiny cell and even though the practice of slopping out is finished, toilets in the cells grant hardly any privacy. Bullying is common and any new young inmate who arrives with smart trainers or a branded tee shirt will seldom keep them for long.

Along the echoing corridors, the routine sounds of metal doors clanging, keys rattling and metal buckets being dragged across the floors imprint themselves deeply in the memories of the inmates. For years later, these sounds bring back vivid memories of being banged up for hours on end while prison officers and orderlies go about their normal duties. At the same time, this relentless cacophony offers familiarity and a strange comfort in a world of uncertainty, frustration and fear. The noisy routines connected with food and cleanliness are important landmarks when life offers no variety nor freedom nor outlet. People who write outraged letters to national newspapers suggesting that prisons are like holiday camps would only need to spend a day in one to correct that view.

It was in this world of keys, locks and metal buckets that Nick began living out the consequences of his decision to follow Christ. He was not given an easy time of it when his new-found life style became known. Teasing became a way of life and everyone was watching him like a hawk for any slip-up. 'In the God Squad now, Nick?' shouted an inmate.

'You're a con man, Nick,' laughed an officer, 'but you won't con me.'

'Charlie Pook's got religion – never,' muttered a man on the wing.

Nick was often called Charlie, but in the past it had been a sign of fear and respect. Nick now had to earn those things again, and everyone was talking about him.

It was all particularly difficult because Nick really had no idea how a Christian should behave.

We had to make sure we did not pass on mere cultural differences as spiritual truths, which was a huge responsibility, but Nick had to learn how to live his life taking account of his new-found Saviour and Friend. Each thing we said was taken on trust and acted on precisely. We tried to impose as little as possible and trusted God would continue the work in Nick which He had so clearly begun.

Nevertheless, however much we may have worried about Nick it was clear that Nick did not share the same degree of concern about himself. He was used to handling tricky situations, having been a major player on the wing. Prison inmate hierarchy is highly structured and your place in it is a key to survival. Prior to Nick's conversion we had prayed hard for an opening onto this difficult wing of the prison. Nick's change of heart was a significant boon and opened up the wing so that the Good News of Jesus could take root here too.

The day dawned when Nick agreed to give what he called his 'testimonial' in the chapel. Nick came up the winding metal staircase to service that Sunday as usual. He nervously shook hands with the welcomers at the door and sat on the right-hand side. He cleared his throat a few times and twitched his shirt at the collar from time to time. David went down to see him during the opening hymn.

'OK, Nick – ready for it?' asked David.

'I'm not sure I'm ready for this,' was Nick's response.

David thought quickly – he was worried for Nick. No one knew he was going to speak, so no harm would have been done if he'd bowed out; but

Nick would have been so cross with himself – that was a certainty. At the end of the chapel service there was always coffee and biscuits and a chance to talk to the various Christians and speakers who were visiting that day.

'It's Jaffa Cakes today, Nick,' said David. In the monotonous world of prison, small treats have a significance way beyond their actual value. 'No talk – no Jaffa Cake,' he said half-jokingly, placing his hand on Nick's shoulder and smiling.

'All right,' grinned Nick, 'all right – let's go.'

Nick stood up at the front of the chapel and gave his brief but hard-hitting testimonial. 'I found God in this place,' said Nick. 'I've changed my life and am going God's way now. David prayed with me and my blood pressure changed, my life's different now for sure.' Nick then looked up and took the assembled lads into his gaze.

'Now all you young men here listen to me. I'm thirty-two. I've been around. I've been a naughty boy over the years and I've ended up in here. It's not a good place to be.' Nick continued in his usual clipped tone and short sentences. 'Now you make up your minds and find Jesus. There's plenty of time for you. You don't want to come back here. I found God; so can you.'

With that Nick raised his arm and said, 'That's it.'

There was a brief silence and then David said, 'Well done, Nick; let's give him a clap.' The men and visitors clapped loudly, a few whistled and all were taken aback.

'Hey, Nick!' shouted David as he began to move down the aisle. 'Well done, here we are!' and a chocolate and orange missile sailed over the heads of the front inmates. It was caught with care and eaten by a very cheerful and relieved Nick Pook.

News of Nick's chapel speech sped through the corridors of the prison. A secret is a very hard thing to keep in prison and this gem of information spread like wildfire. Everyone now knew without doubt that Nick had joined a new cause and there were, of course, consequences. At first many officers found it either amusing or astounding that Nick had 'found God'.

When it appeared not to be a mere passing phase, attitudes began to polarize. Some refused to acknowledge any real change and others believed there was some advantage for Nick somewhere, but pleasingly, one or two began to use his unusual 'talents' to sort out problems on the wing. Before all these events, of course, Nick had always been at the centre of any trouble and both he and his cell were often searched for drugs or evidence of dealing. Now these searches were increased because some officers felt Christian prayer meetings or Bible studies must be covers for some more undesirable activities. Surely this regular client of the punishment block must soon re-offend? There was a group of officers who enjoyed having Nick on the run. He was searched again and again, not allowed to take up more rewarding jobs which were granted for good behaviour and threatened with a move on numerous occasions. Much of it was part of the rough-and-tumble of life on the wings and in spite of frustrations Nick strove to take it well. All in all it made him stronger.

'I'm praying for you,' Nick said to an officer who wound him up regularly. 'David told me that when people sense God is around they get angry and sometimes react like you do. So I'm still praying for you.' Nick was talking to the officer who had barged into his room a moment before. The officer was obviously annoyed at this attempt to delve into his motives. He looked around the tiny cell and viewed the little group of men gathered there for a Bible study. 'What's going on in here?' he questioned.

'We're just praying and reading the Bible,' said Nick cheerfully. 'And if you keep interrupting, I won't be able to help these new Christians at all.'

The determined officer picked up the small black Walkman from the bed. 'What's in here?' he asked, still convinced there was some scheming and plotting going on.

'It's just a Bible tape,' said Nick innocently.

Unimpressed, the officer pressed the 'play' button only to hear a strong dramatic voice speak out on full volume. 'And Jesus said ...' boomed the voice. There was a sharp crack as the Walkman was guiltily dropped and with a grunt the very surprised officer left the inmates to their own devices.

Nick recounts many such instances as he learned the meaning of simple persecution for his faith. Some incidents were more unpleasant than others but his most serious test was yet to come. He was about to learn the true cost of his discipleship.

Nick was due to stand trial for his various offences. His lawyer advised a plea of not guilty. There was only evidence to convict him of being a drugs courier, while the more serious charge of dealing lacked sufficient substantiation.

'Two years, Nick,' promised the lawyer, 'and you've done some time on remand already. Just plead not guilty.'

Nick had a lot to learn about Christian principles but he was quite convinced already that expediency was not one of them. There may not have been enough evidence to convict him of dealing in drugs, but he knew he had done it. Determined to tell the truth in court, he pleaded guilty.

To the despair of his solicitor Nick stood before the judge and confessed, 'I am guilty of being a courier. The £8,000 in my flat is also not really mine. It was not earned honestly, but is the result of dealing and should be confiscated. I cannot lie before God any more.'

I wasn't in the courtroom myself, but my mind can well imagine the scene and I know that such honesty cuts no ice with the judiciary.

Any idea that Christians can gain shorter sentences by being honest is simply not true and Nick is a prime example. The judge sent him down for a sentence of four years, instead of the two years he had been expecting.

Nick came back to Lewes knowing he'd done the right thing. He obviously had not wanted this result but he'd been true to his new convictions. The verdict had deeply shaken him, however. 'Why have I got so long, David?' the chastened Nick asked.

'I don't know, Nick,' said David gently, 'but I guess God wants you to spend more time here growing in faith so you'll be stronger outside.'

Nick seized hold of this interpretation of events and had no idea that his truthfulness was to be the catalyst that would propel not only Nick but also ourselves into a flurry of publicity and excitement. The press could not resist this one and David was asked to receive a visit from a reporter from the *Observer* newspaper. Nick was also to be interviewed and before four months were out we were to be visited by two British TV stations, Dutch TV, BBC World radio and several other radio and newspaper journalists as interest spiralled through the media.

So it was, of course, that David came bursting into the bedroom that Sunday morning.

The article in the newspaper was tremendous. The friendly reporter had come to see David and had done his job conscientiously. He had interviewed the men, asking relevant questions and earning their respect. The article was not sensationalized at all and was in the restrained *Observer* style. We were relieved because we had wanted to avoid overdramatization and misrepresentation. David took a few copies into the prison and they were soon all down the wing and, of course, everyone was interested.

The only previous time Nick had made it into the press was when they reported the seriousness of his crimes. This time he was elated beyond words. There was a large picture of Nick, Keith (another inmate) and David behind a set of prison bars. They were reading the Bible in an obvious set piece, but the most interesting element was the inmates' faces. Men inside jail show various emotions – fear, worry, shame, anger and resignation; but happiness is not usually a feature of that list. Even via the printed page these men managed to look peaceful, joyful, even content. Their previous crime-laden lives had been so very dark that perhaps the change was all the more dramatic for it and there can be no doubt that they now looked strangely out of place behind those bars. To those of us who have the privilege of visiting them the changed faces are truly remarkable. However unworthy society may feel these men are, it is quite clear the God of new beginnings does not view them in the same way. He is prepared to offer even them a new start, a new hope and a new outlook. No one is beyond redemption – that is surely the Good News we proclaim.

'I never thought Charlie Pook would be in the paper for something good,' said one inmate.

'How much money you get, Nick?' said another.

By Monday a red-hot photocopier ensured nearly everyone had acquired a copy and the gossip lines were alive with the story. We later found that prison headquarters had been well saturated with copies too. This was certainly something different in prison circles. Nick took his new-found fame in his stride, although we did explain that becoming a Christian didn't normally attract international press coverage.

'I guess they're interested in my changed plea of guilty,' he said wisely, 'the longer sentence was noticed, then.'

When BBC World radio picked up the story some weeks later Nick told a potential audience of some

40 million people worldwide that he was now a Christian. By then he was used to the attention and commented only that everyone seemed to ask him the same questions!

Whilst all this excitement was going on, it was obvious that Nick's personal life was being affected. Many of the men have quite complicated and often sad backgrounds, and Nick was no exception. At this particular point his girlfriend was Helen, who also had a young child to care for. She had been very supportive of Nick and they were fond of one another. Fairly early on, Nick had wanted to share his good news with Helen.

'I've told her, David,' Nick said with a serious expression one day when David was walking through the wing.

'Oh good,' David replied. 'How did it go?'

'Silly cow,' exclaimed Nick, 'she used up twenty phone units laughing.'

Of course, phone card units are at a premium in prison. Out of very meagre allowances and token pay, men buy the cards, and the time for contact with loved ones that they provide is precious. Once convicted, a prisoner may only have two visits a month, and often distance prevents some even receiving this number of home contacts. Consequently, phone cards are a highly valuable commodity and there is a fair bit of trading, swapping, pinching and general aggro over them. Twenty units were therefore no mean loss to Nick and he was not best pleased with Helen for her response. Nevertheless, he resolved to pray and 'work on her' and he was true to his word. Indeed, he put a lot of us to shame, as he prayed himself, requested others to pray, and patiently explained his decision to change his life to his girlfriend.

'I don't want to go to Heaven without her,' Nick told David determinedly.

'Well, why don't you tell her just that?' replied David sympathetically.

'Right, I will,' grinned Nick, 'and can I tell her to come and have a chat with you when she's ready? I've already told her you'll sort her out.'

David gulped a little at both Nick's trust in his suggestion and in his faith in him to 'sort her out'. The work was obviously beginning to spread out and the prison walls were not going to represent barriers to God's activity within this place.

It was a sunny afternoon when I parked the car and wandered up to the huge prison door at Lewes. There had been a recent case where an overseas visitor had been frisked, temporarily deprived of his Polaroid camera and mobile phone, and placed in a waiting room for a whole hour before it was discovered that the visit he wanted to make was not to an inmate called Castle but rather to Lewes Castle, which is an attractive but rather inadequate building in comparison to the imposing ancient edifice which is Her Majesty's Prison, Lewes. It was not the first time this had happened and the poor Spanish tourist was no doubt relieved that British security round tourist attractions is not quite as severe as he'd first thought. Thankfully he eventually found the true object of his search, although interestingly, he had not questioned the rather brusque reception he had received when he had first knocked on the huge wooden door that I now approached, although a feeling of inadequacy is not uncommon in many as they lift the massive knocker and request entry to visit some loved one inside.

Outside, I saw the usual group of dedicated women, some of whom had had difficult journeys without the benefit of private transport, and who when questioned would declare that they still loved and supported their wayward menfolk and were longing for them to be released. One of these women that particular afternoon was Helen. She was a slight, dark girl of cheerful disposition, although she looked very nervous and rather frail against those huge and secure stone walls.

David collected Helen a little later and brought her up to the chapel whilst he went to fetch Nick. Chapel visits don't count against an inmate's allowance of two visits a month and are greatly appreciated. David may grant them to men for special reasons when he needs to mediate between people in trouble, for example, or help to break difficult news. This was a special event, as Helen had indicated that her initial laughter-filled response to Nick's decision was a thing of the past. Now she too wished to become a Christian.

I sat and looked at Helen as she waited to see Nick. I asked about her child and we traded problems which trouble mums everywhere – childcare and getting about with a buggy. I made her grin with my tales of baby departments on the first floor and my poor efforts manipulating a double buggy. Helen went on to chat about Nick. 'I like what's happened to Nick while he's been in here,' she said. 'He's got very fit and he's changed, gone gentle, I like it.' She said she'd seen the press reports and was very proud of him. She looked round at the bright blue chairs and the cheerful posters round the chapel. 'It's nice in here,' she continued, 'but I don't like those bars.'

At this point we were joined by Nick and David. We let Helen and Nick have a period of precious time together from which it was easily possible to see how devoted to each other they were. We made them a cup of tea and they sat and sipped it in a manner not unlike millions of other couples do every day, except, of course, in this case the normality was an illusion. In a very few minutes they would be separated once more as Nick paid the price of his crimes.

David took Helen to the other end of the chapel and I chatted to a rather nervous Nick. I took the opportunity to speak to him about his life on the wing and to help him select a Bible-reading aid. We chose the one mentioned elsewhere, *Abundant Life*. Nick liked the easy style, with the answers printed in the back so he could check his own answers. He talked in his usual clipped style and his strong accent. As I spoke, I couldn't help but think that apart from him having been sent here I would never have spoken with such ease to someone like him. We would never naturally mix in the same circles or frequent the same social gatherings, yet here we were totally relaxed in each other's company chatting about reading the Bible. God certainly has the means to turn our presuppositions around, I thought to myself, for I found myself moved with affection for Nick and experiencing a deep-seated yearning for his welfare, I was aware that he had done some pretty dreadful things and that it was not for me to declare him 'an all-round nice guy'; neither could I offer my second-hand forgiveness on behalf of all the people whom he had wronged in the past. Nevertheless, I felt a burden to see this man fully committed to the Lord and became convinced that there was a valuable task for him to do in the future. Of course, all our men are special in many ways and I am sure God has jobs for them all to do, but from that day I began to believe that Nick would contact us on release and share his story outside the prison walls. Interestingly enough, soon after and quite unprompted, Nick began to express the desire to do just that.

We were rejoined by David and Helen, and Nick stood up smiling. Helen had been talking to David at the other end of the room in a simple and straightforward way.

'Do you notice a change in Nick?' David asked.

'Oh yes,' she replied, 'he's much kinder and gentler now.'

'Would you like the same to happen to you?' David questioned.

'Yes, I would,' was her simple response.

Nick had obviously prepared her well, for he had described many times how he had found God for himself and how he longed for her to join him in his discovery.

The two people bowed in simple prayer and Helen was gently led to confess her sins and express her need for God. She invited Jesus into her life and was as sincere as she knew how. Just as David had done for Nick and for so many others before, he laid hands on her head and asked God to fill her with His Holy Spirit. No one watching would have witnessed anything particularly dramatic that afternoon. There was only quiet prayer and expectation and there were no loud noises or movements. Nevertheless, God was there, and He made Himself known to Helen. She looked up and said, 'I feel wonderful.'

'You are now a Christian,' David said. 'Go and tell Nick.'

So it was that Helen came across to Nick as he stood up, and told him her own good news. His smile grew broader and he gave her a huge hug. 'I told you He'd get you,' he said. 'Now we'll have lots to talk about on the phone.'

David and I chatted on the way back to the car later that afternoon. We were thrilled, of course, that Nick and Helen now had 'something to talk about on the phone', but we were concerned, too, because we knew just how much the odds could be stacked against them if we thought in purely human terms. Not least we worried about how they would cope in any typical church situation once Nick was released. Many local churches regularly support our work with prayer and giving, and promise to befriend prisoners once they are released, yet the reality is that it is extremely hard for people with little education and with traumatized and even violent backgrounds to feel at home in the respectable, middle-class atmosphere of our churches; however, we acknowledged that we had to leave these things in God's hands and do only what He had for us to do right now and put our trust in Him alone for the future.

Sadly for us the day came when Nick was moved to another jail to serve out the rest of his sentence. Even on his last day he was searched for drugs, as some still doubted his conversion. He used to try to help those who were coming off drugs by visiting them in their cells and praying for them, so the rumour went around that he was still supplying drugs under cover of his new-found faith.

'I see your star pupil's off,' said one officer to David. 'Can't say we're not glad about that.'

Another laughed and shook his head. 'Well, he certainly conned you, didn't he. But he hasn't changed, I'm sure of it.'

David was used to such comments, and had discovered that it was no good rising to the bait every time. However, this time it was a bit different, for Nick had paid quite a high price – two years' extra imprisonment – for his new life and this remark was unwarranted.

'Who made you judge and jury over a man's heart?' David asked the man seriously. 'I always tell the men that they can con me, they can even con themselves but they can never con God. Let God decide whether Nick belongs to Him or not, not either of us.'

The surprised officer fell silent, for there is nothing for any of us to say when we are asked to cast the first stone.

As for Nick, well, he left prison with special permission to take a complete set of Bible cassettes, a huge box containing every book in the Bible in large print and a massive quantity of Christian literature.

'Thank you, David, for what you've done,' he said as he shook David's hand warmly. 'I won't waste my next stretch in prison. I'll keep up my study so I'm ready for release.'

He already knew the first four Bible tapes by heart, and he intended to learn far more in future months. 'Keep in touch, David?' he asked intently.

'You'll get a visit, Nick, and letters from Christians and lots of prayer,' David reassured him.

'I'll work with new Christians,' promised Nick. 'I like doing that. I'm hoping to use my large house for new Christians when I get out.' David could hardly believe his ears. He knew a support house was greatly needed in the area. God never fails to surprise us with His provision even in this exciting work.

One thing was quite clear to Nick on that day he said goodbye in his cell. He did not regret what had taken place in Lewes; he was not ashamed to call Jesus his Lord in very difficult circumstances; and he was proud to have had the opportunity to tell many people worldwide about the difference God had made in his life. Finally he recalled his decision to face up fully to his past in that courtroom where he had confessed to unsuspected crimes and had received the full penalty.

'I know other blokes think I'm off my head,' he said, 'but I want to go on with the faith. My life has changed and I'm glad that on that day I told the truth, the whole truth and nothing but the truth.'

CHAPTER 9

✳

On Which Side of Calvary's Cross Are You?

Nick had hit the headlines and his big story caused great interest. Here was someone who'd taken on the cost of discipleship and two extra years behind bars was quite a cost.

Nick spoke to local and BBC World radio reporters and along with others appeared on both BBC and ITV local evening news coverage. Lots of magazines and local papers picked up the news and began reporting on various inmates and the story generally. Sometimes, of course, we were concerned at misreporting or being aligned with various people or experiences of which we knew nothing, but usually we enjoyed the media attention, especially since it gave such a boost to the men.

Kenny appeared in the *Telegraph* holding a cassette box in his hand and listening to the Bible on tape. He'd been thrilled to tell the surprised reporter about his previously violent life style and how he was now a real Christian who had turned over a new leaf, and seeing himself in the paper encouraged him more than I can say.

A freelance TV programme-maker had visited the week before and he, too, was so surprised at the openness of the inmates to his questions. The Christians seldom seemed embarrassed or frightened to announce their change of heart and challenged us all on the team to question our comparative lack of confidence in explaining our faith. Perhaps it was bound up with our social training not to impose our religious beliefs rather than with any genuine or useful reticence to appear overbearing. Interest in the story continued to grow and expanded to include even journalists from further shores, as already stated.

'You'll find the men sit mainly in the centre aisle. So I should set up over here if I were you.' I was speaking to two Dutch TV journalists who, armed with modest cameras, had been granted permission to film our Sunday morning chapel service. 'There's nothing really dramatic going to happen,' I went on, 'it's quite simply evangelism, and the inmates respond.' I was never quite sure what visitors were anticipating when they came to chapel to share a service.

From various sources we had learned that some were expecting to see evidence of a movement – a kind of irresistible power of God that we couldn't control. We did not see things from that point of view at all. We felt God had called us to do this work of His and that we were merely reaping where others had sown over many years. As we have heard, members of Prison Fellowship and others had covered that prison over a long period of time with prayer. Some, like Maureen, had prayer-walked the walls – stopping to pray at each corner that God would bring people to Himself within the prison. So it was that in the fullness of God's time men began to respond to His call, and we were simply His servants proclaiming the simple power of the Gospel as faithful Christians have always done all down the ages since the early Church began. Of course, this was a move of God's Spirit, for only He can draw people to Jesus, but the work was not out of control in any way, neither was it spectacular. We were fully aware of what was happening and we were just thrilled to be part of it all.

The couple there that Sunday gave us no clue as to their particular expectations, but we later found that they themselves were evangelical Christians from a Dutch church who worked for a major TV company and had heard about Lewes from the BBC World Service. They had resolved to report themselves on the conversions at the prison and knew that there would be great interest in the story in Holland.

They promised to be unobtrusive and set up quietly in the corner and we took little notice of them after that. We were used to visitors of all kinds by now and even the inmates knew that there were often strangers in our midst.

The chapel is an attractive place to be on a Sunday morning. As Nick's girlfriend Helen had found when she first visited us and became a Christian, it's only the bars that give away the fact we are in a prison at all. Bright Christian posters adorn the walls, the deep blue seating strikes the eye and a large simple wooden cross dominates the wall opposite the entrance. On the dais a drum kit waits to leap into action and an impressive keyboard similarly awaits a player. All along the back, rows of Christian books, often given to us by local Christians, fill the shelves, and the coffee mugs and biscuits are set out in one corner ready for the oh-so-important after-service fellowship and chatting time.

The prison bars at the entrance began to rattle noisily as the key of an officer searched for its niche in the lock. The simple prayer group of visitors broke up at the front and we quietly found our places to receive our keen and ever-changing congregation.

The inmates are brought up by officers in small groups from the various wings of the prison including the hospital and Segregation Unit. We are aware that in some prisons inmates have been known to abuse their time in chapel by using it to pass information or other items to one another. We prayed constantly against this and everyone always seemed to be fully involved and concentrating as far as we could see. The group from 'K' Wing, where vulnerable prisoners are kept, sat alone at the back, for we always tried to co-operate fully with the demands for security. We had no intention of making the jobs of officers more difficult. While we expected every man to be allowed to come to chapel if he so wished, and would challenge any obstacle put in his way in that regard, we knew that we must be realistic about where we were working and must demand the highest standards of behaviour from the men.

'If the alarm bell is rung,' said David sombrely, 'it will be the officers who seek to rescue us.' We were never anti-establishment intentionally and generally found a high level of co-operation and help in return.

This particular morning a group from a local church was leading part of the service. The men enjoyed seeing a short drama sketch and joined in singing choruses and hymns. As usual, we sang 'Majesty' with David leading lustily from the front. It had become rather a joke with many visitors and regular inmates that this chorus was so often on the agenda, but its inclusion had a very serious side. As you looked along the rows of men – some in their own casual clothes as they were on remand, and others in the red and grey tracksuits of the convicted – it was easy to spot those for whom literacy was a major stumbling block to worship. 'Majesty' is a memorable piece that can be joined in with gusto by nearly all the men. Unfortunately it was so easy to disenfranchise many of the congregation by selecting hymns which require a reading age of fifteen-plus to follow, let alone appreciate. Similarly, some groups who led worship for us were keen to teach 'new ones' on a regular basis, which, although enjoyable in a normal church context, is quite pointless in our swiftly changing scene and denies the men their simple enjoyment of joining in enthusiastically.

That morning there were mutterings in the second row from the back. The choice of 'How Great Thou Art' was causing dissension. 'Can't read this,' muttered one large, blond and unsettled inmate.

'Discrimination,' replied his mate. 'I can't join in this one. We can't all read.'

We are used to a general level of vocalized comments coming from the men and sometimes they are unnecessary intrusions, but these were, I believe, genuine concerns and had to be faced. We knew that it was all a matter of balance, for some Christians genuinely needed more complex songs but that particular morning was one where we had missed the mark and some could not take the overload of both complicated and new hymns.

Nevertheless there was a good atmosphere in the chapel as there often is. People who visit us often remark on the presence of God they experience in that place. It is indeed a haven in an alien culture, a place of freedom in an establishment of restraint, and a focus of prayer that witnesses to the power of God to those who have taken a path away from Him.

David spoke that morning about the cross, and Howard was asked to lift down the splendid simple wooden symbol that our next-door neighbour John had so skilfully carved for the chapel. When we had arrived, there had been a smaller dark cross with the figure of Christ upon it hung on that back wall and it was the first thing we had wished to change in the chapel. We knew it meant a lot to some people and we had no wish to offend some of our 'higher-church' colleagues and friends who found it of deep spiritual significance. Nevertheless to us it was a stark barrier to our own experience and ministry. We felt called to this place to declare that Jesus had died for us all and that He had died once in actual history for our redemption. The reality of the suffering and cost of that act was pivotal to the Good News of Christ and we could not deny that He experienced the cross for us all. However, Jesus is no longer on that cross, for His offering of Himself was accepted by God and He was raised from the dead and is alive for evermore. By the power of God's Holy Spirit He will now live in us and transform our poor lives into ones useful to God and His glory. We wanted to offer that power of the risen Christ to the inmates of that prison and to declare, 'He is not here – He is risen. He is no longer on the cross but can live in your life and mine. Will you let Him enter?'

We felt no need to express faith in God in a particular way. We seldom used phrases such as 'born-again Christian', 'converted' or other perhaps misunderstood terms. We also avoided any contentious issues such as denominational preferences of any kind and were keen to send those of renewed faith back to any church background they might already have; but for some reason we felt terribly strongly about that cross, perhaps because the risen Christ was the main focus of our mission in that place.

John, our next-door neighbour, was a carpenter and wood turner. We approached him to make us a new focus for the chapel and he acquired a magnificent piece of oak from which to construct a cross. His talented hands created a wonderful new symbol and it was this simple piece of wood that Howard held in his strong hands that morning as David declared its message.

Due to the brief stays of some of the prisoners we always had to work fast. In an ideal world, perhaps, there is time for 'just looking' groups and 'thinking about ourselves' programmes. Here in prison the introduction of such schemes would mean many prisoners never being offered the Gospel. We did not feel we had the right to take that risk. We wanted as many men as possible to be faced with Christ and would reject any suggestion that the only true conversion is one that is arrived at via a long complex road of reasoning and understanding. Many of our men were in crises of a type many outsiders could never know.

To imply that decisions made in the midst of a crisis were invalid was quite clearly wrong. We believed we had excellent precedents in the Gospels for our work. Jesus spent a great deal of time with some people such as his disciples, but with others there was only a brief encounter. Zacchaeus transformed his life after a meeting with Christ of apparently short duration and the Gospels are full of momentary relationships that must surely have had lasting effects. The most significant incident for us was that of the exchange between Jesus and the thief on the cross and it was because of the swiftness of his choice to follow Jesus that we came to call our work 'Thief on the Cross Ministry'.

Even *in extremis* Jesus had the desire to bring men to Himself, and the picture we have of those three crosses on the hillside is as stark an image of the Gospel message as any in the Scriptures. David was explaining that message in simple terms that morning in the service. There were three men sent to die on that Friday and the cross of Christ was significantly placed between those of the two thieves who were due to die with Him.

This cruel Roman means of punishment was designed to be the worst kind of drawn-out death penalty possible, and to be a horrifying deterrent to any who would challenge their complete rule and dominance.

There were those there who railed at the men hanging midway between life and death and taunted those they believed were receiving their just desserts. One of the criminals hurled insults even at Jesus too. 'Aren't you the Christ? Save yourself and us!' (Luke 23:39 NIV). He was in serious trouble and had obviously lived a life of crime for which he was now paying. He met with Jesus and he chose to reject His offer of acceptance. He couldn't save himself but he preferred to keep his anger, bitterness and pride rather than find a new reality with Christ.

The man on the other side of Jesus' cross saw it differently. He was in the same position as the first man, for he'd done wrong, been caught and was suffering the same penalty. However, he was different in a very important way because he recognized Jesus for whom He was – the only hope in a hopeless situation, a good man in a place where only evil men should be. 'Don't you fear God?' he said, 'since you are under the same sentence? We are punished justly, for we are getting what our deeds deserve, but this man has done nothing wrong!'

He recognized that Jesus was suffering unjustly and although I doubt he had any idea at all what was taking place or had any concept of the redemptive nature of Jesus' death, he nevertheless realized that Jesus was there for him.

Even in his personal crisis he tried to reach out to the personhood of Christ. If there was any hope at all in this bleak universe then it had to be in this man. He didn't know why and he didn't know how but he turned to Jesus, this good man, and pleaded, 'Jesus, remember me when you come into your Kingdom.'

The atmosphere in the chapel was electric. Every eye was fixed on that cross, every ear trained on David's words. Here were men who knew about crises, who had experienced choices, received judgements and lived through punishments. They all had a heightened sense of fair play, which to an outsider seems extraordinary because they are all in prison, but to those inside is perceived as only right and proper. Being sent down for an offence you haven't done is seen as a hideous injustice of immense proportions, even when by their own admission the law has failed to catch up with other genuine misdemeanours.

'But I didn't do this,' a prisoner would proclaim, 'I really didn't rob that house.'

'But how many others did you steal from?' David would ask in his straightforward manner.

There would be only a hunch of the shoulders or a grunt in response as the point was grudgingly taken but inside there would be no real submission to the argument. It quite simply wasn't 'fair'.

This story of Jesus therefore strikes so many chords for the inmates. They can picture the scene very readily and can enter into the emotions much more easily than many of us.

This man, this Jesus on the cross, had done no wrong. He was dying for something He didn't do! No chance of a successful appeal here – no early remission for good behaviour. This was final – the real thing – for something He didn't even do. What's more, He was dying for someone else voluntarily. It was a set-up, yes, but He'd chosen to go down that way, hadn't He? He could have escaped, surely? These ideas struck home to those men. They would see the deep horror of the situation. Then they would hear the way Jesus listened to the other men in the same position. Men with whom they could identify – robbers, thieves – bad men. Jesus had time for them, didn't He? He cared for them, didn't He? He offered them a new chance, didn't He?

Jesus wasn't just for the educated, the wealthy or even the ordinary. Jesus cared for the criminals, the bad guys, even the total failures – like those you found in Lewes Prison. Oh yes, these men understood this story. They listened to every word, drinking in the significance of it all – hoping against hope that they might avail themselves of this situation too. God obviously chose to speak to these men as they sat and listened to that simple Gospel message as He has done to many others too down the ages. The Holy Spirit prepared their hearts in ways which we can never understand but the results of that preparation are all too clear.

'So you have a choice before you today,' continued David. 'Are you like the first thief who laughed and scoffed at Jesus and turned His offer down and lost eternal life because of his decision,' – David looked round at the row after row of inmates listening intently, the group of volunteers praying silently at the sides, the officers standing staring quietly, giving nothing away about their thoughts, and the Dutch TV crew with the camera quietly whirring, and then went on – 'or are you like the second thief – the one who saw what his predicament was, recognized Jesus as his only chance and begged – not to be let off – but just that Jesus would remember him when He came into His Kingdom? I can tell you this morning that Jesus not only remembered him, He actually took him with Him. "Today," He told him, "you will be with me in paradise." '

'So it is a simple choice before you today: On which side of Calvary's cross are you?'

Everyone knew where the talk was leading – everyone had seen the pattern emerging – but the relief when the good news was spelled out that the man was saved was almost tangible and certainly immensely satisfying.

David invited any who wished to choose to be on Jesus' side to see him after the service. He had made his point, he seldom laboured it. However, something that morning made him go on. Usually men would wait behind and chat to him individually or David would approach inmates and ask if they'd made a decision for Christ yet. All was orderly, quietly done, almost understated. Sometimes, however, he would feel led to make a simple altar call and today was just such a day.

'If you'd like to choose to be on this side of the cross this morning,' David said, 'if you'd like to ask Jesus to remember you then step up to the front here and we will pray for you this morning. We will sing our next hymn while you come forward.' The first chords of 'Great Is Thy Faithfulness' sounded through the chapel. That morning while the music played and the rest of us sang and prayed, seven men came forward to ask Jesus to remember them when He came into His Kingdom. They made a choice to be on the right side of Jesus' cross and the angels must have rejoiced well that day, because we certainly did, I assure you. One man who had found Christ just two weeks before saw his friend move up to the front. He stood up too, went forward and rubbed his shoulder in support. He had learned so early in his Christian life the joy of seeing his friends come to Christ.

Seeing conversions on a Sunday became a very natural thing. Each week before the service the volunteers would gather to pray for the proceedings and each week after the inmates had been led away we could group together for a two-minute word of thanks and prayer.

'Three men came to faith today and I have two other names to follow up,' David would say – or – 'Four men accepted Christ this morning, let's praise God.'

We started to expect God to work in this positive and rewarding way and quite forgot that this was not a usual happening in outside services. We really were most privileged but we had so much still to learn, of course.

Sometimes the Gospel would be preached but the people converted would be met on the wings and not even have attended the service. It couldn't, therefore, just be the strength of the words that was bringing people to faith. Sometimes we had a visiting band or minister who wasn't as straight with the message, but men still found faith that morning, so it couldn't just be 'who was on', though it must be said that David preached in a powerful and effective style. Sometimes the men came wanting to find Christ before the service had even begun so it couldn't be emotional sway. Oh no, we couldn't say we understood it at all – but it *was* happening and we were there and it was great!

After a time the chapel became a very welcoming place. Yes, it was well fitted out and had bright posters and books round the walls and that super cross above the altar but it was much more than that. It became a place where many prayers had been said and where many prayers had been answered. There was a sense of God's presence in that place so that you felt quite uplifted by just sitting there a while. Some visitors with a strong gift of discernment were especially struck by the power of the Holy Spirit in that room and it was quite certain that the bars on the door and on the windows were no barrier to His presence and power.

We did, of course, share the chapel with the other denominations, and the chaplaincy team were most supportive. Father Barry, our part-time

Roman Catholic priest, worked most of the week on a difficult Brighton housing estate but came in twice a week to minister in the prison. He must have thought it rather quaint that David insisted on changing the cross, for he continued to put back the old one for his Saturday Catholic Mass, but he took it in good grace. He knew we didn't try to poach his members in any way and would send back to his care any Catholics who found new faith unless they insisted otherwise. We had witnessed bad denominational relationships many times and we certainly didn't want that at Lewes. Nevertheless, it was obvious that the chaplaincy was taking on a distinctly evangelical feel and some tensions could easily arise.

Each month the chaplaincy team would meet to discuss issues. There was the Salvation Army minister, Stan; the Methodist chaplain, Kevin; Malcolm, the High Anglican, who was David's substitute, and Barry, the Roman Catholic priest. One morning there was a rumbling in the ranks. The chapel was looking a little too evangelical for everyone's taste, as there was a large poster with a text everywhere you turned. Now we were very grateful for the splendid posters the Scripture Gift Mission had given us. They were bright, magnificent photographs with Bible texts on them and they cheered the place up wonderfully while passing on the Word of God at the same time. However, we knew we'd perhaps overdone it a bit once they were practically double-banked along the walls! Interestingly, this reaction at the meeting had been anticipated and we'd felt convicted about it prior to the discussion. It all went to prove just how much God's hand was upon the smooth running of that place.

I teach in a Roman Catholic school where I work with children who have special needs. It is a wonderful job to have as it not only keeps a roof over our heads – as there is no chaplain's house at Lewes – but it is satisfying and rewarding work. The secretary of our school is Theresa Bevans, and I grew to have a wonderful friendly relationship with her because of her deep-seated and devoted Catholic faith. We would chat over our beliefs in great honesty and openness in spite of obvious huge differences in our perceptions – all I knew and recognized was that here was someone devoted to Jesus and her faith and with whom I could find a unity of spirit which surmounted any doctrinal differences. Her husband, Gary, was also a man of profound faith who had visited Rome as part of a personal pilgrimage. As an artist he had been thrilled at the beauty of the Cistine Chapel and had gazed in wonder both at its construction and its inspirational qualities. 'It's like being in Heaven,' he had told Theresa. Once back home he had made a remarkable resolution. 'Why can't we have such beauty here?' he had said.

So it was that five years later he completed the only copy in the world of the pictures in the Cistine Chapel on the ceiling of English Martyrs Roman Catholic Church in Goring-by-Sea in Worthing, West Sussex.

It is a remarkable work and quite famous, having been shown on television and made open to the public. It is certainly well worth a visit and is inspirational not only in its execution but also its significance. It is an uplifting and spiritual experience to sit a while and gaze at the glorious colours and huge figures set across the span of that ceiling.

After he had finished he was, of course, invited to paint many other places, for his talent is outstanding. Nevertheless, he only takes on work for which he believes God wants him to use his talents. He does not use his gifts for his own pecuniary advantage but for the greater glory of God.

I took David to see the splendour of his work and he stood speechless at the glorious sight before him.

'It tells the story of redemption to those who cannot read,' I explained. 'It lifts up the spirit to think of God in the same way as the high vaults of a cathedral are meant to do. We see our smallness – our insignificance in relation to Him – and realize our true need of God.'

'Then I will ask him to do the same for our men,' determined David, 'for many of them cannot read or write and they certainly have need of God, don't they?'

We hurried round to the school and asked Theresa to ask Gary if he would take on such a task, bearing in mind just how many tasks he had turned down over the years.

A few days later we received our reply. Gary was very excited about it. He felt it was a good and right project. He would paint something in the chapel at Lewes Prison. However, he didn't want to paint the same spectacular scenes again.

'He's looking for a chance to paint some New Testament pictures,' explained Theresa. 'Could he do something like that?'

Our hearts leapt inside. Could he? – Oh yes, he most certainly could. It was exactly what we had wanted. We envisaged not scenes of creation or judgement – but rather pictures of hope in a hopeless world – scenes perhaps of Jesus' miracles and His power over our natural lives – a glimpse of heaven in a place of degradation and despair. Oh yes, Gary's vision was most definitely in tune with ours. Just when would he start?

Gary came into the prison one day and looked around – and the problems soon came into view. The ceiling was basically unsuitable not because of its shape or the nature of its construction but because of the profusion of lights and sprinklers dotted all over its surface. David approached his governor, Mr Steve Ashworth, and he was very keen that something should still be done. Steve's arrival in itself was a true blessing. Early in David's chaplaincy his immediate governor, the one in charge of inmate activities, which include education, sport and the chapel, had moved to other duties. It was a big blow because he'd very much left David alone to develop his chaplaincy department. Just who would replace him, we wondered? Would we now find someone in the post with a much greater, perhaps not altogether benevolent, interest in the chapel's activities? David had no desire to work against the best interests of the prison but there was no doubt that a helpful governor would be a boon.

Steve had worked in several prisons throughout the country and was on an accelerated promotion scheme. Having won a position in one establishment at a Governor Five level he was awarded a swift and unexpected promotion to Governor Four level and had to change prison immediately. The promotion system may seem unusual to outsiders, but once you have obtained recognition at a certain level, you are then responsible for applying for suitable posts yourself. This can be very difficult and stressful as Steve found out. He had moved to a village near Tunbridge Wells to take up one post and now found that there were no local positions available at his new grade. Then suddenly the post at Lewes was advertised. The head of inmate activities had moved posts, leaving a gap which was immediately taken by Lewes' own head of custody. The resulting vacancy was duly notified and Steve leapt in with an application, as did seven others simultaneously. In spite of the strong competition, however, Steve was awarded the position, to the great relief of both himself and his wife Sarah. A second immediate move was avoided.

Steve turned up for work on the first morning at Lewes to be greeted by a change of plan. There was no longer a vacancy in this department and Steve would now have to be head of inmate activities and would he like to start now with a tour of the relevant departments? Steve is a dynamic, bright personality who could take new situations on with ease and so he readily took on the new post, little knowing just what was in store for him.

His programme that morning involved meetings with the head of education and the head of physical activities. He saw the relevant rooms and inspected the gym and sportsfield. Before lunch, however, he made a request. Why, he wondered, had no appointment been made for him with the chaplain? If Steve was to be responsible for all inmate activities then a chapel visit was just as important as meeting the head of education. A slightly frustrated manager immediately requested a meeting between Steve and David, the relatively new chaplain.

'Good afternoon,' said David as he stepped apprehensively into the new Governor Four's office, 'I'm David, the chaplain.'

'Sit down,' replied Steve. 'Nice to meet you. I'm a Free Church man.' David duly sat down and was for an instant unusually taken aback. The two men then began to chat and struck up an instant excellent rapport. The amazing timing of God was just to be wondered at. How good it was of God to make this provision, for both men had hard and demanding jobs, and mutual support was a real joy.

Steve had had real personal problems up to three years previously. He's been a high-flyer, yes, but a very stressed one for all that. He'd thrown himself into his job but had taken release via a substantial intake of alcohol. His wonderful wife Sarah, who was so supportive, found herself stretched to her limit in maintaining the relation-ship as Steve came in later and later and drank more and more. In the end there was little time for real communication and the marriage seemed almost certainly doomed. Fortunately, Sarah met up with supportive

Christians and eventually – loved and prayed for – she became a Christian herself. Of course she then longed for Steve, too, to find faith, but it was a long and difficult road she had to follow. Eventually Steve found the facts of his own inability to cope by himself and he met with Jesus after a powerful evangelistic service at the local church.

His problems did not disappear in a moment, but the corner had been turned and he now had a new purpose and a new power in his life. God's hand was now firmly on Steve's life and, as with so many of us who follow Christ, the coincidences began to mount up so much that they could no longer be regarded as mere coincidence any longer. So Steve and David now felt God had led them unexpectedly together at Lewes and that it would all work out both to God's glory and their own good.

Steve was therefore thrilled with the idea of the chapel being painted in such glorious style. He'd supported the general revamping of the chapel itself – its new programmes – its volunteers – and even began himself to support outside speaking engagements by giving his own testimony. He never knew what was to happen next as he was called on to speak to various TV and radio crews and respond to media interest. It was all very exciting and he was pleased to be part of it all. So when the painting was mooted he took it well in his stride and came up with various suggestions.

Through discussions among the three men it became obvious that the ceiling was not a real possibility but there was a new idea. Why not paint the side wall? On one side the chapel windows looked out on the beautiful rolling hills of East Sussex and offered a glimpse of beauty for the soul on each Sunday morning, but the other side offered only grim reminders of the prison – blank grey walls and rolls of barbed wire. Here was an idea that would be no security risk, simple to complete (as no tower to raise the artist to ceiling level would be required), and would provide all visitors to our chapel with an uplifting experience without having to gaze upwards to appreciate it.

Back at that chaplaincy meeting, where it had been noted that the chapel was perhaps less than ecumenical in its appearance, there was a stunned silence as David explained the plan. A devout Catholic was to illuminate the chapel walls – well, it was all quite stunning and definitely all part of God's provision.

Gary began work that spring and under his skilled hands the atmosphere in the chapel was transformed. Some willing inmates became involved as the artistry evolved and soon we could only gaze in wonder as we were transported in our imaginations back to those first days that the Gospels recall. Right across the front of the chapel, behind the table where Holy Communion was celebrated, appeared the scene at Galilee where Jesus met those first disciples and suggested they cast their nets on the other side of their boat. The symbolism of those nets, bursting with their surprising catch of fish, leapt from the wall and the grouping of the simple but chosen men led the eye effortlessly to the new position of the wooden cross, now rehung further up and to the right.

'They're now looking heavenwards,' explained Gary. 'They have a brand-new direction for their lives.'

We knew this work would add a new dimension to visiting the chapel. The vast expanse of sea and sky so vibrant in colour would surely lift the heaviest heart Godward, and the simple message of those Gospel miracles down the side wall would offer hope to the most downtrodden. The pictures summed up all we were trying to say and their witness to every person who entered that chapel was loud and clear that the message of Jesus is as relevant today as it was when those first fishermen left their nets to become fishers of men.

The Dutch TV crew who visited our simple morning service and heard the usual message of the Gospel made a splendid short film. We later found it was in fact broadcast over the whole continent by satellite. They interviewed Howard, Kenny and Nick as well as David and Steve Ashworth. They discovered that each man in his own way and time had chosen on which side of Calvary's cross he was going to stand. There was no difference really between them, for whether they were behind bars because they worked there or because they were sent, there the important thing was their own personal relationship with God. We all experience life in different ways and travel down different paths. Some of us end up in more trouble than others, and some of us appear to glide through, while others wade through the sloughs of despond and despair.

The choice for us all is, however, the same in the end. We must all face the cross of Jesus either now while we have time yet to make amends or later when we die and it is all too late. We will be asked that question by God himself: 'On which side of Calvary's cross are you?', for that is His chosen point of decision for us all. We can scoff and refuse His offer of life and acceptance if we will, but we can also choose to accept Him and ask Jesus to remember us when He comes into His Kingdom.

This book has been a brief glimpse into the lives of some people who have chosen to be on the right side of the cross, have chosen to follow Jesus and believe in Him. As we've seen, Howard has changed paths and wants to work in the halfway house for ex-prisoners, to help bring others to Christ. Kenny wants to start up self-defence classes with Bible studies for lads he knows who might otherwise end up as he did in prison, and Nick, well, he wants to be a Christian leader telling folk about the Gospel and helping others towards a deeper faith. God took these criminals and transformed them into something special for Himself, just as He took all the other people in this book and has used them for His glory. Every reader of this book can join in such exciting adventures too, for the invitation to belong to Jesus is for everyone.

If you have already chosen to follow Christ then perhaps this book is a challenge to your commitment to spreading the Gospel to all people everywhere, and God might inspire you to take up a new task or role for yourself today. Our greatest task is to spread the Gospel, whilst our ultimate hope is to meet with God face to face one day. How sad if, when that moment comes, we must confess that we brought no one else with us, because Jesus' great commission to evangelize is addressed to us all. If you have not yet found God to be a reality in your life, perhaps the experiences of others you have read about here may make you realize the closeness of God to you right now. You can ask God to enter your life by yourself or ask another Christian to help you. The important thing is that you are able to answer the question, 'On which side of Calvary's cross are you?' with a confident 'On the right side – because I belong to Him!'

We have only to accept our failings and wrong-doings, confess them to God and ask Jesus Himself to enter and transform our lives. He then gives us the strength to change our lives and serve Him instead of ourselves. The result is a glorious liberty and purpose which we can live out in friendship with all those who also belong to Him. It is indeed wonderful Good News that has changed people all down the ages since the first disciples began to spread the Word, and it is Good News we can all learn to experience and in our turn pass on to others. We never know where God will lead us, just as David and I never knew we'd end up in prison one day, but your journey will be just as fulfilling as ours once you begin.

We have discovered that the cross certainly does have a place between thieves, and indeed between all other types of criminals, and we have been honoured to be part of what God is doing amongst convicted or remand prisoners alike, although we have also learned that the cross divides, for as our title suggests, it is *between* thieves. Unfortunately, not all choose to follow Jesus and that is a cause of great sadness to us all. However, St John says:

> Yet to all who received him, to those who believed in his name, he gave the right to become children of God – children born not of natural descent, nor of human decision or a husband's will, but born of God [John 1:12–13 NIV].

We have been honoured to witness so many people discovering the truth of these verses, in spite of difficult and criminal backgrounds, but perhaps we should not really be surprised.

Jesus appeared to spend a disproportionate amount of time with the rejected of society and perhaps it would seem that in these days He is finding a greater acceptance there once more. There are great needs in our world and certainly in Britain there is a huge disillusionment due to unemployment, negative equity and job insecurity.

People may be ready to respond to God's message in a way they haven't for years if only we'll tell them. Our simple message to Christians would be to focus outwards on the world not inwards on the problems inside the Church. In the end our primary instruction is to spread the Gospel and our job is to fulfil that role. It is very exciting to be part of the expansion of the Kingdom. I wonder just what God has for you to do? There is a huge temptation to want to be filled and inspired and excited by spiritual experience for its own sake. We all have problems we need to solve but if we concentrate on them alone we will never move out of ourselves and fulfil God's will for our lives. Forgetting what lies behind and getting on with new tasks is vital or we start to wilt and suffocate in our own desires. The Christian life should be a great adventure and challenge and incorporate an ever greatening desire to bring others to Christ, whether amongst our relatives, colleagues, the sick, the poor or even amongst thieves.

*

Prayer of Response

God our Father wants us to approach Him in spirit and in truth and the actual words we use are of no real consequence. Nevertheless it is sometimes helpful to see how others have approached Him for the first time. This simple prayer below is one way to offer ourselves to God if we feel He has been drawing us to Himself. If you pray this prayer and would like assistance in any way either tell a Christian friend or contact the address that follows. We wish you every blessing as you respond to God in your own way.

David and Gillian Powe

Heavenly Father
I realize I have a real need of you and that you are calling me to your Service. Please forgive me through Jesus for all the wrong things I have done. I am really sorry. Please come to live with me by means of your Holy Spirit and fill me with his power to live a brand new life of service for you. Thank you for loving me so very much. I really mean this prayer, in the name of Jesus Christ your son. AMEN.

THE
FINAL
VERDICT

THE SEQUEL TO *THE*

CROSS BETWEEN THIEVES

TO DAVID
MY HUSBAND AND VERY BEST FRIEND

✳

Contents

CHAPTER 1

✳

Mission Impossible?

Underestimating God's ability to break down barriers is not really a very good idea.

Lewes Prison Chapel was busy that lunchtime. The finishing touches were being made to the splendid painting behind the altar table, and paint, cloths and brushes were strewn haphazardly across the chapel floor. The prison orderly was tidying up as well as he could, but the air was heavy with the buzz of unfinished activity – and a distinct smell of paint.

Six visitors sat nervously at one side of the bright if chaotic room, trying to take in the nature of these unfamiliar and slightly frightening surroundings. Many months previously it had seemed a rather splendid idea to put their names down on a list. A simple action at the time, but one with far-reaching consequences for all of them. These five young men, in training to be Anglican vicars at Wycliffe Hall, Oxford, had volunteered to be part of a mission team to Lewes Prison in Sussex and, in spite of growing anxiety, they and their tutor had now arrived to begin seven days of practical evangelism experience.

Anyone who has been to college will know that confidence and a surfeit of conversation are hallmarks of the Common Room. However neither of these was present in the chapel that morning. In their place were nervous dispositions and the odd hesitant verbal exchange. Back in college, talk about evangelism, or telling people about Jesus, would have seemed serious but not really threatening. The students would have gone over possible responses that people might make when the subject of Christianity came up. Furthermore, each man would have been fairly sure of his own faith, not so that he would appear naïve or over confident but so that he was secure enough to inspire others and indeed to offer himself to the Church for full-time service. Now the crunch had come. The five were here in a prison setting preparing to walk out into those long and dreary wings to proclaim their message of hope to a rather difficult audience.

William was there, cultured, educated, a former barrister, matured by his own experiences of suffering and trauma. His confident speech and powerful faith would surely provide an ideal grounding for work in the prison, but his compassion and care for the inmates were to be the attributes my husband, David, the Chaplain, and I would most readily recall after his departure.

Chris was an open, friendly and street-wise student. We imagined he might have struggled to maintain his individuality in a college environment, but in the prison he was to be in his element. He had a keen heart for evangelism and a rejection of social taboos that might render a religious discussion inappropriate. He had an obvious desire to see a task through to the end and a real heart of gold.

Christopher was, on the surface, more self-assured. He was determined not to be flustered, was slow to worry and quick to pray. Through the week he rose to the occasion and had opportunity to reveal a sensitive heart and a care for the inmates.

Simon was the deep-thinking one who was aware of the spiritual battle raging on all sides. He felt driven to prayer for the situation and people at Lewes Prison. His quiet nature was a calming, reassuring influence when excitement was high.

Matthew was tall, dark and studious, and his nickname of 'Joe 90' suited him well. His calm exterior belied his enthusiasm and interest in the work with prisoners, and he was totally involved in the task set before him.

Philip came as tutor and leader of the group. A very well qualified Old Testament lecturer, but new to the college, he rose well to the very difficult task of being responsible for others in a situation also new to himself. His serious approach to the mission served both him and us well, and his concern not only for the men but for the nature of the mission itself was reassuring and affirming. He later wrote that the team had not so much come to run a mission but to take part in one that was taking place daily. Nevertheless, he and his team of young men did make a real mark on the chaplaincy, and we appreciated them greatly.

So this gifted but apprehensive group waited for David to issue their first instructions. Each clasped a neatly typed daily programme of events, enclosed in a new blue plastic wallet David and I had purchased hastily from W.H. Smith's the week before. Grouped in pairs, they were to be assigned to different members of the chaplaincy team to experience the breadth of activity that regularly took place in the prison.

Every prison has an Anglican chaplain by law, and although some vicars might feel that such a 'patch' might not be very strong ground for a meaningful ministry, David had found the exact opposite. With a simple message, even more simply expressed, he had gone to the cells of the prison offering men the opportunity to start again with God and begin a new life as Christians. Hundreds of men with a desire to meet God and change the course of their lives found new spiritual direction. You can read more of their stories in my book *The Cross Between Thieves*. It is unlikely that many of them would become instant middle-class, educated and totally responsible citizens, but change was very real and very obvious. Many gave up their drug-dependent existence, established more long-lasting relationships, studied the Bible, learned to pray and attempted to join up with Christian groups once they had left prison.

Each chaplain in one of Her Majesty's Prisons works in a team, with ministers from other denominations – Roman Catholic, Methodist, Salvation Army, etc. Other religions are represented by their spiritual leaders, and all operations are co-ordinated by the Anglican Chaplain. Outside visitors and Christians from various denominations often come in to assist the chaplain, and to meet prisoners in religious services and meetings. David had built his team up well, and volunteers came in daily to lead Bible study and prayer groups. As there were so many responding to the Christian message, there were always more inmates to follow up with support, teaching and advice.

It seemed good, too, to invite our ordinands, or 'trainee vicars' as they became known, to experience prison ministry, so that some might feel drawn to similar work, and all would broaden their understanding of working with such men as prisoners. Trainee vicars are no different from the rest of the community. They arrived with their preconceived ideas, prejudices and fears about the criminal world. Most people tend to class all those 'doing time' in the same category – men or women who are getting their just desserts, deserve no sympathy and are best forgotten. The reality is, of course, far more complex. The man incarcerated for non-payment of his poll tax is banged up with the man steeped in crime, the income tax evader with the drug dealer. As in society at large, the prison populations are as varied as the communities they represent. Some prisoners seem to be quite frightening and even wicked, but others appear very unfortunate or even sociable and responsible.

Working in a prison with the hope of bringing people to God would seem to be a real 'mission impossible'. Are such people open to, or even worthy of, redemption? Society may respond, 'no' and of course, all of our inmates had been judged and rejected through their trials in courts of various kinds.

So each man had had to face the reality of his deeds, but maybe it is right to draw back and look at the whole picture for a moment. Just what is the case for the prosecution against these men in the moral sense? Are they the dregs of society worthy only of exclusion? Are we right to spend so much time working with these people? How strong is the case for leaving them to their own devices – for shutting them up and throwing away the key? Was it worthwhile bringing these students to experience ministry amongst such men? Consider some of our cases for a moment before you respond to these questions.

Many reasons for the rise in the crime figures are bandied about – poverty, decline of the nuclear family, poor education, job insecurity, and lack of morality are all cited and there is probably a little truth in all of them. However, time and time again we were to come across individuals who were inside not because they wanted to rob but because they needed to eke out yet another day's existence, supported by an ever-burgeoning drug habit.

Roy Kybett, one of our more longstanding and experienced volunteers, was helping a young man fill out a questionnaire from health care rehabilitation in order to place him in appropriate care after prison. Roy began to go down the list:

'Did you take drugs then, Mike?' he asked the young, almost waif-like boy in front of him.

'Oh yeah,' replied Mike readily, shrugging his shoulders a little and sniffing.

'Heroin?' questioned Roy.

'Yeah,' was the response. 'Three or four times a week.'

Roy carefully filled in the form.

'What about cocaine?' he queried.

'Oh yeah,' said Mike, 'I take that regular.' Then seeing a further clarification was expected, 'Well, most days really.'

Roy filled in the information.

As he carried on down the list Roy failed to find any substance not used regularly by Mike. Finally the ecstasy question seemed different.

'Well, no,' said Mike, 'not really. I only use that for special occasions – you know, parties an' that.'

Roy tried not to look fazed, and moved on to the alcohol section. There again Mike had a huge dependence, as he also proved to have on amphetamines and other pills. There was no area Roy could leave blank. Mike was just 19 years old. The expense of serving such habits can only be guessed at, but it's certain no 19-year-old could ever earn sufficient income to cover it all. Crime and plenty of it was the only alternative, and Mike had hundreds of offences both behind him and up for consideration this time. At least his attempt to enter 'rehabilitation clinic' was a move forward – perhaps a few less folk would wake to find their homes ransacked and their hard-earned possessions removed in order to fund a young boy's drug habits.

Joe was a fence. He acquired stolen goods from the likes of Mike and sold them on in pubs, clubs and at car-boot sales. He made his complete living this way, and was quite indignant at being caught and imprisoned. David tried to reason with this essentially likeable, easy-going chap when he began to talk about his family one day.

'You love your son, do you, Joe?' asked David.

'Sure,' replied Joe swiftly, 'I love him a lot.'

'Has he got anything in line for Christmas?' queried David.

'Sure, he's got a brand new mountain bike to come. It's the real biz.'

David smiled at Joe's happy face, and went on.

'Will he like it, then – this bike?'

'Course he will,' responded Joe vehemently. 'He'll be so proud, I know it.'

'Would he be sad if he woke up one morning and someone had nicked it?' asked David innocently.

'Sad? He'd be sad,' responded Joe swiftly, 'and I'd sure be mad if I found who nicked it – I'd kill him, I really would.'

David paused as he saw the enormity of the idea settling over Joe's previously jocular features.

'So do you think the parents of the boys whose bikes you fence would feel any less sad or mad then?' he questioned.

The nature of the sting crept slowly up on Joe, who coloured deeply and eventually replied, 'No, I guess they wouldn't. I've never thought of it at all like that.'

'Well, perhaps it's time you did,' said David, 'because I don't feel your son will grow up to be too proud of you if you carry on doing these things, do you?'

'No, I guess not,' responded Joe slowly.

David left him pondering this new thought about his life's activities. It would certainly take some time if he were to choose to change, and David assured him that he would certainly need God's help if he wanted things to be different.

Simon's career wasn't concerned with either drugs or fencing because he believed in the 'direct approach' to money procurement. He regularly committed armed robbery, with Securicor vans being his speciality. He was an older, well-built chap when David met him. Strong and tough-looking, he had dust-like hair and was no man with whom to argue. An Eastender, family was crucial to him, but, outside of his close knit circle, he was also a dangerous man.

He was suspected of robbery with extreme violence, as he had used a baseball bat to 'slow down' a couple of guards who chose to flee the scene of the crime. His apparent total disregard of the gravity of his crime was very obvious when he met David to request prayer for his sick daughter. He cheerfully explained his way of life, and boasted of his knowledge of the best places to set up a robbery.

'For example,' he volunteered, 'never do a job in Kingston.'

'Well, why not?' asked David, unable to resist the question in spite of its obviously dubious nature.

'Because there ain't no outers,' answered Simon. 'You can't get out of Kingston, you just go round and round the one-way system – it's not worth the hassle.'

When David later related this tale I could picture Kingston as well as he could. David had worked in a large store there before we met, and I had trained to teach in the town. I could well recall my father driving round and round the town centre, trying in vain to get into the necessary lane to leave for Kingston Hill. The shops seemed all too familiar the third time round!

The stories of these three men symbolize the nature of the lives of those with whom we work, and of course there are also those who have committed far worse crimes of all kinds. The case for the prosecution would appear to be rather strong. These men have contributed little to society, shown no degree of responsibility, and could well be labelled unworthy. Is this how we are going to think? If it is, then we fly in the face of the Bible. Make no mistake, many members of society do totally reject such men, and fiercely resent and resist attempts to rehabilitate or reform them. Even some Christians hold these views.

'They are bad people, you know,' David was told by a member of our local church. 'They deserve their time. Is there any real point in what you do?'

Another member of that church was an enthusiastic participator in the prayer line, but told me sadly, 'I'm so enthusiastic but I keep quiet about it here. Several people are not at all interested, they think it's a bit of a waste of time.'

The Bible, however, is full of hope for the worst and least in society. Nowhere will you read about the greater worthiness of the educated, rich and famous – quite the reverse is true. The pages are crammed with stories of those who found, or had been kept by, God, in spite of disobedience or crime.

Moses the great leader committed murder before leading the Jewish nation to the promised land. Samson's love of a woman nearly destroyed him, but he went on to a final act that demonstrated the power and authority of God. David stole Bathsheba, had her husband murdered, and spoilt his sons by self-indulgence, yet he is hailed as the greatest king and even as a forerunner of Christ himself. Saul was a wicked persecutor of Christians, causing many to be arrested, and standing by as Stephen was martyred. He went on to be the greatest evangelist the world has known. Matthew, a disciple of Christ, was a notorious tax collector, one of a group renowned for fraud and extortion, but he was a close friend of Jesus and the source of one of the gospel records. Indeed there is much precedent for regarding crime and immorality as no bar at all for a change of heart, and plenty of evidence that God shows no prejudice against bad men and women.

Jesus' teaching is full of directives not to judge others but rather to look at ourselves. For example, there is the story of the Pharisee and the tax collector, where pride in social position is deprecated, and we are warned not to value ourselves too highly. Jesus himself socialized with the disreputable and rejected, ate with tax collectors and sinners, and when a criminal crucified with him turned to Jesus he was assured of his forgiveness.

Our students from Oxford had to confront these issues that spring mission time. They knew the text of the New Testament, had even read it in the original Greek, and were well aware that Jesus' great and final commission was to go out into the world with the Gospel. They were also used to arguing the case for Christianity in response to the great issues of life, but here, in this cauldron of crime, despair and ignorance, all their knowledge and skills could swiftly prove to be irrelevant.

So it was some very nervous and awkward men who went on to the wings. Chris went with David down to the hospital area. On the way he talked about conversions and his worry about what to say to men such as these. He felt out of his depth. The hospital wing is long and thin, and lacks the normal busy atmosphere of an average hospital. Along with those who have broken limbs and other normal ailments, one finds those withdrawing from drugs, attempted suicide cases and the mentally unstable. Withdrawn from the rest of the prison, inmates are usually very pleased to see visitors of any kind, representatives of the chaplaincy being no exception.

'Well, what do we do now?' whispered Chris as he stood at the entrance with David, taking in the strangeness of the atmosphere and feeling rather ill at ease.

'Less of the we,' replied David. 'What are *you* going to do?'

Chris looked rather shocked. 'Me?'

'Yes, you,' responded David. 'Let's start with Barry over there.' With that he motioned towards the end of the ward where a huge inmate was standing, hands on hips, observing the two men who'd just come in. Barry, whose arms were heavily tattooed, made a striking picture in that doorway. Yet he had a twinkle in his eye as he bellowed down the corridor, 'Hey, come and convert *me*.'

Chris looked at David anxiously but got no reassurance there.

'He's talking to you,' said David. He had met Barry before and the big man obviously knew what was going on. Chris wasn't really being cast to the lions.

'You know his name,' David went on, 'so you can't ask that. Go and ask him if he'd like God to help him in his life. Go on.'

Something drove Chris to comply, but he wasn't sure what. He approached Barry hesitantly, and looking up at his towering frame he flustered, 'Well, hello there, Barry. I'm Chris. I'm working with the chaplain this week. Errm, have you thought ... I mean do you think ... I mean does God mean anything to you?' he finished lamely.

Barry looked mildly amused and suggested helpfully, 'You're supposed to ask me if I want God in my life.'

'Oh yes,' replied a very embarrassed Chris. 'Well, would you like God to help you in your life?'

'Yes,' was the firm reply. At this point Chris's mind went blank. He could think of no appropriate response. Instead he turned to David and mouthed, 'What do I do now?'

David approached the two men and suggested they all go into a side ward. He knew it was now time to take over.

An astonished Chris sat beside the large man as he explained his need for God to the chaplain. Within a few minutes David led Barry, like so many others before him, line by line, in a simple prayer. It went something like this:

'I am really sorry, God, for the life I've been leading. I'm really sorry. I can't cope any more. I want Jesus to come into my life and make a new start. Please help me. I really mean this. Amen.'

David laid his hands on Barry's head, prayed for him and asked God to fill him with his Holy Spirit.

Barry looked up slowly.

'My wife will be pleased, you know, she's been a Christian for years,' he smiled.

David asked Barry gently if he'd like to ring his wife and tell her the good news. 'Yes, I think so,' said Barry.

Getting an outside line, David rang Barry's wife and let the two speak.

'Hello, love,' said Barry, in a remarkably soft voice. 'I've been talking to the chaplain and I've become a Christian.'

There was a silence before a voice was heard saying 'I don't believe it!'

After a while, David took over, but he also had no real success in persuading her that her errant husband wished to change his ways. Obviously, even years of prayer had not prepared her for a positive answer to her requests. The change of circumstances was going to take a while to sink in!

Later, in the chapel, Chris admitted that he felt quite disoriented by the speed of Barry's change of heart. There had been no long-term counselling or discussion, but rather just a man in need of responding to the Gospel. The event challenged his whole expectation and training, but excited him too.

On another occasion William was with David, walking through 'B' wing looking for inmates to chat with. A very concerned officer approached David.

'They've got a ouija board in there, Chaplain,' the officer confided. 'I saw those things in the army, nothing but trouble, I don't like it.'

The man pointed nervously to one of the cell doors and looked for a response. David knew this officer had no faith of his own, but realized he obviously had a very healthy respect for the dangers of the occult. It was not uncommon for inmates to be involved in such practices – the prison librarian had admitted that she was often asked whether books on the subject were available.

'OK,' David responded. 'We'll go and check it out. Don't worry ... and thanks for telling me.'

Later on that night William recalled the events of the morning. Sitting on the edge of his chair he told the others, 'It was over in three minutes – no, it wasn't – it was all over in two. I've never seen anything like it – it was incredible.'

He went on to describe the events as David had opened the door of the cell. Inside the cramped room four young offenders were sitting round the tiny table, concentrating hard. On the table they had carefully marked out a ouija board and, using a regulation mug, they were asking it questions.

The four were startled by David's abrupt entry, and all looked up. William stood behind him, possibly more surprised than the inmates themselves. David strode the two steps necessary to reach the table, picked it up and said firmly, 'Why are you doing this? This is very wrong. You are playing with fire, and who knows where it will lead? Would you let a child play with a nuclear bomb? Of course not – and neither will you play with this.'

He turned round and threw the offending object out of the cell door. By now the first officer had been joined by another, and they stepped back to avoid the table as it was propelled through the door.

'Throw it out and destroy it,' ordered David. No one argued. It was obvious he meant what he said. David turned back to the astonished men and declared, 'Don't you ever do that again. Now, we're going to pray.'

All four men looked down and began to comply, possibly out of astonishment.

'Hands together,' commanded David. 'Right, let's pray.'

He said a simple prayer asking God to forgive the men for playing with the ouija board, and casting out any wickedness that might have entered the room because of it. When he had finished he and the men looked up.

'Now,' he said, 'you all need God to help you. Would anyone like him now?'

One terrified man raised his hand, 'I would,' he said.

Ignoring the three others, two of whom had recovered enough to begin to snigger, the young man prayed with David, expressing a desire to become a Christian. Before he left, David told him to put his name down for chapel on the following Sunday.

'Oh yes,' he said quietly, 'I will.'

David and a shell-shocked William left the cell and returned to the chapel.

'Let him settle,' David told William, 'then go down and see him this afternoon with a Bible and tapes. Pray with him and we'll all pray for the others.'

After William had explained this astonishing event to his colleagues they all felt a burden for these young men who had chosen a ouija board to help them through prison. The students prayed earnestly. The prayer line was kept busy too.

The next day two of the others became Christians under the ministry of those students, and on the third day the final one decided that he too would like a better path for his life.

For him, James, this day turned out to be highly significant – firstly because he began a new Christian life on what was also his birthday, and secondly because he was 'shipped out' that evening to another prison, and we never saw him again. His name was passed on to Christians in his new prison, and we can only pray that what God started at Lewes, he would bring to completion.

All week the students prayed hard for and worked with the other three men, rejoicing to see them in chapel on the final day of the mission. William was especially thrilled to see them.

'I shall never forget it,' he confided in me. 'It was unbelievably thrilling. I really saw the power of God.'

That mission week 17 people became Christians, and the students were especially challenged and encouraged. They left with sadness on Sunday, after the service, and reported back enthusiastically and at length to fellow college members.

Chris went on to serve a curacy that had prison work involved, and William joined our prayer line to continue his commitment. All of them said they valued their experience, and felt it had affected their own ministry, especially in not underestimating the power of God in difficult lives, and in inspiring a boldness for the Gospel they had not felt before.

The experiences of these students have a relevance to our prosecution case against these criminals. Seemingly poles apart from the men they were serving, the students had found common ground in the love of God. These inmates were especially open and ready to receive Jesus compared to the trainee vicars' own non-believing contemporaries. Any prejudice just had to be laid to one side. God could work, and indeed was working, with such people. The case for the prosecution was just not that strong, as the chinks in its armour began to reveal. The finger of accusation could even be said to be turning round to face both them and us.

If these men were so obviously open to change and receiving the love of God, just why weren't there more of us in there telling them about him?

CHAPTER 2

✳

God's Bizarre Guest List

Jesus replied: 'A certain man was preparing a great banquet and invited many guests. At the time of the banquet he sent his servant to tell those who had been invited, "Come, for everything is now ready".'

But they all alike began to make excuses. The first said, 'I have just bought a field, and I must go and see it. Please excuse me.'

Another said, 'I have just bought five yoke of oxen, and I'm on my way to try them out. Please excuse me.'

Still another said, 'I have just got married, so I can't come.'

The servant came back and reported this to his master. Then the owner of the house became angry and ordered his servant, 'Go out quickly into the streets and alleys of the town and bring in the poor, the crippled, the blind and the lame.'

'Sire,' the servant said, 'what you ordered has been done, but there is still room.'

Then the master told his servant, 'Go out to the roads and country lanes and make them come in, so that my house will be full. I tell you, not one of those men who were invited will get a taste of my banquet.'

(Luke 14:16–24)

Speaking at churches, functions and organizations began to be a very regular event. Many people heard about the experiences at Lewes Prison, and David and I, together with various team members and Howard, an ex-prisoner, were pleased to share the news for two reasons. Firstly, we knew it was a great encouragement to Christians to hear of God working, and secondly, we were funding the purchase of literature.

It was obvious that people loved the stories of the individual men, but I was particularly determined to set the testimonies in a scriptural base. I began to be aware of certain passages that were especially relevant to our ministry, and would construct a format for a talk that would unify the passage and the work. David and I would work together on such a message, and then because we were talking to different groups all the time, were able to use it over and over again.

One of these passages was the parable of the great banquet in Luke, when Jesus tells of a man who was preparing a great banquet and who invited many guests. The invitations went out and notice of the date was given. When the great day dawned, messages were sent out to call the invited ones in, but instead of heading for the feast, one by one they made their excuses.

Jesus told stories that were set in his own time but which have meanings for all times. The man with the banquet is clearly God, who invites us all the join him in his Kingdom. Many today make their excuses as to why they won't join in too, just like the people in this passage.

The first said that he had bought a field and that he had to pay it all his present attention, so obviously he couldn't come to the banquet. How like today; many of us have possessions ludicrously beyond our needs, and looking after them is a huge job. How could we spare time to worship, and meet Christians, and even think about God when the car needs cleaning, the house needs painting, and the caravan and boat need getting ready?

The second man said he had just bought five yoke of oxen and would have to see they were set to work. He had a real job to do and he couldn't possibly spend time out now – maybe later! Similarly today many have demanding or interesting jobs that take up so much time they can think of little else. Unfortunately, people are valued in our society simply by virtue of the job they hold. 'He's a teacher,' we say, 'or a doctor or a company director. She's an engineer, an MP or a solicitor.'

For those left outside this world of work there is only disenfranchisement, low esteem and even despair but yes, the man in the story lives in our society too.

A third man claimed he had just got married so he couldn't be expected to think about God. He had his relationship and a new life to build. Well, we all know how much time and effort we put into relationships – they can be a great distraction. We may choose not to attend the feast on these grounds too.

Back at his master's house the servant messenger reports, and what is the response? 'Go back and persuade them'? 'Tell them I need them'? 'These are the people I want'? Well, actually no. The response turns out to be quite different. The master is angry – these people were clearly invited and have chosen not to come. Now the servant must go into the streets and alleys, and bring in the poor, the crippled and the lame.

Never mind the well-to-do, invite in the ones everyone else has forgotten: those with no money to buy possessions, those who do not have high-flying jobs, those without any supporting relationships.

What a message for today! As we went round churches together, David and I often saw people putting hours and hours into trying to persuade their friends and peers to find God and become Christians. We all want our nearest and dearest to come to God, and must go on trying, but the message of this passage is clear, even if in some cases unwelcome. Go and offer the Good News to others. Bring in the rejected, the poor and the sick. Make sure you tell them about the Gospel too. Furthermore the story goes on, because there is yet more room at the banquet. So the servant is sent out again, this time to the roads and country lanes so that there would be a full house for the feast.

So we too must go further from home, into the most undesirable places, where we least expect to find candidates for Christianity, in order to fulfil God's command to bring everyone in. Perhaps if we dare we may even have to enter prisons, to see if there are any there who would like to come to the feast. Of course the amazing thing, in both this story and today, is that all these unexpected people did come. They weren't full of excuses about whether or not they could fit in the occasion. We are only given the impression that they took their places with gratitude.

Talking about the passage often struck home forcefully with audiences and they would begin to own up to their own prejudices and presuppositions. It did seem that God was choosing a very different guest list than ours for his table.

Mick was an almost wild character whom Roy Kybett met in the hospital wing. He obviously suffered from some mental problems, and was being helped by the doctors and psychiatrists. He was a man of immense stature and long, unkempt dark hair. Roy and David both knew that Mick had as much right to be offered Jesus as any other inmate, and David duly paid him a visit one afternoon. His response was as surprising as it was immediate: he needed help in his life and was not afraid to admit it.

Later that week Roy went in search of Mick to help him with a Bible study. He knew this was going to be difficult, and he just had to trust that Mick would be calm and receptive. Mick was not on the hospital wing when Roy called, but was reported to be in education 'doing pottery'.

Roy made his way to the education department, wondering if his help was going to prove worthwhile. On arrival he looked round the room, glancing at all the inmates attending studiously to their pieces of clay. There was no sign of Mick's wild and woolly hair and his huge frame.

Roy approached an officer and asked for Mick. 'Oh yes,' he replied, 'he's over there,' and pointed to the centre of the room. There was Mick sitting at a potter's wheel working hard to comply with whatever instructions he had received. Roy was startled. Was this really Mick? Roy was momentarily thrown as he realized that Mick had cut off virtually all his hair, leaving only the merest covering, commonly called a 'dust cut'.

As Roy approached he saw that Mick was dealing with his clay in a rather aggressive fashion, lifting it up and pounding it on to the surface of the turntable, making the whole structure jolt under the strain. Mick's concentration was total, and although his demeanour was somewhat threatening, Roy knew that the object of the aggression was indeed the clay.

Gulping hard, Roy set out to make some sense of his mission. Obviously the Bible study was out, but Roy wanted Mick to know he had had a Christian visitor that day.

'OK, mate?' ventured Roy nervously, standing by Mick's side as the pummelling of the clay continued.

'Umph,' was the only reply, but Roy took it as an affirmative response, and went on, 'Well, that looks good, Mick. What are you making?'

Roy waited. A full minute later Mick replied, 'I'm making a dish, a clay dish,' and carried on battering his potter's wheel.

'Well, that's nice,' said Roy. 'I can see now it's a pot.' Roy was struggling, and realized that this conversation was not going to be of a sustained and meaningful nature. He made one more attempt. 'Who's it for then, Mick?' he asked, with as positive a tone as he could muster.

There was a further silence, but Roy could see that Mick was planning his reply.

Finally the huge man said, 'I'm making it ... for you,' and with that he stopped thumping and turned round to face Roy. '... for helping me,' he concluded, and resuming his potter's task he turned away once more.

'Thanks, Mick, thanks very much, mate,' stammered Roy before threading his way back through the class to the door. Once outside he started to allow himself to think about what had happened. He was concerned about Mick, and somewhat threatened by him too, but there was no doubt this man had made a glimmer of response to God. He'd tried to tidy up his appearance and was making Roy a clay pot. Only God can gauge the significance of such actions, but I would dare to guess they are of equal value with some of the noblest efforts some of us have made, we who have had every advantage over Mick in so many other ways. Just as I was thrilled with my own son's genuine first gift to me, so God is pleased with the tiniest step in the life of a man such as Mick. God had asked Mick to the banquet and he had responded.

Brian was an altogether different character. He was an astute and street-wise contract killer, who would deal with or 'sort out' problem people. When David met him he was working as a cleaner on the segregation wing. This is the part of the prison put aside for those who have broken prison rules and are too dangerous to be on the ordinary wings. A squat, stocky man, he had a short haircut and a very creased face. 'Like a creased ironing board,' another inmate once commented.

Brian had no front teeth as they had been knocked out during various fights. His reputation ensured that he was feared and respected on even the segregation wing, and his inability to either read or write was no bar to his holding the highest position. He had taken part in incidents involving razor blades in toothbrushes, and in knee-cappings using a baseball bat, selected for its lightness and ease of swing. So it was no wonder really that most inmates gave him a wide berth.

Nevertheless, David felt he was to be offered the Gospel just like everyone else, and so when he got the opportunity he took it. 'Would you like God to help you, Brian?' asked David cautiously one day.

David was used to people turning the offer down as well as accepting it, but he had also grown to realize that trying to guess a man's response was an empty task, so it wasn't a real shock when Brian replied, 'I could do with some help right now.'

Brian went on to repent of his past and to find Jesus as a new friend. David asked, 'Why have you decided to do this today, Brian?'

'Well,' replied Brian thoughtfully, 'I never thought about it before. Well, not for me, anyway. My sister's a Christian, I think. She lives abroad. But I didn't realize it was for blokes like me. I'd like a new start.'

In the weeks that followed Brian was a regular chapel-goer, and attended Roy's Bible studies in his corridor. He told David he felt better and that the Bible studies helped him.

'But you can't read, Brian, can you?' David gently questioned.

'No,' replied Brian, 'I can't, but I listen to learn, and talk of course. You know something?'

'What's that?' asked David.

'I hold this Bible in my pocket,' said Brian, pulling out his small brown New Testament, donated by the Gideons and given to him on his first day as a Christian.

'When I'm tempted,' Brian continued, 'I put my hand in my pocket and I feel God's Word right there. I feel the pages and I think of God's love going right through me.'

In the early days of Brian's conversion, officers kept asking him what he had in his slightly bulging pocket, because of course they always had to look out for any trouble, but after a while they remembered that Brian always carried his New Testament around and stopped asking him.

One day he asked to see David, who found Brian was beaming with pleasure.

'I wanted to tell you how I'm getting better,' Brian declared. David sat and waited for the tale to unfold.

'Well,' said Brian, 'there's this little tyke who fell out with me over some burn. [A prison term for tobacco.] Well, he wound me up, and in the end he wrote a note saying he hopes my mother dies of cancer.' Brian paused and David winced. Both knew Brian's mother had succumbed to that dreadful disease only months before, and although the man could not have known this it made the appalling insult worse. Brian continued his story.

'Well, of course I wanted to sort the bloke out – no one says that and lives.' David sat up and took careful note of this suggestion.

'Well then, I did something incredible,' pronounced Brian, this time pausing for effect and hoping for a response.

'What was that then?' questioned David.

'I warned him,' said Brian, triumphantly. 'I *really* warned him,' his voice hit a high note of satisfaction before dropping lower to add, 'I've never done that before, never, not just warned someone! So I guess I'm getting better.' Brian sat back and waited for an acknowledgement.

'Well, that's very good,' said David, shaking his hand firmly. 'Well done, Brian, that's a real step forward'.

David just couldn't wait to recount this story to us all, and found it hard not to grin, although he knew that this really did represent a step forward for a man such as Brian.

That afternoon Brian went on to ask for help. He had a brother whom he hadn't seen for some time, and Brian wanted him to visit him. He needed someone to contact his brother. So it was that Roy found himself driving up to a rubbish tip, seeking out a man who worked there, who was related to Brian. Roy alighted from his car and approached a couple of men emerging from a caravan in order to shunt piles of junk from place to place.

'I'm looking for Jim,' said Roy, as he approached the two men.

'Who's looking for him?' was the reply.

'Well, I'm a friend of his brother's, and I've got a message for him,' replied Roy, feeling uneasy.

'Who are you then?' One of the sturdily built men stepped towards Roy.

Now Roy was no wimp. An ex-heavyweight wrestler, he was often mistaken for an ex-inmate himself, and he would even joke about being out on licence now and then. Nevertheless he could spot danger when he saw it, because he knew Brian was inside for an unpleasant incident concerning baseball bats and a certain local rubbish tip. He took a step back and, taking a deep breath, he declared, 'I'm a member of the chaplaincy team at Lewes Prison, and Brian asked me to get a message to his brother to see if he'll visit him!'

He finished and looked up at the men. He never knew what had eased the situation; it could have been the message itself, the unlikely nature of this religious man, or even just his tone of earnestness, but whatever it was, it worked. The men looked hard at Roy and one said, 'We'll pass the message on.'

Roy knew when he'd outstayed his welcome, turned swiftly round and paced quickly back to his van.

Three days later the larger of the men turned up to visit Brian, who was very grateful to Roy. Although he was not half as relieved as Roy that the incident was over.

Brian grew as a Christian, and on his release linked up with another Christian in Birmingham for help. He wanted to make a new start far from his old haunts. With determination like that who's to say he won't succeed? We certainly pray that he does.

Would you say Brian was an odd selection for the royal banquet? If you did I would have to agree, but fortunately it's not you or I who draw up the guest list!

So I could move on to tell you of other men whom God was to draw near to himself in Lewes Prison, all of whose lives make untidy and in some cases disturbing reading. Why did God call Jake to be a disciple in prison, for example? He was accused of a multi-million pound fraud, and had travelled the hotels in Britain using false names – a real con man if ever there was one!

And why was Ted chosen? He planned the armed robbery of an off-licence, dressing up in combat jacket, army boots and balaclava. He made a plan of the area and timed the offence carefully – except that, forgetting that Wednesday was half-closing, he got caught outside the shop.

Dave tried to rob a fish and chip shop of its charity takings, needing the cash for drugs. However, the owner had glued the box to the counter, and rendered Dave near senseless with a huge piece of cod he had been battering. Staggering outside Dave and his friend were caught because they drove the wrong way down a one-way street and crashed their vehicle.

André found faith too. Very quiet and composed, he kept himself to himself and would sit listening to tapes and reading his Bible in his cell. One evening a group of five men pushed their way in at 'association time', because they were after the simple gold chain he always wore round his neck.

It was only then we discovered the truth about André. He wedged the door behind them and broke the first four men's noses in the ensuing fight. Then he calmly opened the door and threw the last man over the landing rail on to the safety nets below. He then turned to an officer and quietly reported the incident. It turned out he had been a trainer in the South African equivalent to the SAS – not a man with whom to trifle.

Later André was moved to the Isle of Wight, where he was followed up by our Korean volunteer, Bruce, who enjoyed fellowship with him and tried to ensure that André was set up on a good future path.

Ted was an abused child who turned abuser. Married to a woman with two children from a previous relationship, he abused them and her until she finally turned him in. High on drugs, he assaulted and committed acts of indecency against her. Yet he found God in his prison cell. Could this be possible?

Can men such as Ted and André, Dave or Jake, find God? Can the Brians and Micks be part of God's great planned banquet? The simple answer is

Yes. The power of God is not limited by our understanding, neither is his favour extended only to
'nice' people. The Gospel has the power to offer
a new start to everyone, including people such
as these examples from prison. These men are
sincerely invited to God's feast even if the final
guest list strikes us as totally bizarre.

CHAPTER 3

✳

A Day in Court

Howard had been our orderly at Lewes for many months, and he had taken his job very seriously. Quite apart from cleaning up the chapel and serving at the various services, he had brought many men to the chapel and helped them on the wings when they became Christians.

When his story came out in *The Cross Between Thieves* he was thrilled to read about his life and the change of lifestyle that took place in prison. He had, however, one reservation. 'It's all so out of date,' he said when he had finished the book. 'So much more needs to be said.'

Since his time in Lewes he had been dramatically moved to the Isle of Wight, and had his Christian commitment thoroughly tested by a tighter regime and by other Christians who doubted the reality of his faith. But he pulled through, obtaining an earlier parole than expected, taking up opportunities to tell churches and other groups about his new faith and trying to encourage support for the work inside Lewes Prison.

Howard once explained to me how it felt when you are sent for trial at court. 'Once you get in that van,' he said gravely, 'your life is out of your own hands. It's all up to other people now. You feel so powerless. There's nothing you can do about it.' It is interesting that he centred round the idea of powerlessness. Many prisoners are used to feeling in control because their crimes make others afraid of them and give them an illusion of self-esteem. Coming into prison is a huge shock, giving them a more realistic new perception of their status in the eyes of society.

Joe picked up the idea later that week, as he chatted to David.

'The judge is everything,' he claimed. 'If he gets to know you it can mean trouble. If I do something in Judge X's area I'll move to London and get caught for something there. Then the local charge is brought up to the London court and dealt with. It can save years off a sentence. Believe me: I know.'

Especially difficult, I've been told, is the lot of vulnerable prisoners whose turn comes to go to court. Due to the risk of other inmates attacking them because of the nature of their crime, they have to be protected as they go in and out of the common parts of the prison. One man from the protected 'K' wing, called Shane, shared with me his experiences of attending court.

7.00 a.m.   **Bang. Bang. Bang!** 'Jones, come on Jones, time to get up for court. What did you say? Talk like that and you're nicked boy!'

258

My pad [cell] mate tells me to push off as I've woken him up with a brew [cup of tea]. Ungrateful bloke!

7.15 a.m.   I've washed, cleaned my teeth and dressed, and I'm ready to go to Lewes Crown Court. I know I'm going to prison 'cos otherwise I wouldn't be in front of 'Send 'm down Brown'.

7.30 a.m.   Door opens. Two screws stand there. As a protected prisoner I need a guard.

7.35 a.m.   A brisk walk out of the block to Reception. Loads of people milling about changing from prison clothes to their own (they're going to court, to a hospital – or they're going home).

7.40 a.m.   The changing rooms are clear. The two screws guard me. No one speaks to me, just knowing looks all round.

7.50 a.m.   I'm searched and ready to go into the box. That's a room with a bench for the Rule 43 prisoners [those named '43' are given extra protection under the 43rd rule of the prison system].

'Do you want breakfast, Jones?'

'No,' I reply, and have a fag.

The time drags slowly by.

9.30 a.m.   The long wait is over. The door opens and I'm ready to go. One last search – no cuffs as I'm in the sweat box [prison vehicle]. I get into the van. They put me in a cube [term used to describe each section in the prison van] so you have to sit.

9.40 a.m.   The engine roars into life and we go for our ten-minute drive to the crown court. I've waited two hours for this. We could have walked in twos, just like school, but they have to waste a grand of tax payers' money.

9.50 a.m.   So we get to Lewes Crown Court and they off-load us. The other prisoners into a large holding room and me into a Beast Box [tiny, separate room for segregated prisoners, often known as 'beasts' due to the nature of their crimes].

9.55 a.m.   Then you get a brew and settle down to wait for your barrister to come. In the meantime you read the walls and find out how much of a slag your bird is, 'cos you find out she's been having sex with what seems like half the prison. Then you write on the walls too. The door opens and some bloke who looks about 19 says, 'Mr Jones, your barrister's here. Come this way please'.

In the old days the screws took you. It was just, 'Jones, your barrister's here.' Now it's Mr this and Mr that. It's a joke. We mess them about and there's nothing they can do. I plod along to see my barrister and pass the holding room. An inmate sees me and shouts, 'Jones, you've had it, bacon.' [This term of abuse is derived from bacon bonce = nonce, and is used to threaten unliked prisoners.]

'I'm gonna kill you,' shouts the man.

Then everyone is at their door joining in with their pound's worth. They kick the doors and shout abuse about my bird and my mother, and the bloke from the security company is scared stiff.

I'm in the interview room and a guard stands at the door, although as it's glass, they can all still see me. My solicitor and the barrister await me. My solicitor asks me, 'How's it going?'

I answer 'Great,' but not meaning it of course, because I can still hear them yelling 'beast' through the door.

10.00 a.m. The barrister tells me what is going to happen today. 'Right, today it's pleas and direction. You are going guilty on the handling and the theft and not guilty on the burglary.'

Of course I'm not asked my opinion during all this. 'You will get JR'd [Judge's remand].' I argue with him. I want to keep my present remand status. I stand my ground because I know how it works. My solicitor pays this barrister and I kinda pay him, so he's sacked if he doesn't pay attention to my instructions. The two professionals have a bit of a row and my solicitor wins.

10.30 a.m. We are going to court at 3.30 p.m., I'm told. So as it's only 10.30 a.m. I have to trek back to my box and wait. I sit here alone with nothing to do.

12.30 p.m. They bring my dinner. It's microwaved rubbish.

3.25 p.m. I ring my bell. The guard comes. I am desperate for the toilet. They don't want me to go as I'll be late in court.

3.40 p.m. I arrive late in court and my barrister shakes his head. The judge enters. 'All stand,' says the clerk.

I look at this man who can take my freedom away, and watch him smile at me. The judge doesn't appreciate me pleading not guilty when I'll obviously plead guilty at the end of the day. I don't respond.

3.50 p.m. It's nearly over. I plead not guilty anyway and I'm put on the list for two months' time.

'Take Jones down,' says the judge.

3.55 p.m. I'm back in my box.

4.05 p.m. My guard comes to get me.

'Is my barrister here?' I ask, eager to find out what's going on next.

'No,' replies the guard. 'You're going back to prison all by yourself.' With that the cuffs are on and I'm placed in a Ford Fiesta and driven back to prison. I'm cuffed to a bird who works for the security firm. She rambles on about my nearly causing a riot back there. I swear quite a bit at her.

4.15 p.m. I arrive at reception and for some reason I'm sent straight down the block to a strip cell. The search includes me having to squat. I'm told to dress.

4.45 p.m.   I get back into my cell with a cig and a brew. I tell my cell mate my day's been a total waste of space. I get little sympathy but it made me feel just a little bit better.

Time after time this idea of powerlessness in court is mentioned. The judicial system is a world apart from most of us, with its own language and code of practice. The uneducated or unable often respond by using language and behaviour which only serves to bring even more trouble on their heads. They often simply don't have the language either to explain their feelings or articulate their needs and questions. However, they all have one thing in common – they will tell you all about it. In prison someone who listens is a very rare person indeed.

Most of our prisoners were on remand or waiting for a decision about their future. If found innocent they never returned to us but were released into the community, but if declared guilty they knew they would not only be returned to prison but more than likely be sent on to a new establishment. We often witnessed that tension the day before a final court appearance, and knew that they felt quite unable to think beyond that next day. We always offered prayer on such occasions if we were aware of the event, and asked God for justice to be done in that court room. We could often only ask for this, as frequently we did not know the facts of the case in hand.

The men usually felt content with this approach. Sometimes we felt it right to pray only for mercy, since no other plea was appropriate, and occasionally we made a strange and individual request. Andy was such a case. He was due in court to face burglary charges. He had been interested in Christianity for some time, and one day came to chapel where he found a true and living faith. To say his appearance was unusual was an understatement. Standing six foot two in height, he was a large, imposing figure whose hair was bundled up behind his head in a huge lump. He told us that when let down it reached his legs. However, his hair was almost unnoticeable compared to his general appearance. There was no need to ask him his profession – he was a tattooist who had practised his art almost exclusively, it would seem, on himself. There was barely an inch of his limbs not covered with skilful tattooing. He was the sort of character you just couldn't help staring at, and the fascination of seeing tattoos on eyelids, ears and well into the hair line could not easily be ignored.

Andy knew this, of course, and actually was neither cross nor anxious about being the object of such attention. Nevertheless, on this Sunday morning he was worried.

'I'm a Christian now,' he said. 'I know I've done wrong, I admit it. I've made a new start but I know I must pay.'

'That's good,' said David, 'you're doing fine.'

'Yes, I know,' said Andy, twisting his hands together anxiously, 'but I know what everyone thinks, I don't think anyone will believe me. They'll think I'm all bad because of this.' Here Andy indicated his tattoos, pointing at his face, and sweeping his hands across his brightly coloured arms. 'What can I do? What can God do?'

'Let's pray,' suggested David, uncertain of what to say, but trusting that the words would be forth-coming.

Andy gratefully sat in an attitude of prayer, obviously waiting for help, and David looked at this trusting figure who just wanted a fair deal. And, from somewhere, the words came.

'O God,' he prayed, 'we ask for mercy for Andy. Please may he appear quite white when he's in court. May the people in that court just see his orig-inal features and colour.'

David continued to pray for a few minutes more, and then the two sat up and looked at one another.

'Is that possible?' asked Andy.

'I guess it is,' replied David. 'Our God can do anything.'

Andy seemed satisfied and left the chapel that morning, telling us his case was on Friday and that he'd see us next Sunday before he was shipped out, and let us know what happened.

We never did see Andy again. The next Sunday no tattooed face appeared at the chapel entrance. We could only guess at what had happened. We just prayed that all had been well and that God had helped Andy out in the way we had all hoped.

Two months later David told this story in a church in Burgess Hill. At the end of the service a woman virtually ran up to David as he packed his books and papers into his small black briefcase.

'Excuse me, I'm a probation officer. I was there,' she blurted out. 'I saw Andy – we all saw Andy in court that day.' Here she grew quite excited. 'He just looked normal! No one noticed anything. The judge was remarkably lenient. He seemed to take to Andy and believed he was sorry and had made a new start. He got sent to a probation hostel in the north.

'It was only after it was all over we noticed his face. I couldn't believe it. How could I have missed those tattoos? He looked so – well, strange. If I'd noticed I wouldn't have been able to see anything else. How did I miss them?'

She looked at David, waiting for a confirmation of what she had already guessed.

'It was the power of prayer,' stated David, quietly wondering to himself at the amazing result of that prayer. How good it was too that God had allowed us to know what had happened!

The story ended satisfactorily for Andy, and he was relieved to be given what amounted to a second chance. For many, of course, the story is different, not only because they end up imprisoned, but because they feel let down, confused and exhausted by the whole procedure.

For instance, I talked to Dan, sent down for his part in a very unpleasant fight which ended in a tragic death.

'You cannot bear the suspense in the end. It goes on and on and you get more and more confused about it all. You can't wait just to know,' he said.

Inmate after inmate confided the same information. The tension and sheer length of time before the resolution of a case caused the worst stress. Many of us will know that the cases we witness coming to a close on television refer back to incidents many months, sometimes even years, before.

These gaps have to be borne by everyone involved in the case and can seem interminable.

Jack told me he found all the evidence upsetting because he could not answer when the things being said weren't true, but this distress paled against the awful waiting, the not knowing.

Once convicted many are able to come to terms with even long stretches – at least then they know the result and can mentally prepare for the future.

Perhaps it was this powerlessness and the period of tense uncertainty about which we have spoken, that rendered so many men ready to respond to the offer of help and purpose that comes from God. Some might argue that only those who find God in a careful, reasoned way during a stable time have made a genuine decision to become a Christian. I do not believe the gospels record this, or that it can be universally applied today either. For many it is a point of crisis, deep searching or uncertainty that wakes us from our apathy or indifference and causes us to face spiritual truths. A few may approach God out of pure intellectual desire, but most of us recognize our own sin, inadequacy and need, and turn as a child does to its parent, hardly knowing what changes will be ahead once we have dared to allow God to enter our lives.

Whatever the theory, our evidence was clear: man after man chose to follow God before or during their time in court, and we certainly rejoiced that they were not alone, either in the dock or later in their cells once sentenced. Of course, any decision was only the beginning, and the journey of

faith would be long and hard for many – but everyone has to start somewhere!

Sometimes people would question the men's
change of heart, and insist that Jesus called us to be
made disciples, not just converts, as if men could
become disciples without first choosing to follow
Jesus Christ. Our reading of the Bible is that faith as
small as the tiny mustard seed is acceptable to God,
and it is a concept we hang on to, both in prayer
and action.

Of course the experience of court is threatening
and distressing to all – victims, witnesses and relatives alike – and the defendants are usually the only
people who can be said to deserve to be there.

Few of us will stand accused in a court room,
and we can be thankful to God for that, but
however strange it may seem, this awesome experience has been used by God to bring people to
himself, and for that we can be very grateful too.

CHAPTER 4

✳

Angels in My Peter

In court, prisoners are aware of the authorities that hold sway over their lives. They are not islands on their own doing as they please, but are answerable to other people and organizations. However, these earthly institutions are not the only elements to assert power over their, and indeed over our, lives. Even in this highly materialistic and earthly-centred society we are aware of a degree of 'other' worldliness. For most people their busy and relatively stable lives often crowd out spiritual things, and they might even be led to regard them as meaningless or at least irrelevant. However, prison, possibly like other crisis situations, has a remarkable power to concentrate the mind on the true nature of reality.

Unfortunately, probably due to a lack of Christian witness and example in their lives, prison inmates are drawn to the darker side of the spiritual world. As the incident with the ouija board in chapter one illustrated, there were plenty of opportunities to look into the unpleasant side of life. David routinely asked inmates whether they had had any dealings with the occult, although he didn't use that term, as it was often not understood. Laurence was one such new Christian to whom David posed that question.

'Have you had dealings with ouija boards, Laurence?' asked David. 'If you have, we'll need to pray it through and out, so that God can change you fully.'

'No,' replied Laurence confidently, 'I haven't touched a ouija board at all.' He shook his head vigorously and then screwed up his eyes, obviously thinking hard.

'I've done satanism in graveyards,' he added, 'does that count?' David paused, looked at him straight in the eyes, and said quietly but firmly, 'Yes, it does count, Laurence, it really does count. I think we'd better pray over this one right now.'

Another lad called Jason became a Christian the same month. He was a sad, lonely person who had become involved in drugs and crime at an early age.

'I want a new start,' he declared, 'I really do.' As David was praying with him moments later, he felt he should ask Jason a question. 'Do you have a pain in your neck, Jason?' he asked, 'and somewhere else?' He paused, 'But I don't know where.'

This word of knowledge had slipped into David's head and he knew he had to ask Jason. The young man started and sat upright.

'How did you know?' he asked David. 'I do have a pain there, and I've got a pain in my big toe – just there,' he added, bending down to indicate which toe was hurting.

Jason had denied involvement in strange practices prior to praying with David, and the source of the pain was unknown. David tried once more because he had learned that persistent inexplicable pains were often linked to evil events.

'Are you sure you've had no links with ouija boards, Jason?' he asked carefully, and then, 'or your family? Is anyone in your family linked to these things?'

Jason looked straight at David and light seemed to dawn. 'Oh yes,' he replied, 'I've not done anything, but my sister's a witch, she used to say things over me all the time. She's been doing that for years.'

The innocent look on his face made David resolve to explore more broadly in future. Jason was being straight – after all, he'd been asked if he had ever been involved in occult practices and *he* hadn't, but his sister ... well, that was a different question altogether.

These simple stories reveal the astonishing vulnerability of people to become involved in evil without realizing it. Perhaps it also explains why some of them were so responsive to the Gospel. The idea of the other-worldly, the inexplicable, being possible was not totally alien to their experience. For them the world was not restricted to a rational series of events, all of which result from simple cause and effect. Yes, they were used to controlling their own destiny on the streets and resented the authority of the law and state infringing on their activities – but strange events and the power of the paranormal, that did not really surprise or horrify them as it generally would more law-abiding members of society.

Jason's pain left him after prayer, and he was relieved. Now he was to start a new life no longer controlled by such evil forces, and only the presence and power of the Holy Spirit would keep him safe in future. Without God's help we are all open to strange forces, however materialistic we may consider ourselves to be. The presence of God in our lives is the only means by which we can be sure that we are safe from evil influence. This may not be modern thinking but it is certainly Christian thinking, and we have witnessed the reality of it.

However, although we are aware of a significant amount of involvement in the occult in the prison, there was activity of a more wholesome kind too. Some of the events could be dismissed by a sceptic as wishful thinking, but we believe that God was working in that place, and that the 'coincidences' and remarkable events were too frequent and persuasive to be dismissed lightly.

Doug was a mature, quiet man whose arrival at the prison had thrown him into utter turmoil because he was charged with offences of a sexual nature. He was placed in the special part of the segregation unit set aside for vulnerable prisoners. Here, any who needed segregating for their own protection would spend their term, hoping never to be the victim of the other prisoners' surprising hatred for those who had committed what, in their eyes, were unacceptable crimes.

Doug was unlucky. Someone had read about his alleged activities and was quick to establish his

presence on that wing in Lewes Prison. The segregation unit is set in a low position in the establishment,
close to the inmates of 'F' wing. These convicted
prisoners are often older and more settled than
other inmates, and in this case a group planned their
own scheme for retribution. Doug was subjected
to night after night of verbal abuse and threats.
Working in shifts, the prisoners would shout across
the courtyard dividing their part of the prison from
Doug's. Insults included threats against his family,
accompanied by strings of expletives.

Dave was Doug's cell mate. His sleep was of
course non-existent during this period, although he
was not the actual target of the victimization. Dave
had become a Christian a few weeks before, and
he suggested to Doug that he ask David for some
advice. Doug duly sent in a wing application, and
David went down to see him late one afternoon.

As David entered the room he realized he was
dealing with a very troubled man. Doug's torment
was proving unbearable. Sitting up, he brushed
back his silver-grey hair. Although short in stature
he didn't have the appearance of one easily intimi-
dated, but David could see that he looked a lot
older than his 50 years, probably the effect of the
continual abuse he was now suffering.

'Can you help me?' asked Doug in a desperate
tone. 'I don't think I can take this much more.'

David listened carefully as sorrow and fear
poured out of this terrified man's lips. Doug
declared himself innocent of his alleged crimes and
David did not argue. Many of the men protested
against their imprisonment or their sentence.

Pleading innocent was the norm. David often half-joked that he had 350 innocent men under his care! Nevertheless we knew that some of the men were indeed innocent of all or part of their indictments, and that stitch-ups were a reality of life for part of the criminal world. For this reason David left the judgements to God, supported by what he felt was sound biblical backing, and dealt with the more immediate needs of each individual he met. After he had prayed with David it was obvious there was a sense of relief in Doug's voice and a glimmer of brightness in his eyes.

'So this is what Dave, my cell mate, was talking about,' said Doug. 'I sure feel different but I don't know why.'

Douglas certainly looked calmer, but David realized that his present anguish would continue unless something could be done about the aggression from 'F' wing.

David had two options. Firstly, he could request that this man be moved to another establishment on compassionate grounds, although of course the grapevine would inevitably catch up with him, and his flight prove pointless – furthermore, the man would then be beyond David's further assistance. Secondly, he could report the incident and attempt to pin down the perpetrators. This option was fraught with problems, not least of which was the possibility of an intensification of hostilities.

David thought for a moment, when into his mind slipped an amazing third suggestion. Praying silently for courage, he faced Doug and said confidently, 'We're going to ask God to help you, Doug.

I'm going to pray that angels will watch over you. We need a real miracle here.'

The bewildered inmate looked hopefully towards the chaplain.

'Is this possible?' Doug whispered. He had certainly never heard of any such thing before, but then he had never heard of praying to God and feeling a real buzz from it before either. He decided to go with it.

'Can you do that?' David's faith that he should act on this idea did not waver, but he later admitted he would have appreciated a change of orders at that particular moment if it had been possible ...

David stood up to pray and asked God to post two of his largest angels in that cell – one at the door and one at the window. His prayer grew with confidence as he spoke, and by the time he said Amen his conviction was solid.

The next morning David visited Doug in his cell.

'You'll never believe what happened,' enthused the excited inmate as David entered the room. 'There wasn't a sound last night. No sound at all. I slept right through for the first time in weeks.'

David gave a broad cheerful smile and sat down on the hard bed.

'That's just great, Doug,' he said. 'I think we had better say a prayer of thanks, don't you?'

'Oh yes,' replied a very grateful Doug. 'I really do, it's truly amazing.'

'I had an angel in my Peter, a real angel,' said Doug ['Peter' is prison slang for a cell, after Peter's enforced stay in prison]. From that moment on there were no more threats or abuse hurled towards Doug's cell, and he and his cell mate had much to talk about. Doug was greatly affected by this event and brought inmate after inmate to David's attention in the following weeks.

There were many other such amazing incidents of a seemingly coincidental nature. But, as they say, although answers to prayer may seem coincidental, strange occurrences stop when the prayer does. Here we were covered by prayer and involved in a very real front-line ministry, and God's help was just flowing on and on.

Pete, for instance, was adamant that he didn't want God as he had no evidence that God existed. He decided to throw down the gauntlet, which in our dealings with God, is often a very rash thing to do.

'I'll believe if my sister chooses to visit me,' he said firmly.

Pete and his sister June had fallen out many years before. June lived in a sleepy Devon village many miles and thoughts away from East Sussex. Now that Peter was inside he had time to reflect on his lost years of sibling contact, and regretted the fact they didn't talk. Real people are unable to resolve their differences as easily as characters in soap operas do week by week. Perhaps that's why we all like to watch the neighbours in Ramsay Street apologizing to each other regularly and sincerely, because we know in reality that people will hold on to resentments, jealousies and slights for many a decade, and even die without resolving the festering wounds, usually caused by the tiniest of incidents. Indeed, soap-watching could be perceived as a national exercise in wishful thinking!

Pete obviously wished this awkward silence with his sister could be broken, and he was adamant nothing could be changed and that he'd only consider God if it did. Three weeks later his bluff was called – June turned up to visit him.

David met up with Pete the next day, and he was so overwhelmed and overjoyed that he responded instantly to the offer of a new start with God. Days later he was still seen shaking his head with disbelief, but with a tiny smile on the edge of his lips that would burst into a full toothy grin whenever David walked down the wing.

'It's amazing,' said Pete to anyone who would listen, 'just amazing.'

Roy met a relative of a prisoner one day outside the prison walls. He had gone out to his van to pick up a book he'd promised to show an inmate, when he looked past the rows of cars neatly parked in the drive and saw a woman sitting under a large tree, which stood on a slope leading down to the main road.

Roy was concerned, because the woman was curled up with her head between her knees, and appeared to be crying. As he approached her, however, he realized there were no sobs or indications that the woman was in distress, but he felt he should speak to her anyway, and ventured, 'Hello, can I help you?'

The woman started and glanced up at Roy. He sensed she was a little alarmed at this disturbance, and aware that his muscular appearance might well have given her extra cause for concern, he added quickly, 'I'm a member of the chaplaincy department in the prison. We are available to help people. Are you all right?'

The woman pushed her long hair back from her face and explained, 'I'm praying. My brother is inside the prison and I don't know what else to do. I came here to visit him but when I arrived I just felt I should sit under this tree first and pray for him.'

Roy spoke to the woman for a while, and promised that the team would look out for her relative. Then the woman stood up and went into the prison to visit her wayward brother.

The next morning Craig became a Christian, and was able to ring his sister to tell her the good news.

'And all because a woman sat beneath a tree to pray,' reported Roy that afternoon. 'It really was quite a coincidence, wasn't it?' said Roy, winking, knowing full well it was more than that.

'A real coincidence indeed!' David answered.

One Sunday after the morning service, David was walking through the wings with a message for an inmate. Suddenly a man called out to him across the landing. David saw a thin, dishevelled inmate leaning against his cell entrance and motioning him to come across. David duly approached the man, whose name was Jordan, and asked, 'How can I help you?'

Jordan eyed the chaplain up and down, and David was not quite sure whether he was approving or not of this man he had summoned to his assistance.

'I'm not a religious man,' Jordan began. David took little notice of this opener because inmates and officers used it so often that its impact was negligible. This morning he didn't even respond with his usual, 'God is aware of that.' The comment was usually followed by an excuse as to why its user had not been in the habit of attending church, though seldom, in David's experience, did it mean 'I don't believe in God'.

Jordan went on, 'Well, as I said, I'm not religious at all, but since I've been in here I've been thinking. I'd like to get to know God. I've tried to get to chapel but I've never made it somehow.'

David knew that some of the inmates found getting to chapel a problem. It always meant putting your name down the day before, and often missing other tempting activities. Sometimes there were limits to numbers too.

'Anyway,' continued Jordan, 'I've been praying in here,' indicating his cell, 'and I felt I was meant to stand outside here and ask the next bloke who came along.' He gazed up at David as if looking for a reaction, but waited only a second before adding, 'and it was you! So could you help me find God ... at all?' he finished, almost lamely.

So David prayed with Jordan, and a volunteer later read the Bible with him and taught him to pray. He grew as a Christian quite swiftly, and displayed a real drive to find a new purpose for his life. His faith had obviously been kickstarted that Sunday morning on the wing.

We were surrounded by remarkable things happening to the men, and often amazed how God used events to spur us on in our own faith. A day late last year was one of these rather special events. David and I were in a train returning from London, and it was about midnight. We were chatting about the evening we'd just experienced. David had been invited to speak to the Christian fellowship at the Houses of Parliament. As well as committed Christians there had been many interested guests – to say it was an honour and a thrill to have been there is a gross understatement. We were really on a high. In spite of obvious nerves we had felt so up-lifted by prayer that the whole event had gone like a dream. We had met Douglas Hurd, Lord Longford, Emma Nicholson and numerous other household names at the buffet held in the Speaker's apartments. David had spoken well and clearly, and had pulled no punches about the need to change men's hearts if we really wanted a drop in the crime rate, stating that no amount of tinkering with sentencing policy would make the slightest difference to men who felt that a request 'not to do it again because we, the middle class, don't like it' was an insufficient reason to start going straight.

It was a bold speech, and we had felt we must be true to what we really believed. I had drafted the speech with great care after we had talked at length together about this opportunity, and David had put across the message in his usual witty and anecdotal style.

I had watched him delivering his speech, standing in front of a vast and impressive fireplace, with the rows of chairs facing him, each with an elegant and important person seated upon it. The lifesize portraits of former Speakers looked down from high on the walls, and the rich red and gold décor formed a stylish setting for this impressive scene.

The huge banqueting table was covered with plates from the preceding meal, and everyone there was remarkably attentive, listening to this ordinary chaplain who was used to addressing a very different audience.

David relaxed into the talk, and as usual took questions from the floor with both ease and humour. Asked about officers he responded with a story about one who had recently approached him about his fear of dying. David told how he had taken the man's fear seriously, and reminded him that it was well founded, as statistically one out of one people die ... David went on to explain that he had firmly, but kindly, confronted the officer with the Gospel's message – 'Those who believe go to Heaven. Those who don't have chosen Hell.' The listeners, almost hanging on every word by now, were relieved by David's revelation that the officer chose at this point to become a Christian.

In the vote of thanks an elderly and obviously experienced member thanked David heartily for his forthright yet humorous approach, and expressed a wish that more clerics would be as clear and direct in their message.

We were greatly relieved. The straight approach could have backfired but it didn't. Each guest had heard the Gospel clearly that night, as well as learning what was happening to the inmates and staff of Lewes Prison. The opportunity was one given to very few, and we could only pray it would have lasting and meaningful effects. Sufficient to say that Viscount Brentford, who as Chairman of the organization had sent us the invitation, was thrilled with the occasion and reported that many had felt they had had a thoroughly good and stimulating evening. We thanked our prayer partners in our hearts as we left that building, and could hardly believe where this work had led us.

So obviously on the train that night our conversation was centring round the events and conversations of the evening, when we were suddenly interrupted. We were in a carriage with a corridor running beside it, and suddenly there was a sharp tapping on the window. We looked up, breaking off in mid-sentence, and sat upright as we rather nervously found ourselves staring at a young, dirty face looking at us through the glass. Behind that face stood the taller, heftier frame of a second young man, also peering in at us too. The first man placed his hand on the door handle and began to open it. By now we could see his rather untidy style of dress and the tattoo just below his right eye.

He stared at us and fixed his gaze on David 'Where do I know you from?' he asked. Though our hearts were thumping, there was a tone in his voice that indicated he was not really threatening us.

David thought quickly. He knew he must respond with care. 'Lewes?' he replied. 'Do I know you from Lewes?'

He deliberately only referred to the town in case his first feelings were wrong, but he need not have worried.

'Lewes Prison,' responded the young man. '*That's* where I know you from. You're the Father, ain't you? The Father in the prison. Here, Mick.' With this, he stuck his head back into the corridor and addressed his friend. 'It's the Father. You know, from the prison.'

The second man ventured the tiniest of smiles before retreating down the corridor. The first man opened the door of the carriage fully and stepped in. He sat down opposite David and pronounced, 'I'll have a word with you. I'll sit here.'

We had mixed feelings. At least we knew where he was from, but we still had no idea about his intentions or what he wanted to have a word with us about!

'I remember you,' he started. 'You gave me a radio. I was desperate. All alone. You gave me a radio.' He grinned from ear to ear obviously recalling the situation.

'You gave me a radio ... and I've still got it.' He triumphed almost as if it were the only item he'd managed to take care of in his short but obviously eventful life. 'They sent me to Wandsworth,' he went on. 'I was banged up 23 hours out of 24. It was hell. But I had that radio. I'll never forget that, or you,' he said looking straight at David.

'So you're out now?' said David, stating the obvious. 'What are you doing?'

'I'm out with my mate seeing a friend at Gatwick,' replied the man. 'Paul's the name. Paul. Do you remember me?'

'Well yes,' said David, 'but I had forgotten your name. Glad to be out?'

'You bet,' he responded, 'I can't get over this, you know. I haven't got a job yet but I've still got that radio. I'm off now,' he declared as swiftly as he had announced his intention to stay.

'I hope you get a job soon,' I said, as he turned and reached for the door handle. 'Good luck,' I added.

'Yeah thanks,' said Paul and slipped out to join his mate again, still muttering about the radio.

'I've never been so glad that I gave a man a radio,' said David after Paul had gone. 'It obviously meant so much to him.' He hadn't responded to the Gospel as far as we knew, but he had to a simple act of kindness.

'Someone gave us the money for that radio,' mused David. 'They'll never know what they did.'

Then we started talking about the irony of this event: the Houses of Parliament one moment, an ex-inmate on the train the next. Kipling's poem, 'If', about being able to talk both to princes and the common man, sprang to mind.

We knew that here was our real calling – of course, we had thoroughly enjoyed the glamour and excitement of the evening, but nothing could beat the thrill of offering the Good News of Jesus to men like Paul, or the joy of knowing that the simple gift of a cheap little radio in the name of Jesus could have such a profound and lasting effect. We knew too that when we all face God we will be answerable as much for those tiny things we do as we will be for the greater events of our lives. It is in the giving of a cup of water to a stranger that our real faith is revealed.

＊

CHAPTER 5

The Defence Team

Working with prisoners is exciting and satisfying. It can also be tough and frustrating. There have been times when the frustration of being unable to meet both the demands and the opportunities of the ministry has been almost demoralizing. A never-ending stream of new inmates coming into the prison and responding to the Gospel sometimes meant we didn't have proper time to cover their needs. Criticisms that there was no point in offering people a change if we couldn't follow it up, so that they became lasting disciples, were often expressed by those we believed should have been more open to a move of God, and who would have done better by offering a hand of help rather than an unconstructive put-down.

But those who chose to get to know these prisoners found that in spite of the difficulties of bringing men into a growing faith, the rewards of the activity were huge. As in any Christian work people have fallen by the wayside, and many have stagnated in their faith. After all, outside we often meet Christians we have known for years who appear to have gone no further down the road to commitment than when they first believed. So it is for some of the Christian inmates, and we believe the principles of the parable of the sower apply equally to a prison ministry as they do to any outside church.

> While a large crowd was gathering and people were coming to Jesus from town after town, he told this parable: 'A farmer went out to sow his seed. As he was scattering the seed, some fell along the path; it was trampled on, and the birds of the air ate it up. Some fell on rock, and when it came up, the plants withered because they had no moisture. Other seed fell among thorns, which grew up with it and choked the plants. Still other seed fell on good soil. It came up and yielded a crop, a hundred times more than was sown.'
> When he said this he called out, 'He who has ears to hear, let him hear.'   (Luke 8:4–8)

If the seed represents the Word of God in the form of the Good News of Jesus, just how often and how intensively have we taken part in the spreading of it? We yearn to bring people to Jesus Christ, but if we're honest, we often work to help those we love the most and those to whom we are more readily drawn, with little real desire to help those less attractive. In our work we often meet those who pay lip service to the need to evangelize widely, but who feel it is not their own calling, and who are not prepared to enter into any commitment to it, be that in a prison, a housing estate or overseas.

The seed that fell on the path came to nothing, and all those who have decided to respond to the call to evangelize will know that a proportion of seed will fall into the lives of those who show no interest at all in the things of God. In the prison this is a reality too.

'No thanks mate,' said Bill, who had sat through a clear and concise presentation of the Gospel in chapel one morning. 'I don't want to offend you,' he said to David, who had just asked him if he wanted God to help him in his life.

'You haven't offended me,' replied David, 'you have offended God, but then you will answer to him one day and not to me.'

Bill was taken aback but still resolved that the cost of discipleship was too high for him.

Steve was another case in point.

'I believe all roads lead to God,' he stated when asked a similar question. 'I believe in a life force, an energy – I'll plug into that.' For him the Gospel had fallen on a barren path and the uniqueness of Christ passed him by.

Some of the seed in the story fell on rock and began to grow, but withered because there was no moisture to keep it going. Every work of evangelism will meet the people represented by this type of ground. When I was younger I was part of a flourishing Bible-based youth group that met the needs of hundreds of teenagers, and urged them to submit their lives to God's service. Over 20 years later it is obvious that a fair number of those teenagers never went on to maturity of faith. No leader to whom I have spoken will dare to hazard a guess as to which characters in their present groups will come into this category, but they are sadly forced to admit that there will be some. Only God knows people's hearts, and we cannot presume to say this one will stay the course rather than that one. It is not for us to know, and we prejudge at our own peril because we are clearly warned in Scripture not to do so.

Jim responded to the Gospel one Sunday in the service because he felt he needed help in his life. He prayed as all the others had done, and said that he felt the power of God inside as David ministered to him. Nevertheless he was already wavering by the next week, and by the following Sunday he was not only missing from chapel but said he no longer wished to have chaplaincy visits.

Why did this happen? It is rare for someone to slip away so swiftly, but it does occur, although we could see no reason why Jim's heart was such stony ground. There was no difference in his approach that could be discerned, and we were left with no satisfactory explanation.

Of course we were disappointed, but what should we say at this point – 'Let's give up? People like this don't understand enough. Stop the ministry. Don't preach the Good News'? No, because this parable prepares us for the possibility of it happening. Inevitably, some will respond with what seems a very real initial commitment, but they will still fall away.

Other seed fell among the thorns, which grew up with it and choked it. Mark's gospel adds that because of these weeds the seed could not bear fruit. This ground represents the ineffectual Christian who has experienced the things of God and enjoys the benefits of a clear conscience and the hope of heaven, but whose life is filled with other activities which allow no room for maturity of faith or service of others.

Toby became a Christian, and he appeared regularly in chapel on a Sunday, where he sang lustily, prayed unselfconsciously, and chatted to visitors gladly. Nevertheless, he showed little interest in prayer and Bible study on the wing, and his peer group appeared to dominate his activity. None of his friends turned up in chapel with him. They thought Toby just needed a Sunday fix of religion, and knew it had little effect on his everyday existence. Now of course we hope that the spark in Toby will grow to a flame, but we are concerned for him on his release, because only a deep and conscious commitment will keep him on track on 'the out'.

Nevertheless, the seed that fell on good ground yielded a good crop – a hundred times larger than the original. Here is the crux of this parable. We tend to focus on the first three types of ground and major on the negative aspects, but the truth is that we are meant to recognize the joy of the fruitfulness of the seed on the good ground.

The true Christian not only finds God and his peace, but goes on to give service by bringing others to a similar experience. Fruitfulness is the key to reality. If there is no fruit there is no real life in one's faith. This message is a two-edged sword, of course, being both a huge encouragement and an immense challenge.

At this point the strong converts among the inmates come into their own. Yes, we meet those who falter along the way or even fall at the first hurdle, but we are also privileged to meet those who are 'the good ground'. Some of our men cause us to cringe in embarrassment when we compare our faith and willingness to declare the Gospel with theirs.

Mark brought eight or more of his fellow prisoners to the chapel. He was a young man who found faith when he was weighed down by his own failure and lifestyle. I'd met him in the chapel, and he had told me that his Mum always went to church. He committed his life that morning and rang to tell her the good news. Her prayers and thanks must have been very profound, because her 'lost' son came home at last.

Similarly Graham found faith and wasn't afraid to share it. He told many on the wings of his new love for God, and began to express himself and his new faith in writing. One Sunday he burst into chapel and approached David with a piece of paper. 'Can I read it?' he asked, waving the piece of paper in front of his nose.

David looked at the keen, dark-haired young man before him, and saw his enthusiasm. 'What is it?' he asked, gently taking the writing from Graham's hands.

'My poem,' declared Graham. 'It tells what God means to me now. I wrote it myself. I can't stop writing now.' Then he added confidently, 'I know it by heart, you know. I don't need the paper.'

David was sorry to disappoint such keenness, but there was a band in that morning and the schedule was really tight. 'Look, Graham. It will have to be next week. You can read it next week, I promise.'

The look of disappointment on Graham's face was touching. He was a good-looking fellow, and made the best of himself even in prison. He would not have been out of place in any church setting that morning, and he displayed a surprising maturity. Normally inmates want everything 'now', and they are unable to be patient about anything. If one has promised to do something or bring something, they will badger almost hourly until the promise has been fulfilled. Maybe having nothing and being out of control of one's own actions almost wrings this attitude out of them. Suffice it to say it is almost universally the case.

Graham somehow mustered up the willpower to be patient that Sunday and said, 'OK. OK, I'll wait. I wanted to do it. I really did. I'll practise. I'll be good. I'll do it next week.'

All week Graham practised in his cell. He read it so many times to his peers that he really did commit it fully to memory. The next Sunday he was up as early as he was able, reminding us that his turn had come.

'Where's the paper, then, Graham?' asked David.

'Oh, I don't need that,' replied the now impatient inmate, 'I know it by heart.'

'I think you'll need it when you get up there,' said David confidently. 'It's different at the front.'

Graham hesitated. He hadn't thought of that.

'You'll have to wait another week,' said David, frightened that the prisoner would stumble and be demoralized by his performance. A look of utter dejection crossed Graham's face and once again he took his place amongst the empty chairs. But, not wanting to see the lad disappointed any further, David sent a volunteer to his office, where he thought there might still be a copy of the poem on his table. He didn't want to raise Graham's hopes unduly, but hoped he could resolve the problem.

Halfway through the first hymn a breathless volunteer thrust the copy of the poem into the chaplain's hands. 'Great,' whispered David, and crept up to Graham, who was hiding his disappointment well as he sang heartily.

'Here we are, Graham,' said David pushing the paper into Graham's hands. 'You're on!'

Graham looked intensely at David, expressing his thanks with his eyes. His moment had come and he could hardly believe it.

As it happened, he really did need that copy of his poem because in spite of his enthusiasm and confidence, it was scary up there in front of everyone! He read the poem clearly and well, and grinned from ear to ear when he had finished. There was a huge round of applause and a very cheerful inmate returned to his seat.

Some weeks later, just as Kenny, an earlier inmate, had done the year before, Graham was chosen to read his poem at the prison carol service. If reading in chapel is a challenge, then doing so at this major event of the year is awesome. Lots of outside visitors come, and together with governors, officers and inmates, the congregation approaches two hundred.

David at least was prepared. In spite of his earlier experience, Graham still believed in his own ability to remember his own writing. Had he not pronounced it a hundred times since that Sunday in chapel, and without mistakes? Surely he could do it now?

David had placed a copy of the poem on the lectern 'just for appearances', he had told Graham, but when the moment came Graham froze, and was intensely grateful to see that typed sheet in front of him.

When he closed, he raised his palm in acknowledgement of the applause and the cries of 'Go for it, Graham' and 'Well done, mate' which accompanied it.

Here is Graham's poem, which he is pleased to share with everyone who will listen. I am sure you will agree with all who have heard it before that it is a real and moving expression of one man's faith.

ALL THIS FOR ME

I once lay in a tomb of life, dead to rhyme and
   reason,
All purpose gone, no hope of goal, blind
   without a vision.
The walls were made to keep you out, instead
   they kept me in.
The stone was there to keep me safe, to hide
   away my sin.

A small still voice kept telling me, 'I have life for
  you,
I really want to set you free, to let you start
  anew,'
But I felt safe within the dark, the light I could
  not bear.
The fact that Jesus died for me was neither here
  nor there.

The mask I wore was made of pride, to hide my
  haunts and fears
I wore an air of confidence, water-logged in
  tears,
With mouth and eyes in conflict, I tried to play
  the part.
I didn't want the world to know I had a broken
  heart.

One day a man from Nazareth came knocking
  at my door.
'I've come to set you free, my son, and give you
  so much more.'
'But Lord!' I cried, 'can this be true? my chains
  are very tight.'
'Peace, be still, come, follow me, you'll find my
  yoke is light.'

I left my tomb and followed him, and very soon
  I found
That all my sins and hurts and fears, no longer
  had me bound.
My blinded eyes were opened, my shackled
  heart was free,
The liberator, Jesus, has done all this for me!

'Greatest Love'

Graham Pinsent
October 1996

David read a book by Romanian pastor Richard Wurmbrand, and was struck by the point that 'there is no "I" in the Our Father' – he and I know that without others we can neither sustain nor expand the ministry. Of course we are not a church and have no paid personnel, but we know each person can bring a distinct contribution to what is taking place, and that we are totally dependent on volunteers to disciple the new converts.

In *The Cross Between Thieves*, our first team members are recalled and many, though not all, are still with us at this time. However, new people spring up too, and help to expand and enhance the work. Andy, from YWAM, was one of these, and he began to come in on Sundays and to work once a week with inmates. He found he needed to reassess his approach to pastoring situations, as the men were often lacking in literacy skills and unused to reasoned argument, but he enjoyed his ministry and was a fruitful contact for many prisoners.

Jim Greenwood, a real friend from earlier days, began to come in to chapel once a fortnight, and to offer his skills and his faith to pray with inmates moments after their prayers of commitment. Travelling some 50 miles did little to daunt his valuable enthusiasm and, always a man of great prayer, he contributed greatly to the services. For his part, the work ministered to his spirit in a real way, as he had often toiled in the Lord's service in difficult home and church situations and had shown steadfastness well beyond most others. The excitement of seeing the men's response he viewed as God's reward to him, and felt privileged to be part of it all. Furthermore, his infectious laugh and sense of perspective were a huge asset to the group, and we were delighted to have him aboard.

David definitely had great faith in Jim's abilities, and soon grew to pass new converts on to him for prayer. One morning Robert came to faith, and told David he had been playing with the occult on a small-time basis. David summoned Jim and a volunteer to pray with the man. 'He needs to have prayer for release,' he told the solemn Jim.

'Right,' was the answer, and a faithful Jim said prayers with the volunteer over the man, to cast out any evil influence that might have entered him.

'He was so authoritive in prayer,' said the volunteer later, when we were all settled in the chapel with a mug of tea after the inmates had returned to their wings.

'That's good,' said David. 'So you have had lots of experience of this type of thing, Jim?'

A huge smile spread across Jim's face, and his shoulders began to shake as he explained, 'Oh no, I've never done anything like it before. I've never made it to the right team or been sent on a relevant course, but I knew I had to do it. I couldn't let you down... It all seems so right, so obvious and almost, well ordinary,' he continued. 'I guess I really am just learning on the job and where better would I do that?'

We had also developed links with local bands and groups who would attend a service and brighten it up considerably. Because the inmates moved so often, there was no stable community, and each service on a Sunday (or indeed each week on the wings) was unique. Consequently, as long as we knew in advance and there was an element of real commitment by the Christians, we could live comfortably with many short-term visitors.

For example, Terry Tully, a local man who used a sketch board to preach, could establish a meaningful ministry with just one visit every two months – each occasion he visited was equally as valid and valuable.

However, although Sundays were normally well catered for, we had times when only four of us were there and when we were really stretched to meet the needs of the inmates. Still, we had to trust that we had the right people, and leave our concerns in the hands of God.

At Icthus Church in London we met Graham Kendrick, who expressed a real interest in our work. When he began his ministry he sang in pubs and clubs in order to evangelize. As a student in the seventies, I had enjoyed his early tapes, and greatly appreciated songs such as 'Paid on the Nail' and 'No room at the world'.

I chatted to Graham about these songs, and he seemed amused I could remember these very 'ancient writings'. He obviously had a heart for evangelism with the unchurched, and agreed to visit the prison in the next few months.

The week before Graham's visit, David told the men that he was coming.

'Who's he?' asked an inquisitive inmate.

'Well, he's really famous,' replied David, realizing instantly that this was a hopeless task.

'Is he that bloke who plays the guitar on 'A' wing?' asked another.

'No,' responded David, 'he's coming down from London to play for you.'

'Well, that's good of 'im,' interjected a third, leaning back in his chair and placing his hands behind his head. 'I like music and guitars.'

Graham arrived at the prison by 7.45 a.m., and I met him and his companion outside. I thanked them for coming, and knocked on the huge gate to gain entrance. The officer on duty let us in, and began to look with suspicion at Graham's equipment.

Slightly flustered, Graham handed his mobile phone co-operatively to the officer behind the screen.

'Oh good,' teased the officer. 'I need to make a few calls to Australia this morning.'

Graham smiled, realizing this was unlike the usual welcome he received in churches across the country!

The second officer was searching his guitar case. 'These yours?' he questioned, picking out a set of spare guitar strings from beneath the splendid instrument.

'Yes,' replied Graham, 'they're spare guitar strings.'

'Great for this,' declared the officer, drawing his finger across his throat in a mock attempt at suicide. 'I don't think we'll have those in, do you?'

Graham looked aghast at the suggestion, and asked, 'What do I do if I break a string?'

'Come back and see me,' responded the officer, who was warming to the task.

We had all learned a long time before to go with the general banter and teasing of the officers. They had a huge responsibility to handle, and often carried the can for being either too lax or too strict with the interpretation of the rules.

Humour is a huge reliever of tension, and it is certainly rife in Lewes. David always thoroughly enjoys it all, and certainly gives as good as he gets whenever he can. Graham Kendrick was obviously also learning fast, and a glimmer of a smile spread across his features as, horror of horrors, the officer found a 'secret' compartment in the guitar case that lifted up to reveal his screw driver, kept on hand to alter his strings whenever necessary.

Without a word the officer held up the offending item, raised his eyebrows and slowly handed it over at the desk. 'Have a good morning,' he said as he passed the guitar back to its owner.

Graham came up to the chapel and soon felt at home, in spite of the missing typed order of service which apparently other organizers always gave him.

David joked, 'OK, Graham, how's your playing on "Majesty"?'

Graham looked surprised. 'Majesty?' he asked, 'why Majesty?'

'Well, because we always play Majesty, and anyway it's the only one in our book that you haven't written, so you need the practice.'

Graham grinned, and realized that this environment was rather more easy going than usual, and definitely different from the norm!

We did always play Majesty – everyone could sing it, and everyone did sing it, both in chapel and out. It is a deep song easily sung by men, and not very musical men at that.

One day David was stopped outside the prison by a man he failed to recognize.

'Do you remember me?' a voice asked.

David looked back and saw a man sitting on a bench, either having visited or about to visit an inmate inside the prison. Unfortunately David could not recall the man's name.

'Will this help?' asked the man, and with that he began to sing the words of Majesty. The scales fell from David's eyes and with a grin he declared, 'John, John Drake, I remember you.'

David shook his hand, and John went on to tell David how he was now out and living nearby.

'I still can't read very well,' he confided, 'but I can still sing Majesty. When we went to the other prison all of us Lewes men used to sing Majesty. I even asked for it in chapel once, but no one else let us sing it there. I'll never forget that song. I sing it when I want to go back to my old ways.'

So Graham was required to play Majesty that morning he visited the chapel, but he did have to check the chords first! He was brilliant when his turn came to play and sing, and the men were really moved.

Afterwards a man came forward in order to respond to God, and Graham was thrilled to talk to him and show him a new Bible.

After that Graham popped down several times over the months, and each time he saw men become Christians. It was obviously a pleasure to be unknown, to be there on the cutting edge of evangelism, and to see his own songs inspire faith there and then in individual prisoners.

How about us? Well, we were honoured to have him, and so pleased that the men were having this opportunity to hear a man of such talent singing the Gospel to them.

Similarly we are thrilled to have visitors from many churches, who back us in prayer and support so fruitfully. Sending visitors is of course a great help to us, but of even more meaningful assistance is their level of enthusiasm and encouragement. Several individuals are a positive and sustaining influence on us, and we realize how much benefit we derive from the simplest call, letter or visit if it emanates from genuine concern to support and motivate.

We believe this area of forging supporting links will be one of growth for us, and we pray that people will be drawn not only into our own work, but into work with prisoners in general.

The need is great and the workers so few, but those who are involved have gained great benefit from it. I picture all the people who help us as if they were a defence team in a court of law, fighting to give the prisoners a chance, not to escape responsibility but to have a new start. Our plea is that it is not a hopeless cause in which we are engaged, but rather that it is possible for prisoners to find God and make a real contribution, both to the Church and to society as a whole. I believe this to be a fully achievable goal, as long as we all work together to help them to do so.

✳

CHAPTER 6

Advocating Simplicity and Perseverance

'But it's just a Sunday School story,' blurted out a flustered and rather cross Martin.

'I don't wish to offend you or be critical,' he continued, rising to his task and certainly intending to be critical if not offensive.

'They all listen attentively but all you're doing is telling Bible stories – and that's all!'

The critic looked at the chaplain for a response to his comments, but for once found David rather reticent. He stood leaning against the hall listening to this rather intense inmate, wondering at his dismissive tone. Surely this man should have had more wisdom? – after all, he was a long-term Christian himself who, prior to his arrest for a serious offence, had been involved in committed Christian work.

Martin grew tired of waiting for a response, and chose instead to elaborate his opinions. 'I'm also most concerned about your follow-up methods,' he continued, obviously enjoying this expression of his previously pent up views.

David listened as Martin brought up one by one those issues which to us were the old chestnuts. It

was unusual, but by no means unique, to have
an established Christian on the wings, and David
knew that if he could be involved in the work Martin
would be of great service to the other inmates.
Focusing on the shortcomings of the system was
certainly not a productive activity for his gifts. David
spent some time with Martin trying to answer his
questions reasonably. Later he came home and
attempted to work over the conversation as cons-
tructively as possible. Our attention was soon
centred on the phrase 'it's just Sunday School', and
after due consideration we decided to take it as a
compliment.

All the talks in the chapel week by week feature
a simple Bible story, and attempt to explain it in
contemporary terms. Simply expressed messages
they certainly are, but simultaneously profound
none the less. Martin seemed to have missed the
point, because casting light on Jesus' life and
ministry must be the most beneficial thing we can
do for another person during any exposition of the
Bible. However, the notion that spiritual matters
must be complex or technical is not one unique to
Martin. Whether inadvertently or not, large parts of
the Church have rendered themselves incompre-
hensible to the man of average or below average
intelligence. By this I certainly do not mean that
traditional, more formal services are more culpable
in this matter; quite the contrary. Many regularized
services have huge benefits for the less literate
amongst the population – after all, if something is
the same each week you can at least learn it by
heart, and there is great reassurance in familiarity,

as we all know. Furthermore, an emphasis on the visual provided by the use of religious pictures, symbols and celebrations involves the use of the whole of a person's understanding, not just the mind. Even if repetitive liturgy were the problem, there is no solace to be found in those of a much freer habit condemning traditional worship out of hand, because they too fiercely maintain their own ritual, albeit a more expressive and less predictable one. No, I believe we are all equal in this area, since any church, whatever its persuasion, is capable of exclusivity and a non-welcoming culture.

Rick came back inside after maintaining nearly a year outside trouble free. 'I'm so sorry to be back,' he gasped, grabbing hold of David's arm, 'but it's good to see you. Will you help me again? I'll be up in chapel. I do enjoy the services.'

David welcomed Rick back, although obviously sad to see him return, but realizing what an uphill struggle he had faced.

'Did you go to church, Rick?' he asked quietly. 'How did it go?'

'Oh yes,' said the dark-haired and very untidy inmate, 'I did. I used to go to this church in Sussex and I wanted to talk to him [here he motioned upwards] but I weren't allowed.'

'What do you mean?' questioned David in a rather concerned voice.

'Well,' continued Rick, chattering on, blissfully unaware of the effect this was having, 'I was asked to leave. "Here you, get out of here," one bloke said, and even when I kept trying I was always asked to go. I don't know why,' he finished lamely.

'Oh dear,' replied David, 'I am so sorry.'

He knew that Rick looked particularly dishev-elled, but he was also sure that he wanted a new future for himself. What a shame he had felt so rejected.

Rick began to continue his news, 'I didn't have anywhere to go on the out. I can't read much and I needed help. They gave me a room, but I didn't have anywhere to sit. I know I shouldn't have done it, but I stole to get a chair. Can anyone help me next time?' he asked innocently.

David certainly prayed that someone would help him next time, and we resolved to link him up properly on his release and point him in the way of Howard, who used to look after him during his previous spell inside. Hopefully, Howard would help him on the outside as well.

We knew that educating the outside churches was growing into a priority area. Christians are obviously scared of ex-inmates, and find their lifestyles and habits unsuitable bed-fellows for their own preferences. Nevertheless, unless we can persuade churches to 'adopt' our men then many will fall by the wayside, and that would be a tragedy.

One day I was incensed by a Christian's sugges-tion that we couldn't expect churches to pick up these people without training. Although this per-son was a lecturer in a theological college, the idea that we can only minister if we have under-gone a course on a specific area is a fallacy. Which Bible do people read, I wondered? The disciples, who were aware of being uneducated men, went about ministering to vast numbers of people, most of whom were from the lower layers of society. What training did they receive, apart from being with Jesus? It seems that training, although a helpful and valid activity, can sometimes be thought to replace simple discipleship and obedience to God's commands to help people. Of course we need schooling and advice, but there is nothing like learning on the job, and if an absence of specific training means the neglect of whole groups of society, on the grounds that we cannot relate to them, then it is an offence to the power of the Gospel. Stepping into the unknown with God is true evidence of faith, not least in the area of relationships with people to whom we are not naturally drawn.

Speaking about the work therefore has become a central part of our timetable, and we find a real response among many groups of Christians. We want to reassure people that a willingness of heart is the only criterion necessary to welcome the majority of ex-offenders who have declared an interest in the Christian faith.

As part of this aspect of ministry we began to look for Bible passages from which to start, and of course we didn't have to look very hard at all. The Bible is crammed full of references to people put into prison for every reason you can think of. Once one begins to look, the information is everywhere – Joseph falsely accused of sexual assault; Samson seized and incarcerated; John the Baptist imprisoned for speaking out; Peter and Paul caught for being Christians. These particular examples were innocent of their crimes, but there are also plenty of references to criminals who were guilty, not least of whom was Moses, who went from being a murderer to being the deliverer of God's chosen people out of Egypt.

Running alongside these stories are numerous general commands to remember, visit and help those in prison, and it would probably prove very fruitful to take note of all these references. Work with prisoners takes little time to justify from the Scriptures. The theme is starkly present.

So passages began to come to mind to use in outside talks, and a favourite was that of Jonah. He was in a prison of sorts, albeit inside a whale, and he learned to face up to God and his responsibilities whilst there. He had not wanted to spread the good news of forgiveness to the people of Nineveh, on the grounds that … well, when we analyse the grounds they are surely staggering. It appears he did not want to tell the people of that great city to repent, on the grounds that they would respond and then God would forgive them! Here we have displayed the tragedy of the true state of many of our hearts. If we do tell 'the undesirables' about God then they might respond, be accepted and become, horror of horrors, equal to us! 'The Church isn't for people who commit crimes and go to prison, or who live on the streets, or who sell their bodies for money, is it? I don't want them in my "club". It's for people like me, after all.' Now, we may not say this openly, but there is a degree of truth in it. Perhaps we find it easy to criticize when strange or previously evil people convert, because we don't really want it to be true. Just as in the story of the prodigal son, we are the elder brother, jealous of the younger son's return to favour because we were there all the time, and can't see why his restoration now should be celebrated. Even worse maybe is that element of Pharisee about us that will always despise the tax collector, and resist his rise at any cost.

Jonah, however, came out of the whale. He repented and realized his own inadequacy, and went back to do his task. True enough the people of Nineveh repented, and, in spite of all his lessons, Jonah sulked when they did. God had, even then, to remind him that he loved every man and woman equally, and that Jonah's prejudice had no place in God's plans at all.

David tells this story to various churches, lacing it heavily with illustrations about prisoners' lives and responses to the Gospel. Always very funny, the talks draw people to listen, and the punchline or real message is very straight and simple to get across when people are so receptive.

'Are you still in the whale?' David asks, 'or are you ready to go where God sends you, whether that's abroad or to a hospital or a drug rehabilitation centre or the streets, or even to a prison?' Nearly everyone leaves with a desire not to be stuck in their own particular whale, and hopefully with a yearning to find out just where they will go next. If they come away with an interest in or a care for prison work, then that is a huge bonus, and many splendid people go on to offer practical and prayer support through such meetings. It certainly is good to open up the ministry to the outside as much as we can.

Meanwhile, back in the prison we continue picking up Bible passages that are relevant to the men, and explaining them on Sunday mornings. The two builders who chose to erect their houses on either rock or sand in Matthew 7 become two inmates called Brussel and Sprout. They are released and one can't wait to get things going the way they used to be, while the other tries to remember what he has learned about God and put it into practice. Using two chairs as 'inmates' the story is told and the point made. For weeks afterwards the men talk about Brussel and Sprout – the names proving to have been a real inspiration.

The story of Elijah and Baal is expounded, with questions as to why Elijah was not called Remand, so that the story would have been renamed as the tale of Bail and Remand! However, the serious side of choosing whom to serve is forcefully made, and several men respond in faith.

The message of Naaman is frequently chosen because it brings up the idea of doing something very ordinary to find God, namely dipping oneself in the smelly old Jordan, as that officer had to in order to cure his leprosy. Had not his own country got superior rivers after all? Have we not also got far 'superior' ways of finding meaning than just trusting God? The trouble is they all fail when the chips are down – only simple faith in God will carry you through.

So it goes on – taking these stories and showing how they all point to the one and only true helper:

Jesus. Whether they come from the Old or New Testament, the messages all point to our need of God and his ability to help us and, used as illustrations, they serve us much better than any amount of long-winded explanations would ever do.

'Are you doing the story today, David?' asked a very keen inmate one Sunday. 'I do hope so. We talk about them afterwards on the wing, you know. We tell the ones who couldn't come. They all want to hear the stories. They're really good.'

David received the praise cheerfully, because he knows we never have to make up any story or concoct a sermon for the morning, because lifting the message straight from the Bible seems to be effective every time. If people think they are 'just Bible stories' then fair enough, because that's exactly what they are, and if that medium is the best way to explain the love of God to people, then that's what we will prepare. Perhaps it would be good if in some places the practice of retelling Bible stories was restored in ordinary church life, because certainly we find a message expressed in that way is understood and retained very effectively.

Like any teaching or explaining, however, we find it necessary to cover our ground again and again. Of course we have new inmates every week, and plenty of them who have never heard the Christian message before, but even those who have responded need constant repetition of the basics. We are meeting people who have no real knowledge of Christian things at all, so it is hardly surprising really that they need a repetitious diet of knowledge and explanation. When I was at teacher training college we learned about a theorist called Bruner, who developed the concept of a spiral curriculum. This means that every time a subject is revisited one learns more about it in terms of comprehension and development. Without revisiting any area, ground is often lost and previous learning forgotten. So it is with faith. We need to revisit areas again and again, and then we slowly grow. Thus it is we celebrate Easter year by year, but no one claims to have fully grasped the meanings of its message.

The men with whom we work need considerably more 'spiral' than the average, since their starting point of understanding is often nil. Patience when dealing with offenders is paramount, and a grasp of the leaps of understanding and life changes that we require of those who come to faith is central to being able to help. Read here the story of Thomas and consider the progress he has made. Would you be willing to help a man such as this, being aware of course that he could well slip again, and need to revisit those basics many times? Whatever you feel you surely cannot help but be inspired by his obvious desire for faith and the efforts he has made to change.

I AM 37 YEARS OLD.

MY NAME IS THOMAS AND ONE DAY I WALKED INTO BRIGHTON POLICE STATION AND TOLD THEM THERE WAS A WARRENT OUT FOR MY ARREST!

NOW ILL TELL YOU THE REASON WHY I DID THAT. I WAS A RECK THROUGH

DRINK AND DRUGS, I COULD SEE NO OTHER WAY OF SAVING MY LIFE, OTHER THAN HAND MYSELF IN, I WAS A JUNKIE, WHICH I MANAGED TO GET OF AND STOP TAKING SMACK ALL TOGETHER, WITH THE HELP OF A DR FROM AN ADDICTION CENTRE, BUT I THEN STARTED TO TAKE DRINK, AND I MEAN I HIT THE DRINK LIKE NEVER BEFORE, I COULD DRINK A WHOLE CASE (24) TENNIES SUPERS 9% ALC, IN A DAY ON MY OWN, BUT NEXT DAY I WOULD NEED AND I STRESS THE WORD NEED, ONE OR TWO CANS OR SOME KIND OF DRINK JUST TO MAKE ME FEEL GOOD OR SHALL I SAY NORMAL, MOST MORNINGS I COULD NOT SHAVE BECAUSE I SHOOK THAT MUCH. THE BEST BIT, I TOLD MYSELF LIES, BY THINKING IVE GOT THIS UNDER CONTROL, BUT SOON CANS WERE NOT ENOUGH SO I STARTED DRINKING SPIRITS. DIDN'T MATTER WHAT KIND, JUST SO LONG AS I GOT DRUNK, THIS WENT ON FOR AROUND 3 MONTHS. I WAS ON THE STREETS AFTER GETTING THROWN OUT OF A NIGHT SHELTER, FOR UNKNOWINGLY TAKING AN OVERDOSE OF DRINK AND PILLS, SO ON FRIDAY THE 13.12.96 WHILE SITTING IN A DAY CENTER IN BRIGHTON, I LOOKED AROUND ME (I WAS ILL I HAD NOTHING THAT MORNING) AND THOUGHT TO MYSELF I NEED HELP

BADLY OR IM GOING TO END UP LIKE SOME OF THESE MEN, I JUST REALIZED I WAS LOSING EVERYTHING, MY RESPECT, CARE FOR MYSELF, I NEVER WASHED, I ALWAYS WORE THE SAME CLOTHES AND I STANK BADLY. WHAT MADE ME COME TO MY SENCES I WILL EXPLAIN OR AT LEAST TRY TO, OR WHAT I NOW BELIEVE TO WHAT MADE ME DO WHAT I DONE TO SAVE MYSELF, WELL I DIDNT SAVE MYSELF, I NOW BELEAVE THE LORD OUR GOD HAD A VERY BIG PART TO PLAY IN MY DOING WHAT I DID. YOU SEE AROUND 1983/84 I BECAME A BORN AGAIN CHRISTIAN, IT ONLY LASTED A FEW MONTHS BUT THAT VERY FIRST TIME I GIVE ME LIFE TO JESUS, I COULD PHISICLY FEEL THE HOLY SPIRIT SURGE THROUGH MY BODY, I WAS HIGH ON JESUS FOR A COUPLE OF WEEKS, AND I LOVED EVERY MOMENT, YOU COULDNT GET ME TO STOP TALKING ABOUT HOW REALLY GOOD I FELT, BUT SLOWLY I SLIPED BACK INTO MY OLD WAYS, AND THE THING THAT MAKES ME TRUST THE LORD HAD A HAND IN THIS CHANGE OF COARSE, WAS WAY BACK IN 83/84 WHEN I LEFT CHRIST 'HE NEVER LEFT ME' AND HE SEEN I HAD HAD ENOUGH, HE KNEW I WAS READY TO GIVE A TRUE AND (HOPEFULY) LASTING COMMITMENT TO HIM, THERE MUST BE SOME REASON FOR HIM TO DO WHAT HE DID, I DONT KNOW

WHAT AND I DONT CARE I AM JUST SO
GLAD AND FILLED WITH JOY THAT HE
LOOKED AFTER ME AND I NEVER KNEW
UNTIL I CAME TO THIS PRISON, SO ALL
YOU WHO READ THIS DONT BE LIKE ME,
I NEARLY GAVE UP HOPE, AND THE
SAYINGS TRUE WHERE THERE IS LIFE
THERE IS HOPE THROUGH JESUS CHRIST
OUR LORD.

Thomas' letter is both challenging and inspiring,
isn't it? And that's exactly what he wanted it to be
the day he agreed to write up his story. There are
many like him who want the outside world to
understand their faith, inadequate as it might
sometimes be, and accept it for the reality it is for
them. One thing is very clear: we may view their
stumbling and struggling as a sign of weakness
in faith, but they certainly don't. They pick themselves up and go on, seldom questioning whether
God will take them back! Not for them the agonies
and self-indulgence of wondering if they've lost
their way completely – no, once they've met with
God they expect him to be there for them, and are
prepared to try again. This attitude is commonplace
and very humbling. Similarly when things go badly
they seldom seem to blame God for it – seeing even
disasters as mere accidents or 'the way it is', and
not stopping to question God's love because of
them.

Derrick, one of our orderlies, was a lovely man
who found faith in prison. He brought many to
chapel, and helped numerous struggling people on

the wing. However, he fell foul of a few nasty individuals who decided to 'tax' him for his own 'protection'. Derrick refused to hand over his cigarettes or phone cards, as a stand for what is right. It was a decision that cost him dear. Mixing sugar with boiling water, the men entered his cell and 'jugged' Derrick so that he was thoroughly burned, and still not content, they then set about him with two batteries in a sock until he was black and blue. Poor Derrick ended up in the hospital wing a very injured man.

The previous day David had arranged a chapel visit for Derrick and his wife, and together they had come to terms with his imprisonment and his new faith. He had been glad of the opportunity to set things straight, as he had been having some problems over a couple of his fairly large collection of children. David saw him in the hospital the day after the attack, and expected a good deal of trauma, laced with a degree of self-pity.

Derrick would have none of it. 'I am so grateful to God,' he started, looking up from his bed at the chaplain, who would hardly have been surprised to see a far more angry response. 'They missed my face,' he confirmed, pointing at his unmarked features. 'My wife would not have liked that at all. I am so glad I saw her yesterday. God is very good!'

Derrick was shipped out for his own protection, and one wonders at this man's reaction to an appalling crime. I doubt many of us would have been so ready to praise God in such a situation, but to Derrick it was just a natural response.

This simplicity of faith is not then one which succeeds due to any avoidance of trouble, but one which seems to stem from a really meaningful first encounter with God, and which remains with the new Christian through thick and thin. We Christians can certainly learn from such expressions of faith.

In terms of the courtroom theme of this book, we are indeed the briefs and advocates who must put the Christian faith in a favourable light to the world. We have to explain not only God's love, but the pathway to making a response to him. The lessons of prison ministry are clear: to be effective we must be simple in our message, being totally straightforward about the core issues, and rejecting man-made complications and barriers to faith; and we must persevere in our telling so that we do not perceive a slowly developing spiral of faith as failure but as a genuine response to God. If we can be both simple and persevering we will be encouraged by what we find, and learn to take delight in the faith of new Christians, even if their expressions of faith are far removed from our own.

Furthermore, if we feel we want to respond to these elements of Christian advocacy we must be aware that whatever we do in terms of evangelism must be given, continued and finished in an atmosphere of prayer. After all, however sound our presentation of the Gospel may be, we have to remember that we receive our remit from and must appeal ultimately to, a much higher court than any earthly one. Our guiding principle and privilege must surely be that God draws people to himself, and our role is to join him in his own work by prayer and simple obedience to the commission to spread the Good News of Jesus. When we do so the results are often amazing, and all the more so considering the inadequacy of both our prayer lives and our actions. May the stories in this book spur us on to be sound and keen advocates, because it is, after all, God's expressed work that we do.

One final story illustrates our need to reassess our attitude to explaining the Gospel. David visited a church where he was assured, 'We don't get converts here. We can't remember the last time someone came to faith.'

Although interested in the prison work and willing to support it, the members felt it had little relevance for their own ministry, which seemed to be confined to helping the faithful.

After the service one lady approached David with concern. 'I've brought a lad I know tonight. He's been before but he hasn't made a commitment.'

'Have you asked him to become a Christian?' asked David, in his usual simple style.

'Well, no,' stammered the lady, a bit taken aback, 'I haven't.'

David went over to meet the lad, who seemed very open and obviously searching. 'I found all that very interesting,' he volunteered.

David asked him directly to make a step of faith, and the young man did so at once, seemingly relieved that someone was at last going to help him through.

Later David spoke to the lady and a group of other church members. 'He's a new Christian now, look after him. You can have people find faith you know – but you do need to ask them first!'

The group, rather stunned, gathered round the boy, and seemed quite pleased, but David knew that some attitudes would have to change radically if that boy was not to remain the only person to find faith in that particular environment.

That example is rather blatant, but perhaps it points to a truth. Simple faith sharing isn't difficult, but it is costly in terms of effort and sometimes loss of face. If we want church growth perhaps many more of us must be willing to pay the price of having the courage to face possible rejection before we see the fruits of success.

✳

CHAPTER 7

Appeal to a Higher Court

Paying lip service to the power of prayer is not something in which we can afford to indulge. We know that all the response to the Gospel and the demonstration of God's power which we are privileged to witness are the result of prolonged or faith-filled prayer, and by no means only ours. Appeals to a higher court than that of an earthly authority are constantly being made by our own volunteers, friends, prayer line and the relatives of those in prison. We believe that the volume of positive answers we all receive is to demonstrate the Lordship of God over the situation, to encourage Christians and to bring ever more people to faith in Jesus.

For us the answers may seem speedy in coming, but for many, years of faith are coming to fruition as each inmate finds God for the first time. One day David received a letter from a couple who had heard about Lewes from a friend, and now wanted to find out just what was happening.

Keith had lost his way years previously, in spite of his parents' profound faith and faithfulness in commitment. Now Keith's way had resulted in his incarceration in Lewes gaol. His parents were distraught but restrained as they simply requested prayer for their beloved son. They believed he might already have been moved on, and were throwing out a life-line to David to see whether he believed there was still hope.

David looked Keith up on the inmate list, and went off to 'B' wing to find him. On his arrival, an officer told him that he thought Keith would appreciate a visit, as he was going through a hard time. David looked at the rather dishevelled and quiet inmate, and realized just what was meant by having a hard time.

'I see you've had a spot of bother,' he said to Keith, looking towards a very black and bruised eye that was obviously newly acquired.

'Yes, I have,' replied Keith, whose clear and precise speech implied that he was used to pleasanter surroundings.

'They said I'd insulted a mate ... but I don't know why ...' he finished lamely.

Keith's brush with the harsh realities of prison life had obviously shocked him, but David saw his present position as a window of opportunity in a previously solid wall of refusal.

'Your parents are very concerned about you, you know,' stated David calmly.

'You haven't told them about this eye, have you?' interjected Keith very nervously, looking anxiously up at the chaplain.

'No,' said David reassuringly. 'I didn't know you were hurt. They have been praying for you, you know.'

Keith acknowledged this first by the faintest movement of his head, and continued to listen carefully. No doubt a few days previously would have seen him hasten to show disinterest, but now he was obviously open to influence.

'It's time to let God help you, isn't it?' asked David, by now sure a positive response was possible.

'I guess so,' replied Keith, looking dazed but none the less interested.

'I believe God wants you to let him into your life, Keith. You need to become a Christian and lead a new life now,' suggested David.

'I think you're right,' conceded Keith humbly, and then went on to pray a simple prayer of confession and to receive God's gift of his Spirit.

'Do you want me to tell your Mum?' asked David, when the prayers were over.

'Yes, please do,' responded the grateful inmate.

'I expect they will be pleased after all these years, don't you?' said the chaplain, grinning from ear to ear.

'Oh yes,' replied Keith, 'they'll be pleased. I'll tell my Mum myself tomorrow, I promise.'

Minutes later David was in his office, holding a neatly typed letter in one hand and a telephone in the other.

'Good morning, Mr Danes. This is David Powe, chaplain at Lewes Prison. I received your letter this morning.'

'Oh yes,' replied Mr Danes without much expectation in his voice. 'How nice of you to ring. I just wanted some advice really.'

'Well, I have some good news for you,' responded David.

'Really? Have you seen Keith?'

'Yes, I have seen him,' replied David, 'but it's more than that. He's come to faith.'

There was a long moment's silence at the other end of the phone before a further response, 'You mean he's become a Christian?'

'Oh yes,' said David, realizing there was more than a degree of surprise at the other end, 'you have been praying for him, after all.'

There was a flurry of activity as Mrs Danes was brought to the telephone, gasps of joy and amazement were expressed and the happy couple tried to assimilate this new information.

Two days later Mrs Danes rang David once more, 'We have to thank you,' she began enthusiastically. 'We came to see Keith, and when his sisters were at the drinks machine he told me. He told me he had become a Christian. It was all so easy. I can hardly believe it.'

David smiled at the receiver and asked that the family go on to help Keith in his new Christian life.

'Oh yes,' she replied, 'we know that, we must take it carefully, we have so much to plan, we really do.'

So Mr and Mrs Danes saw the answers to their long and earnest appeals to the highest court known to mankind. God had responded so generously, and witnessing that answer was a deep joy for us all, and a spur to faith for everyone who has heard about it since. We pray for Keith and his family, and trust God for his future, and we are also thankful that he has such a supportive family to whom he can return.

So that you can share in just a little of the family's joy at Keith's new beginning, there follow two letters we received regarding the experience from their point of view. They would wish others to be encouraged by their answer to prayer and to be an inspiration to relatives to go on bringing their loved ones before God. Although all the names have been changed in this testimony, the text of the letters has not been altered, and reveals how receiving a positive answer to a request can be quite a journey in itself!

Letter 1

Dear David,

Joe and I have experienced such a wide range of emotions since your phone call to tell us that Keith had become a Christian! The amount of prayer which has been dedicated to that young man by ourselves and others is significant! God **had** heard all our cries of longing ... but was this all too good to be true?

I suppose our feelings after the initial euphoria were, to be honest, of disbelief! You can read in books of wonderful answers to prayer in tragic circumstances but it couldn't really happen to our family, could it? And yet, you know deep down that our God is a wonder-working God and it **can** happen to us. We then said that we'd just wait and see what Keith would say, if anything! We weren't disappointed when we saw him on the Tuesday because, as I told you, he grasped the only few moments we were alone to say he had become a Christian. What an encouragement! However, the doubts still come to the surface. Does he **really** want to change or will life just carry on as before when he comes out? When you said Keith had been filled with the Holy Spirit what exactly did you mean by that? Has he had a very real supernatural experience he can hold on to, which even in the darkest moments he cannot deny? Please forgive me for voicing our feelings … my genuine prayer is, 'Lord I believe, help my unbelief!'

Perhaps a little of the background will show you how we have been very aware of God's fingerprints on so much of what has happened to Keith, and how his time in Lewes seems to be part of this.

Two years ago, while still at Art College, Keith was offered an unconditional place at a college to do an HND. He was very thrilled about this but over that summer of 1995, as he got more heavily into drugs, his interest waned, and by the time September came he had decided he didn't really want to start the course. We were bitterly disappointed because we felt he had been very fortunate to have been offered this place. However, as the beginning of the term came closer, he became a bit more positive and so I took him up at the beginning of October.

We had a horrendous summer with him and it seemed incredible that he had actually gone to College! As I drove home along the M40 I felt very thankful to God that we had reached this point. It was a very wet and stormy day and the sky overhead was dark and menacing. Suddenly the sun came out and in the spray from the numerous lorries on the road I saw thousands of tiny rainbows! A line from a hymn came into my mind ... 'I trace the rainbow through the rain' and I realized that the fact that Keith had started college at all was indeed a rainbow through what had been a very rough storm.

As the months progressed he subsequently got into more trouble, and the whole of 1996 was filled with anguish and heartache. But each day we endeavoured to trace a rainbow, to look for something positive to be thankful for, and when I found I was struggling to hold on to the Lord, he graciously pointed me to the very first line of that hymn, 'O love that will not let me go'.

One Sunday evening, shortly before Keith eventually came to court, the theme of our service was faith, based on the story of the healing of the centurion's servant. Joe and I found a lot of significance in the story. As we worshipped that evening, singing songs like 'Faithful One' and 'Great is Thy Faithfulness', I felt a real sense of joy ... not happiness because I certainly wasn't happy, it was joy, the same joy I had been surprised to feel at my father's funeral ... joy because you know your faith is real and works in the darkest moments of life. We finished the service with the hymn ... yes! ... 'O love that will not let me go'. When we reached the third verse, I sang with conviction from the heart:

O joy that seekest me through pain,
I cannot close my heart to Thee,
I trace the rainbow through the rain,
And feel the promise is not vain,
That morn shall tearless be.

When Keith was given a custodial sentence in February 1997 and he was sent to Lewes, numerous people said to us that God was working in a wonderful way in Lewes Prison. We knew that Keith would only be there for a very short time, and Chris Lambrianou tried to phone you and said that you were on holiday for two weeks. Great! Just the very time that Keith is there, the chaplain is on holiday, so we thought! But in retrospect we can see how perfect God's timing is. Keith had been in Lewes for nearly two weeks, he had experienced the grimaces of life in prison, he had been beaten up the night before and so must have been at the lowest possible point, and you came back from holiday and became Jesus' feet and hands and brought his words of compassion and healing that Monday morning!

As I mentioned in my previous letter, the first Saturday Keith was in prison I saw the article about Lewes Prison in *Renewal* and I wrote to you to order a copy of the tape. The following week I saw a copy of the book, *The Cross Between Thieves* in our local bookshop and bought it. When I returned to the car I browsed through it while I waited for Joe. I was completely 'gobsmacked' (seems the only appropriate word!) when I noticed the title of the second chapter. 'I trace the rainbow through the rain' and saw the whole of my 'special' hymn written out in full. Wow! Lord! Your fingerprint again. I spent a large proportion of Saturday reading the book and what a thrill it was! Could it be possible that Keith could actually be impacted by what was happening in Lewes Prison?

You can perhaps imagine our feelings when you called on the Monday morning with the news! I came rushing down from our bedroom when I heard Joe's excitement! There couldn't really be anything else at that particular point which could have made him so ecstatic! I didn't need to ask him who it was, I think I knew but I couldn't really believe it!

We just need to exercise the faith and trust that, 'He who has begun this good work in Keith will carry it on to completion'. We'll continue to trace the rainbow through the rain because I'm sure there will be more storms ahead. However, we have come to realize that to be able to see a rainbow you need to be looking in the right direction! I'm sure that as long as we keep focusing on the Lord and his

promises then we'll find 'That in Thy sunshine's blaze its day may brighter, fairer be'.

We still don't know how much longer Keith
will be at Lewes and by now he may well have
moved on (I recollect writing this once before!)
but whatever the future holds we want to
thank you for ministering to him at the very
moment of his need.

With our love,
    Mary and Joe

Letter 2 (one month later)

Dear David,

We had a phone call from Keith last night to
say that he is in Dover. Initially Joe and I were
disappointed he had moved on because Lewes
has become quite special for us! We had
started to think that perhaps he would stay
there for his whole sentence. However, as we
thought more and talked about it, we just felt
an overwhelming sense of thankfulness that
Keith had been able to stay at Lewes for as
long as eight weeks!

In the six weeks since he became a Christian
we have been hugely encouraged that Keith's
trust in the Lord is genuinely developing. He
is seeing the Lord's hand in specific situations
… e.g. '… so there has been another miracle!
I can't believe it!' The Bible has also been a
source of strength and comfort to him, e.g. 'I
read a bit of Psalms last night which kept my
chin up a bit,' and then he wrote out the whole

of Psalm 54 which obviously mirrored his own feelings at that particular moment. He frequently writes, 'I hope and pray that …' and he told my mother in a letter, 'I have been to church for the past month, have a Bible and I read a Psalm every day which I find helps keep my strength and faith up.' He has also shown remorse when he wrote in a letter to Joe's aunt, 'I'm ashamed that you know that I'm in here and that you probably can't believe that one of your family is in prison. It is such a dark and chilling word, prison.' It is such a thrill to see the way that the Holy Spirit is opening his spiritual eyes. Forgive us for doubting … the Lord is dispelling it!

Thank you again for all your concern and interest. We look forward to receiving your prayer letter in due course so that we can continue to pray for you all at Lewes. We trust that this is only the beginning of our links with you and that one day we might meet in person.

In a letter from Keith, which was written last Friday and arrived this morning, he says, 'I'll be going to church on Sunday. David is on holiday which is a shame because I wanted to say goodbye, but I can always write to him.' You have obviously meant a lot to him and perhaps you will get a letter one day.

The words which come into my mind as I wrote, come once again from that very special hymn, 'O love that will not let me go' … from the last verse this time …

O cross that liftest up my head,
I dare not ask to fly from Thee:
I lay in dust, life's glory dead,
And from the ground there blossoms red
Life that shall endless be.

Throughout this nightmare the Lord's powerful intervention has always been our source of hope and he has not let us down. Thank you for the enormous part you have played in helping Keith to discover that hope for himself. For Keith, life is beginning to blossom from the dust it had become!

    With our love and grateful thanks,
      Mary and Joe

Not all appeals to God are answered in the same way of course, and sometimes we grow to realize that the result we have so yearned for could lead only to disaster or at least disappointment if it were granted. Most of us fail to see that until much later, but Norman was one man who saw it early on, and whose response to God's seeming refusal should lead us to feel shame at our own feeble foot-stamping when our desires are thwarted.

Norman was in 'K' wing – the vulnerable prisoners unit – where he had been placed awaiting trial for alleged attacks on his own children. Norman hotly contested this accusation, and declared himself a victim of acrimonious false allegations. Only God knows the truth of men's hearts, but some men are indeed accused of false crimes from time to time, with horrendous consequences. Not being able to read minds, we had to take each man's word before God and leave the judgements to him.

Norman was devastated by his imprisonment, and was pleased to see David on his rounds. Norman responded instantly to the Gospel, although he had no background in Christianity and his father had even been an atheist. It was immediately obvious that the reality of Norman's faith was going to be a force for good, and although he couldn't join in Sunday chapel because of his 'K' wing location, he grew as a Christian at remarkable speed.

Most inmates in Lewes stayed only a few weeks or months at most, but Norman was to be there fairly long term, as his case was constantly subject to delay and requirements for further evidence. Quickly aware that Christianity meant changes, Norman set about altering his responses to other inmates. He began to be generous – an attribute virtually unknown on the average prison wing. When others requested coffee or other consumables, Norman would willingly supply them.

'What do I owe you?' the unsuspecting inmate would ask.

'Nothing,' Norman would reply. 'I'm a Christian. I'm meant to share.'

The astonished prisoner would shrug his shoulders and move on, probably thinking he'd found a soft touch. However, over the weeks the news got about, and Norman's amazing response to his possessions, in a world where so little means so much, began to gain respect. Norman had made his mark.

Naturally Norman prayed to God for his release. Feeling unjustifiably imprisoned must be a frightening experience and one in which it would be right to plead for help. Like Joseph in Genesis so many centuries before, Norman knew the pain of false accusation and loss of liberty inflicted by another's scheming. However, like Joseph too, Norman did not waste his time plotting revenge, complaining or blaming God. In fact, Norman's astonishing philosophy could put to shame most of our own responses to unfairness.

'I'm due for an end to my case,' Norman confided to David. 'I'm OK about that. I'd like to be out, but if I get twelve years, well, I'll take it that God wants me in here, doing my ministry.'

The ministry to which Norman referred was his general running of the wing, because in the nicest possible way Norman was the Christian baron of 'K' wing. Over the months the inmates had begun to trust Norman's impartiality and advice. He gradually took on the role of rota-maker, time-allocator and all round organizer of the wing's activities. The officers were pleased. With such a benevolent baron on the wing their job was rendered so much easier, as little escaped Norman's notice and everyone knew he was in control.

At one point three-quarters of the wing were Christians, and there were regular Bible studies in the coffee house – the extraordinary nickname for Norman's cell. When David went to visit him one day there were at least five interruptions.

'Will this tie do for court, Norman?' asked an inmate, anxious that he should look his best when up before the judge. Norman gave his advice and the man went out cheerfully.

'Ready for my reading lesson?' asked another inmate called Steve. 'Hang on, Steve,' replied Norman. 'I'm busy with the chaplain right now.'

Steve shrugged his shoulders and went out, knowing his reading lesson was coming. Steve was a short, thinly built man who could be described as inadequate in terms of education. He had responded to the Gospel in his straightforward way and was now being taught to read by means of Matthew's Gospel and Bible tapes. For me this was thrilling, as education in this country was originally initiated by a drive to allow the common man to read the Bible for himself. Although our education system has largely thrown out any links with making the Scriptures readily available to all, and even with any idea of real religious education, here was history repeating itself in a thoroughly rewarding way.

Steve was proud of his growing but still embryonic skills in learning, and was in no doubt that he was benefiting from being on the wing. 'I like it in here, David,' he told the chaplain. 'When I come back I'll do more Bible stories.'

David smiled inwardly. How could he tell this man that coming back was not a truly noble or appropriate aim for a new Christian – when to Steve it represented a stability of lifestyle he had never known, and a friend and mentor in Norman who surpassed any level of care he had ever experienced.

So David's visit to Norman continued to be punctuated by inmates' queries until it was time to move on to another wing.

'And all this,' David thought to himself as he left, 'without Norman even being able to go to chapel on Sunday or have but the barest structure of follow-up! God is indeed good and alive and leading men in Lewes Prison.'

One of the most humbling experiences for us in our dealings with Christian inmates was their inhibitions in responding to God. They were seldom hampered by inappropriate intellectual arguments about the possibility of divine intervention: if the Bible said something could happen, then it would happen; and if a member of the chaplaincy could pray in a certain way, then so could everyone else. The concept of hierarchy or special roles for ministers or people who were long-term Christians had no meaning on the wings of a prison.

A small group of Christian inmates were in a cell reading and praying when David popped in one morning.

'We're going to pray for Mike here,' said Tim, 'he's got this headache right across his head so we're asking God to get rid of it.' The inmate who'd spoken looked up at David confidently, and no glimmer of doubt crossed his face or echoed in his voice. He knew he was going to get a positive response. After all, why shouldn't he? Mike had gained his headache after a thorough going over he had received one night during a robbery. The pain just went on and on, and had not left him since.

Sure enough, Mike's headache left him and the men's faith and belief was strengthened, because Mike went all over the wing and communal areas declaring his release from pain and extolling the power of prayer! In the innocence and freshness of their faith, the men saw their prayers answered daily. Maybe greater tests of waiting and faith were in store for them over the years, but for now lots of them had no trouble at all in believing that God answers prayers.

We were being driven into even deeper realms of experience by all this, and almost daily occurrences of remarkable answers to prayer were a reality. For those who have the time to write and talk at length about the possibilities of prayer, there is always a satisfaction of the mind, but for those of us experiencing supernatural interventions as quite normal, there is also a sense of wonder, an inner affirmation of the power of God and a deep desire for others to witness the reality of that power.

Back on 'K' wing there was a problem Dan couldn't work out. 'These trainers keep moving,' he said earnestly but very straightforwardly to David.

'What do you mean?' asked David, who was used to having to drag details from inmates one by one, as filling in on minor, or often even the major, details never seemed to be an inmate's strong point.

'Well, they move across the room,' explained Dan, impatient that the chaplain didn't immediately grasp the drift of his meaning. 'At night,' he went on, 'they've definitely moved from here to here.' He pointed forcibly to each corner of the cell he shared with Joe. 'Joe saw it. He knows too,' he claimed.

David wasn't quite sure what was going on, but he had learned that strange things did occur and he was not going to disregard an inmates's concern, however bizarre it may have seemed.

'Well, it's odd,' added Norman, drifting into the cell, having heard that the chaplain was on his territory. 'This whole side of the wing has grown cold. The cells on that side are warm,' and he indicated across the narrow corridor that divided the cells, 'but this side is always cold.'

David now knew that something was up. 'Well, there have been some pretty evil things going on down here, Norman,' he explained. 'These things have their effects.'

Norman nodded wisely, and if he hadn't known previously about these occurrences he certainly wasn't thrown by the idea.

The previous week he had caught Steve with a ouija board, given to him by an unscrupulous and dubiously connected inmate who assured him it would help him find out what God wanted him to do. Not having been a Christian for very long, Steve had been none the wiser, although he was quickly put right by Norman once he found out. Norman was aware of the occult and its bad influence, although cold areas of the wing was a new concept, and he had not yet made any connection.

All the Christians on the wing prayed about the problem, and David brought Roy down, so that they could exorcise the area and ask God to fill the vacuum with his presence. The coldness disappeared, and there were no further reports of moving trainers.

The inmates took all this for granted of course, but David, Roy and I wondered at the way these events were now so commonplace and – well, almost ordinary. The prayers of the New Testament

no longer seemed so distant from our own experience, and we simply had to exclude explaining
away the stories of demons leaving and God's
supernatural intervention in people's lives. It all
served to make us bolder and more confident in our
approach, both to evangelism and to witnessing and
ministering outside the prison. Nevertheless, everything seemed very calm and relaxed, and there was
no sense of whipped up emotions or unhealthy
interests either.

Meanwhile we began to hear how God was
answering our prayers for former inmates who had
moved on or been released. Letters and Christmas
cards began to arrive, not only from all over Britain,
but also from all over the world, and we rejoiced
that men were moving on.

Ken had been on remand, charged with a very
serious offence, but had found Jesus Christ in Lewes
Prison. A year later he sent us the following letter
and poem which did encourage us as he intended,
and which we hope will encourage many others
who read it:

Dear David, friend and brother in Jesus Christ,
   Greetings!
   I write this to you that it may encourage you
and all, of the power and love of our LORD
JESUS CHRIST, and to thank you, for it was on
the 5th, this time last year, that you prayed
over me, and JESUS forgave me, and touched
my life, that it may never be the same again.
I know that I have never felt so much love and
peace as I do now, from that very moment,

there was a joy placed on my damaged heart, which came from life's cruel blows.

Since I was sent to this prison, and felt the reputation in which it does live up to, and all included, I have never seen such wonders to the glory of God in such a place as this. You see men come to Christ, to see them change their hearts, filled with hope, love for their fellow men, understanding and wisdom in words and deeds, is truly a joy to see. Only JESUS can change bad into good. As for me, every day is exciting, my spiritual life has grown, I cannot explain in words how the love of God has touched my life, all I can say is that he is my life, is with me always guiding me, comforting me and teaching me. The fellowships we have are a blessing, the friendship, a closeness is as if I have been given a new family where we help each other when difficult times come. Only good comes from God and forgiveness in love, Amen.

THANK YOU DAVID

Our fellowship has grown, and will continue to do so, for we were all lost souls until we asked JESUS into our lives and believed.

In this prison, all in fellowship with CHRIST join together in prayer at 11.00 p.m., we find there is much power in this form of prayer, which gives us all an opportunity to pray for revival and those in need, at 11.00 p.m. the prison starts to glow, because that's when they turn the lights off. Amen.

God has the perfect plan, and we are all part of that plan, which was given to us by his grace.

GOD BLESS YOU DAVID, in all you do and say,

Ken.

God wants us to plan.
but not to panic ...
To be busy
but not to be burdened ...
To be righteous
but not restless ...
To be working
but not worrying.
He wants us to have our minds on
what we're doing
while our hearts
are fixed on him.

How wonderful it was to receive such a letter and poem, and to witness this man's growth in faith in just one short year. Of course his path will be long and difficult, not only over the lengthy sentence that stretches before him, but also on his eventual release, but this man's hope shines through to us all and should urge us on to bring many more like him to faith. It is also helpful to know that Ken wrote to his victim in repentance and sorrow, and was reconciled to her in a remarkable way. God came into a life of appalling problems and redeemed it into something positive and good. The miracle of the power of the Gospel can be witnessed in this one man's response, and we are privileged to have seen it happen too.

John was now in Wandsworth serving his sentence, but he had become a Christian when David had been deputy chaplain at Belmarsh Prison, in London, prior to his move to Lewes. His letter is both moving and revealing as it indicates not only John's prayers but his concern for other inmates and David himself.

Dear David,

Greetings in Jesus' name. How are you, and how is fellowship in Lewes? I pray God is moving through his Holy Spirit and bringing more of the 'weak things of the world' to himself. Naturally, I mean the 'wanting' children of our world.

You asked me about using something I wrote in my last letter for some purpose (which escapes me). Well, yes of course, please do, if it will help in God's work. I'm too happy to offer a word or two.

I'm especially uplifted right now. Vineyard church visited me today. Well, the talk progressed and conversions were mentioned, particularly the hundreds at Lewes. At that time our C. of E. chaplain pointed at me, saying I had been converted 'at your hands' and was the 49th to be done so. I never forget you making a little note in your note book. From then on I knew I was going to be asked to share, so I did. It's the first time I have shared to any number of people that wonderful experience and the beginning of a life-changing process that is continuing daily – thank God. I'm very uplifted now and feeling so thankful to all he has and is doing. Relationships with my family are improving daily. God is so very good. I just want to keep recommitting myself to him. I recently had a dream that one of my sisters came to visit here. When I saw her I knew something wonderful had happened in her life, yes, she had given her life to Jesus. My heart leapt. It is very close to my heart. I pray it was a prophetic message and not just my emotion thinking. Carol, my youngest sister, has suffered for many years with internal ailments. And she has suffered when she wrote last time, she said that all she wanted was to be free from this constant pain. In and out of hospital she has gone and still the misery continues. I know Jesus can heal her, I know he wants to. If it is her that I dreamt about, I believe he will heal her when she decides to let him in. It only takes a committed 'yes' and that is enough. A family so torn over the years that is not only reconciled to one another but to God in unity as well is more than I could ask – but ask is what I'm doing!!

Over the years I have desired this more than anything. I had visions years ago of a reunited family. I felt that the 'buck' had to stop with me. Someone had to take the initiative or whatever, to change the situation. I didn't know how then. My own part in tearing relationships was very damaging. Fear and selfishness, pride and bitterness crippled me.

But now, a new creation, with the indwelling Holy Spirit and the kind of faith that could lead to all that God and I desire is happening. I am the first in the family to become a Christian. It is my responsibility to testify to them, to show them that God is as real and alive today as in the days when his Word was written. The Lord is pouring out his blessings on the nations, he is revealing himself in a way that cannot be denied. It is happening – today. I don't want my loved ones to miss out on the revelations of his promises.

I read a wonderful line from C.S. Lewis' *Mere Christianity* recently. He put Jesus' words of 'only believe' into another kind of image. Talking of food, he said, 'we don't know how food is nutritious for us, we know it is, but not how, we simply accept that it is'. If only people could accept Jesus as easily, instead of pussy-footing around saying things like, 'well, I'll just check the Bible and see if it says that,' or 'prove that he loves me'. I know it is hard to conceive for a lot of people, but 'seeing is not always believing'. More like, 'believing is seeing!!' I am almost preaching. Perhaps I should save it for those who need to know the truth.

It would be lovely to meet you again. The thought of it is exciting me already, ha ha. Well, David, I have another letter to write so I will close this one for now. I pray that you, your family and your ministry continues to thrive under the Holy Spirit's guidance, and the fruits of your labours are many.

Love in Christ,
    John

I include these letters because they represent the many contacts we've maintained, and answer part of the question, 'Where are they now?' Many of our new Christians are still in gaol, spread over the country in various establishments. Some have found fellowship and help, others struggle to keep their faith. Only time will tell if their faith will stay the full course, even as it will tell if those of us from very different backgrounds will maintain the commitment too. Suffice it to say that they seem to have made a fairly sound start and appear to mean business with this new faith of theirs.

Some of the men of course are out and about by now, and one of our joys is to bump into them unawares. Dave turned up at the launch of my first book, *The Cross Between Thieves*, which our friends, Judy and Derrick, at Hunts' Bookshop had organized in Tunbridge Wells. Queuing up at the end of the evening, he was bursting to tell us that he had been supported by a local church and, by virtue of a series of amazing events, was able to set up his own second-hand shop called 'New Beginnings'. What a thrill to see him and hear him volunteer to come and tell others about his experiences! Here was a man breaking with the mould of his past and choosing a truly wonderful name for his new venture in trading.

At various churches we could see ex-inmates joining in the services, usually incredibly conspicuous because they always chose to sit at the front of the church as in chapel, and were blissfully unaware that many established Christians come early to service just to sit at the back!

Outside McDonald's we bumped into Roger, who beamed from ear to ear. 'I'm glad I came to Lewes,' he blustered. 'I've put my life right. I came to chapel every week and went to carpentry class. I go to college now to learn more carpentry.' Then as he turned to go away, having thanked David profusely for his help, he added, 'I still go to church – the local Methodist, you know.'

'Well done,' we responded in unison as he walked off cheerfully, obviously pleased to have met us once more, although this time in happier circumstances.

Paul was in the local car park working as an attendant when he acknowledged that he knew us. David wished him well before he was ushered forward by the car behind. One glimpse was all we had, but we could see from his smile that Paul was a happier man.

So too was Ryan, who literally ran across a road in Brighton as we were heading towards a theatre to see the Victoria Wood show.

'Can't stop,' he blurted out, 'but thanks for all you did. I'll never forget you.' With that he was gone, but the brief encounter lifted us more than any theatre visit could ever do.

So from time to time we are sent full and encouraging news from ex-inmates, and at other times we are only granted the shortest meeting, but we receive sufficient feedback to inspire us onwards, and we are well aware that for many people work and prayers are given without any knowledge of results at all. We are fortunate and blessed and we know it.

Of course some people are desperate to test the ministry by finding inmates who would 'prove' or 'disprove' the case, and some seem to believe that inmates should show a rate of growth that would be exceptional or even unique inside most churches. This kind of evidence is not granted, and in terms of most ministry we know our prison one can only be said to be in its infancy. Most people take years to develop deep Christian faith, although of course a sizeable number do sprout significantly, and we know our Christians are likely, for the most part, to experience the same somewhat bumpy ride.

We aren't surprised, therefore, when we meet some of our 'men' once more inside the prison walls, for having, as they put it, 'slipped up, Gov'. Most are terribly shamed faced and full of excuses and apologies, but nearly all go on to recommit themselves and re-establish their Christian lives. Of course this happens in all Christian ministries, so why not in prison, too? Nevertheless, it is a sadness when an inmate returns and has to be helped back on the path. It is always taken seriously, but pleasingly the occurrence is remarkably rare.

All these fellows are the subject of much prayer and we shall never know how the appeals to that higher court, made by so many members of our prayer line and interested churches, are the stimulus or cause of the burgeoning faith of so many new Christians. We thank God for the faithfulness of the pray-ers, who seldom know the results of their pleadings but who take it on themselves to lift prisoners and ex-criminals to the heavenly court in order that they might finish the race they have chosen to start when they first find faith in prison.

✳

CHAPTER 8

How Much Do You Think
You're Worth, Boy?

Is a rich man worth more than a poor man,
A stranger worth more than a friend?
Is a baby worth more than an old man,
Your beginning worth more than your end?

Is a president worth more than his assassin.
Does your value decrease with your crime?
Like when Christ took the place of Barabbas,
Would you say he was wasting his time?

Well how much do you think you are worth, boy?
Will anyone stand up and say?
Would you say that a man is worth nothing
Until someone is willing to pay?

I suppose you think that you matter,
Well how much do you matter to whom?
It's much easier at night when with friends and
    bright lights
Than much later alone in your room.

Would you say they'd miss one in a million
When you finish this old human race?

Does it really make much of a difference
When your friends have forgotten your face?

Well how much do you think you are worth, boy?
Will anyone stand up and say?
Would you say that a man is worth nothing
Until someone is willing to pay?

If you heard that your life had been valued,
That a price had been paid on the nail,
Would you ask what was traded,
How much and who paid it
Who was he and what was his name?

If you heard that his name was called Jesus
Would you say that the price was too dear?
Held to the cross, not by nails but by love,
It was you broke his heart, not the spear.
Would you say you are worth what it cost him?
You say no – but the price stays the same.

If it don't make you cry –
Laugh it off – pass him by,
But just remember the day when you throw it away
That he paid what he thought you were worth.

How much do you think you are worth, boy?
Will anyone stand up and say?
Tell me what you are willing to give him
In return for the price that he paid?

'I don't care what you've been told,' said Terry Tully, the visiting speaker, 'you're not worthless.' There was already an air of concentration in the chapel, because the inmates appreciated Terry's ministry. A builder by trade, he had suffered greatly in his personal life, not least by the premature and unexpected death of his son. His immense sorrow over this tragedy was kept in balance by his very real and personal faith.

'If Jesus can't help me through this, then what's it all about?' he said to David and me.

He certainly had the gift of communicating his message to the prisoners, and they knew that his comments were genuine and powerful. Terry went on, 'When I was at school I was hopeless. I couldn't add up and my writing was bad. I was told I was rubbish and I'd never make anything of myself.' He looked round at the assembled men. 'I guess some of you know that feeling. But let me tell you – one day I met someone who told me about Jesus and that God loved me, and my life changed. You're not worthless. Don't let anyone ever say that to you again. God made you and he thinks you're valuable, whatever anyone else may say!'

The men were thinking. You could see from their faces that many were identifying themselves with this man's testimony.

'You're rubbish, no good, worthless', would all have been words used about them, and many would have heard such abuse so often as to be unable to consider themselves in any other way. Low esteem, in spite of displays of amazing bravado, was the norm. Most people outside have suffered from varying degrees of lack of confidence, in spite of having no real grounds for it, but some of the prisoners have experienced year upon year of abuse, failure and rejection. Being of value or worth to themselves or anybody else is quite often a meaningless concept, and certainly feelings of inadequacy are emphasized by being caught up in the judicial system.

When accused defendants stand before the magistrate or judge and jury at the culmination of weeks or months of preparation, they know they will hear the verdict of society upon their lives. In others' hands lie the decisions that will affect their futures. Their autonomy is gone and they can only hope for fate or clemency to deal them an acceptable hand. They tend to know all about court procedure, even if they have not attended one before, because many other men have and information is easy to get. Everyone's life is open and discussed, because for men who have to live, eat, sleep and even attend to basic bodily functions in public, there is little reason to hide the common experiences of a trial.

Consequently the men all know about the strengths and weaknesses of various judges, courtrooms and briefs, and what has happened to every other inmate whose time comes up for the reckoning. Tuning in to local radio is an essential skill, or someone's crime may be secret and their fate unknown. Knowing about everyone else is an almost universal interest, and is naturally immensely satisfying – until of course your turn comes up. Then all the feelings of inadequacy, rejection and uncertainty rear their ugly heads for your own case, and the perception tends to make a 'subtle' change. Now the spotlight of interest fixes on you, and it makes for very uncomfortable emotions of both vulnerability and loneliness.

I can remember a period of my life when I was very vulnerable and feeling alone. I had moved to college – Gypsy Hill College, Kingston – for teacher training. Unlike the apparent mass of students who were thrilled with the freedom of it all, the communal independence was not for me. I was after the qualification and wanted above all to teach, and this endless round of coffee cups, lectures and preparation was personally unsatisfying. I was also removed from my cosy world of church social life and support, and my lack of independence probably shocked me most of all.

Several things kept me going. The first was Mondays, as they were main subject study days. I was very fortunate to be taking Biblical Studies as my main subject – a course only available at Gypsy Hill, which consequently drew many evangelical Christians to study there. I was incredibly influenced by Peter Cousins, Old Testament lecturer and later an editor of Paternoster Press, who opened my eyes to the Old Testament and thrilled me week by week by being simply the most stimulating lecturer I have ever heard. He had an amazing ability to take a sometimes narrow evangelical viewpoint, reveal its flaws in terms of intellectual criticism, and then give really satisfactory answers to questions that many of us had refused to face. Thus serious open-minded Bible criticism became an enlightenment, not a faith-destroying activity.

I shall never forget him for illuminating the Old Testament in that way.

Anne Long was our New Testament lecturer, and she was responsible for the second positive experience at college. (Later she went on to Nottingham and then to be involved in the Acorn Healing Trust.) Anne instigated a dance drama group called Charis, about which she later wrote a book called *Praise Him in the Dance,* and in this group we interpreted the miracles and parables of Jesus' life through the medium of dance drama. Although this experience was in its infancy in terms of being shared by the Church, the members of the group grew immensely in their understanding of the power of the gospel stories, and I shall also never forget the influence of that group on my life.

The third major sustaining factor at college was far more mundane – it was the possession of a cassette recorder. As I write now it is a cause of real amusement that owning such an item could have held such significance, but it certainly did. I had never previously possessed anything like it and I was fascinated by it. My cousin owned one and I can remember being really jealous, hardly imagining that one day I would have one myself. I managed to be frugal in the first term and bought the cassette player proudly one Saturday just before Christmas. I also purchased a simply hideous lime-green canvas bag in which to store and carry this fairly substantial item, and took it back to my tiny room in the digs.

I opened it all up with great care, and although I had no real tapes to play, I took my single blank

C60 and practised playing my guitar and singing into a mike propped up on a copy of Bright's *History of Israel*. What a thrill to play it back – I was truly delighted. However, I was to be more excited still as I began to acquire various tapes to play on my own in my room. One holiday I discovered Graham Kendrick's 'Paid On The Nail' recording, and simply wore it out as I listened again and again to this talented man, who in the 1970s was plainly light years ahead of other contemporary Christian artistes.

Various tracks on this and other tapes were to be hugely important to my Christian life, not least of which was 'In Your Way And In Your Time', basically a prayer of submission to God, that his ways and times are certainly not usually what we expect but nevertheless always the best. I never forgot that song, and sang it with a friend at various weddings and Christian events all down the years, always finding that it would touch each listener with its deceptively simple words and flowing melody. However, it was another track that I was to recall more than twenty years later, when one morning we visited an Icthus church in London and spoke to Graham Kendrick himself about his forthcoming first visit to Lewes.

'Please sing that song, Graham,' I requested quietly, 'the one called "Paid On The Nail". It is so relevant to our men.'

So it was that Graham began to use that song in our services, to extraordinary effect.

'It's as if it were written for prisons like this,' I joked with Graham one morning.

'Yes,' he replied with a broad smile, 'it is, isn't it?'

The song was so powerful in the prison context because it utilized this very concept of worthlessness. Yes, I had felt inadequate and without real value in that college setting, but compared to our inmates I know nothing of feeling unappreciated. Nobody ever shouted at me that I am rubbish, and I have never been totally bereft and overwhelmed by a feeling that no one, literally no one, cared about me. Plenty of prisoners, and come to that probably other members of society, have heard such abuse and felt such utter rejection. To men such as these the words of Graham's song rang a great many bells indeed.

How much do you think you are worth, boy ...
Would you say that a man is worth nothing
Until someone is willing to pay?

Whenever Graham sang all eyes were fixed, all ears trained on the words.

'Held to the cross, not by nails but by love', continued the song – beginning to offer the hope that someone did indeed care for each individual in that chapel.

Then the song moves to its climax. If Jesus loved me so much as to die to pay the price for me, then what is my response?

If it don't make you cry –
Laugh it off, pass him by –
But just remember the day when you throw it
    away
That he paid what he thought you were worth.

The music rose with each line of this challenge, and as it quietened down again everyone was trying to grasp the meaning that Jesus paid what he thought we were all worth when he died – and he deserves a response for so doing. Graham had used this powerful song in the chapel several times before we took him to the vulnerable prisoners of 'K' wing. 'K' wing reminds you of scenes from films where prisoners are interrogated by evil guards and acts of appalling brutality are carried out. Of course the treatment of prisoners is more than fair in Lewes, and life bears no resemblance at all to the films. Nevertheless it must be the low ceilings, lack of real daylight, and sense of being underground that cause the comparisons in my mind, and whenever I step up and out into the daylight of the prison courtyard I can only feel a huge sense of relief that freedom is a reality for the majority of us.

A small group of inmates gathered on chairs, not knowing what to expect, looked up at this stranger. There was nowhere to plug in the guitar, no mike, no music stand and certainly no plans. Graham began to play various songs and received sincere applause after each one. One man in the front row sat seriously consuming his packet of Doritos one by one, before finally screwing up the packet loudly and stuffing it into his pocket. Several got up and left and then returned later. Two radios were playing in the background, and a group of men were a bit grumpy because the pool table was out of use during this impromptu event, and it was their association time being used up. At the end of the wing, two officers stood in the office or 'bubble' looking down at the scene, and behind them the air conditioning unit buzzed regularly, as men trooped in and out of the toilet and wash unit.

Halfway through an alarm bell went off in the wing above, and all the red alert lights down the wing began to flash on and off, much like the blue lights on top of speeding police cars.

The majority of Graham's audience, however, ignored all these seemingly disconcerting events, and listened attentively to this man who had bothered to come and play to them. Obviously it must have been unusual for Graham to say the least, but it didn't show in his ministry. He began to play 'How much do you think you are worth, boy?', and it became obvious that the acoustics were on his side. Everyone was concentrating, moved and inspired, not least David and I, and it was also evident that the singer was totally absorbed and filled with the Spirit of God.

Afterwards this generally rejected group of men shook hands with Graham one by one and thanked him sincerely for his appearance.

'You could take this up professionally, you know?' suggested one inmate helpfully. 'Right,' replied Graham with a smile.

All the ministry at Lewes is working towards the aim of telling inmates that they do have a real value and are in truth worth a great deal in the eyes of God. All the evidence of their lives might work against it, but the gospel message of a new purpose is true. We want as many men as possible to face their earthly judgements in court upheld with the certain knowledge that Jesus is with them. If they know about all the traumas and vulnerability of standing in court, either from past experiences or from other inmates, we wish them also to know that they have a real person in Jesus to stand beside them too.

The idea that Jesus is their advocate and friend is an easy concept to grasp. They all have briefs and people who plead for them in court, but they all also know the inadequacies of the system. They need and want someone to answer up for them, and the concept that Jesus might just be the one has strong appeal. What is harder to grasp is the knowledge that this special person, Jesus, actually took their place when it came to facing up to God's judgement. After all, who'd take the rap for anyone else unless forced to?

David told them one morning about Barabbas.

'Now there was an evil man,' he explained. 'He was due to be executed for his crimes and he was banged up, probably in the segregation unit, with no hope of reprieve. Suddenly two screws burst in the door, "Barabbas," they cried, "on your feet!" '

Everyone in chapel that Sunday sat forward. They were all interested.

' "What now?" thought Barabbas,' David continued. ' "Am I being shipped out, even ghosted?" ' (This term refers to moving prisoners without prior warning to either inmates or relatives, and represents a generally disliked practice.)

The congregation of inmates smiled and nudged each other as the story moved on.

' "No," Barabbas was told, "you're free. Get out now." The prisoner looked bewildered, "What do you mean?" he asked.

' "This Jesus, Jesus of Nazareth, will be taking your place. He has done nothing wrong – but he's going to die. I shouldn't ask questions, just go." So Barabbas left, probably thinking Jesus was crackers, but free all the same. Jesus took Barabbas' place, but he did more than that,' David explained, as everyone tried to take it all in. 'He took the place of everyone – me and you and he will give you a fresh start if you want one this morning. You'll be free like Barabbas – not to go on with your old ways, but rather to find new ways of life – this time with Jesus at your side.' David went on to ask if there was anyone who would like to come to him afterwards and find Jesus for himself. That morning five people responded in faith, because of course Barabbas' story is a very powerful one and God certainly used it on that and many other occasions.

In chapel that morning was Kenny Jones, a really committed Christian whose faith story was told in *The Cross Between Thieves*. After Lewes he had gone to another prison and then on to release. Unfortunately he had been involved in an incident concerning various dubious items and was back in on remand. Although this incident was a far cry from his previous convictions for appalling violence in his pre-Christian days, and he assured us he was not really guilty anyway, he knew he should not be inside at all.

'Sorry, David,' he offered, the first time he saw David on the wing. 'I have kept my faith, you know. It is hard, but I have. My wife's gone and I have custody of one son. It's been tough but God will sort me out I know. I'm going on with Jesus.'

Whatever the ins and outs of his reappearance at Lewes, there was no doubt that this slight, wiry, previously highly dangerous man, with his gappy grin, was 'going on'. Within one week his cell mate Danny came to faith and was off his heroin habit. Within two weeks he was leading a whole group of inmates up to chapel, virtually in a line, to 'come and hear David'; and within three weeks he had organized a Bible study of twelve men, nicknamed the dirty dozen, so that Roy would come and teach them all about the Bible.

'You have to give it to people straight,' he explained to David. 'No mucking about. They'd better come up and find out what God's about if they don't know. So I'll bring them.'

In chapel there was Kenny in the front singing 'Majesty' as loud as ever, and raising his fist in a salute every time Jesus' name was mentioned. One visitor remarked it was strange we were all so pleased to see him again, but we just couldn't help it. He was such an inspiration.

This time the Reverend Stephen Nunn picked him up and welcomed him into his parish in Hastings, and helped him thoroughly through his bail period. Kenny was to join Howard and lots of other ex-inmates in that church, which was a shining example of Christianity in action, prepared to take those whom so many others would not. Indeed Howard became a member of the Parish Council Committee, voted in against opposition from another candidate. We were sure he would have very valuable insights to offer that no one else would be able to share in quite the same way!

Kenny's story, however, brings us to a very important point. Instant middle-class conformity and value systems are far from the grasp of lots of prisoners. If we set targets which exceed the bounds of reasonableness, they will fail miserably, and possibly give up. We do see inmates again as they battle against years of habit and overwhelming temptations, but it doesn't mean they are no longer in the faith. I'm not tempted to steal, so I can't really pride myself in not doing so. I am tempted, however, to be very impatient, and will often fall to that 'crime'. Do I then castigate myself and believe my faith is no longer valid? Of course not. I perceive it as a falling down, a slip up, a regrettable occurrence. Many of my failings will never be known to others, and I won't face public recrimination for them either, but in God's eyes they are just as bad, as Jesus made clear when he said hate was of the same nature as murder and lust a degree of adultery in God's sight.

Similarly, although we want our new Christians to grow and expand in their faith, we have to be realists, not only about their lifestyles but also about their ability to fit into the average church grouping. Time after time we meet ex-inmates who have become Christians in prison and who are now out and about. Always they greet us, always they shake our hands, and thank David for his prayers, and always they have the light of God's love in their eyes.

Those who work in prisons know that generally the eyes of inmates are sad or bad or downcast at least. The change in the eyes of those who meet with God is quite remarkable. A sparkle, a glimmer, call it what you will, is present, often right from those first precious moments of new life. This light in the eyes continues and is in evidence whenever we met ex-inmates.

Maybe we notice it in them especially because of the dullness or lifelessness that held sway there once before, but whatever the cause, you just can't miss the power of that witness.

In C.S. Lewis' mighty children's story *The Lion, The Witch and The Wardrobe*, the children ask the professor how they will know if other people have been to Narnia – the magic land that represents the essence of Christian experience to so many readers. The answer is that there will be something about the eyes of someone who has been there and experienced meeting Aslan the Lion – the Jesus figure from the book.

For us this has been the case too, and as we've bumped into those often young men while going about our business, they have that certain something about their eyes. Often they have not linked up with a church, although some have, and we want to encourage them to do so. But we have had to learn to let them go, as Jesus obviously did in the gospel stories, not knowing where they were ending up but trusting their lives to the Father God who drew them to himself in the first place.

Now some Christians may be dismayed by this, finding it inconceivable that anyone could go on with God without being a fully-paid-up card-carrying member of a local Christian group. But we all need to broaden this view, offering help and encouragment to all who are open to faith if we wish to reach some of the outer edges of society with the Gospel. You cannot apply the same rules to a highly educated, middle-class, articulate and socially acceptable convert as you can to the average prison inmate. Their interests are poles apart, their skills and abilities totally diverse, and their needs as different as chalk and cheese. The challenge for all of us is to find ways of opening our churches to such people without forcing them into our preset mould. We must focus on the true elements of spirituality and help them to grow in those, rather than demand that they interest themselves in certain limited activities. Of course some churches are brilliant at welcoming, supporting and nurturing converted prisoners, but while they are few and far between, we can hardly be surprised if substantial numbers of inmates cannot take the pressure of some fellowships and have to plough a rather lonely furrow. Obviously this is not a desirable state of affairs, but it is still a reality for many. The surprising and indeed joyful thing for us is to see men still glowing and trying to put things right in their lives, in spite of little or no support, and the crucial thing is to pray for a greater understanding and willingness to help on the part of church groups everywhere.

Sitting at the back, way behind Kenny during the service on Barabbas, was Paul. He knew all about feeling worthless because he had experienced weeks and weeks of regret and remorse when he first came into the prison. One day he had completely lost his temper at a gathering and attacked a man with whom he had disagreed. Grabbing the first thing that came to hand, a large and substantial saucepan, he had used it to settle his grievance in an uncharacteristic but very violent manner. His poor victim suffered real damage to his head and was hospitalized immediately. A full recovery was unlikely and Paul found himself under arrest for grievous bodily harm. David met him early on entry and offered him God's amazing offer of forgiveness and a new start, but Paul would have none of it.

'I'm not worthy,' he wailed, leaning over his knees and obviously grief stricken. 'I can't forget it. I don't know why I did this. No one can ever forgive me.'

Later in court Paul displayed considerable grief in front of the judge, confessing his crime openly and with shame. He was placed in the hospital wing because he was suffering from debilitating stress, and eventually, but very slowly, he began to accept the love of God, even for him, by regularly coming to chapel. One day he took up God's offer of new life and became a Christian, and the effect was almost instant. Still smitten by his deed, he now knew he was forgiven, and his shining eyes were seen every week in the chapel, as he joined in the service fully and with joy. God had eventually spoken to Paul's heart and convinced him that he was not worthless after all. We doubt he will be in trouble again, although of course he will have to live with the effects of his crime for the rest of his life.

Jake was another inmate in that chapel scene who was struggling with the concept of worthiness.

A young offender, he met David on the wing and had a chat with him in his cell.

'I'm not up to much,' he said, 'I can't even get my life right either.'

'Why's that?' questioned David.

'My mother is a witch,' declared Jake, a very straightforward and unimaginative lad, 'she's put a curse on me and I'm not sure why.'

'She might have done just that,' assured David, 'but God can remove it, I promise you.'

Jake indicated both surprise and interest. 'Really?' he asked.

'Yes,' replied David calmly.

Bowed in prayer, Jake became a Christian, and David denounced the curse placed upon him. It was all quite calm and meaningful, and afterwards Jake looked very relieved. The next day Jake told his mother on the phone that he was now a Christian, and she was not a happy woman. There followed a stream of abuse; calls to David's office and threats of revenge were to follow. Jake, however, went on in faith, and became a strong Christian on the wing. His feelings of worthlessness were dissipated, and he had found a new sense of value in his relationship with God.

As we work with the men we realize there are no real barriers to being welcomed into God's family and finding worth there, apart from those to which people wished to cling. Everyone's need is different and results from any one of a huge number of causes, but Jesus, the only real friend and advocate of all, is able to give new purpose and relief to all who seek Him.

This is true, of course, in every walk of life, not only in prison, but is probably more obvious there, because of all the sad and difficult backgrounds. Just as he did on earth, Jesus is giving value to these rejected members of society and is declaring them worthy. Many find that their new friend is with them when they go for their cases to be heard, and face the consequences of their actions, and many too will have the further and much greater thrill of seeing Jesus by their side when the time comes for them to face that final and ultimate judgement at the end of their lives. Every reader of this book needs to be sure that they find their value in terms of their relationship with Jesus too, because it is the only value or worth that will count in the end. It is easier for those of us outside prison to perceive our worth in terms of our job, power, education, money or human relationships. Valuable and attractive as all these things are, they will count for little when God assesses the state of our life's work and experience. He will wish to know how we stood in relationship to his Son and we will stand or fall by that alone.

Yet it would seem that it is the prisoners who have a truer picture of their position before God, and realize their need of a saviour more readily than others. This could seem an unacceptable message for many, who will feel grossly superior to people who are banged up in a prison. Nevertheless the gospel message is that everyone has fallen short of God's glory and needs the forgiveness and acceptance of Jesus to be able to reach God. The question, 'How much do you think you are worth?' is one for us all to answer honestly, and is a clear reason for us all to make sure we are in a sound relationship with God himself.

CHAPTER 9

✳

The Ultimate Court Appearance

All prisoners have one momentous advantage over those of us who have never been part of the penal system, namely that of experience. Inmates comprehend the emotions involved in passing through the hands of the judiciary, and the frustrations and consequences of failing to convince a jury of their innocence.

It is neither fashionable nor 'spiritually correct' today to talk about religion in terms of judgement. One could be justified in believing that the wheel of Christian understanding has turned a full 180 degrees from its position in other ages, and now concerns itself only with aspects of God's nature that refer to his all-embracing love and forgiveness. Any sense of being called to account for one's deeds is seldom, if ever, the subject of serious consideration.

The truth would appear to be that the theology of God's universality of embracing love is interpreted to require any concept of guilt to be quashed as unaffirming or exclusive, and any perception of duty to the lost to be regarded as at best slightly misguided and at worst positively embarrassing. One can imagine that a glance at the Bibles of some Christians would reveal scores of passages removed or crossed out, especially in relation to some of Jesus' own sayings regarding facing God and the final judgement.

Inmates in our prisons seldom develop such sensitivities to the idea of being answerable for their deeds. The vast majority of them do not complain about the legitimacy of the court trying them, as their attention usually centres on either pleading their innocence or on emphasizing mitigating circumstances. They know that their chances are spent and that they can no longer run away. Facing the music, or rather the judge, is all that is left, and the feelings are not comforting.

One Sunday the 'story' in the chapel was centring on God's call to each man to face up to himself.

'When you come to the real court after you die,' David was explaining simply and seriously, 'you will have to face God and the books he opens. In these books will be all the things you've ever done and all the things you haven't done. You will be judged by these things.' David looked around the room and could see he had everyone's attention, with every eye upon him. After a short pause he continued, 'You'll be on your own then. No brief will plead for you or explain your circumstances, and there will be no co-defendant there to either support you or take the blame. God knows all about you. You won't be able to hide at all. He won't let people get away with things.'

369

The mood was serious but not heavy, and everyone was following the argument with no difficulty.

'But there is another book called the book of life,
and if your name's in there, then you won't be
judged at all. It's Jesus' book – the one that holds all
the names of the people who've asked him to take
over their lives. Let's look at the Bible together!'

David told everyone to open their Bibles at
Revelation 20:11–15. As usual this took some time,
and various volunteers helped some inmates find
the appropriate page. Sensibly and with a great
deal of effort on behalf of some, the passage was
read aloud,

> Then I saw a great white throne and him who
> was seated on it. Earth and sky fled from his
> presence, and there was no place for them.
> And I saw the dead, great and small, standing
> before the throne, the books were opened.
> Another book was opened, which is the book
> of life. The dead were judged according to
> what they had done as recorded in the books.
> The sea gave up the dead that were in it, and
> death and Hades gave up the dead that were
> in them, and each person was judged accord-
> ing to what he had done. Then death and
> Hades were thrown into the lake of fire. The
> lake of fire is the second death. If anyone's
> name was not found written in the book of
> life, he was thrown into the lake of fire.

After the congregation had finished reading there
was a short pause and then David added, 'Jesus

was grassed up, you know. He died even though he'd done nothing wrong at all. The truth is he took the rap for you and me.' He pointed round the room ending with himself. 'Everyone who wants a new start this morning can have one because of what he did. If you'd like to go to heaven when you die and have a new life right now too – then you'll need your name to be in Jesus' book of life! Come and see me afterwards if you'd like that.'

The closing part of the service took place quietly, and afterwards men began lining up for tea and jaffa cakes as usual.

Dick, a young man from the back, remained still. David approached quietly and sat beside him. 'OK?' he questioned.

'I'd like my name in there,' said the pensive inmate, 'in that book of life you were talking about. Does it mean even me?'

'Oh yes,' replied David, 'it certainly does.'

Several others that morning found faith in the Good News that Jesus could help us to find God, but no response was more rewarding than that of Dick's.

He was not the only inmate to have responded to this passage, and although of course it is only used from time to time, there is no doubt that the Holy Spirit uses it to bring people to Jesus. One can almost see the brains of the inmates ticking over, and several reported just what they had been thinking: 'Fancy my experience being in this book. How did they know how I'd feel? These books of life sound just like I've seen in court. Those briefs seem to have all the answers about what I've done and

I guess God knows it all too – though I've never thought about it before. Judgement at the end – that sounds awful. I know what it'll be like. I really do. I'd better do something about it right now.'

Now some people seem to think that the only legitimate approach to Christianity is made by someone who has carefully weighed up the pros and cons, probably attended a course, and has made a decision in cold, emotion-free circum-stances, fully aware of all the implications for the rest of a lifetime. To them the sheer rationality of God's love must drive the decision, and any swift and therefore 'dubious' response to God should be the subject of the greatest suspicion.

In reality people respond to God for an infinite number of reasons, just as they did in the times of the Bible, and just as they have done ever since. Who, after all, can put their hand on their heart and say that their relationship with God started and indeed continue with only the purest and most cerebral of motives? Or perhaps go further and even question whether cerebral motives are the only ones that count anyway?

Some people gradually move into Christian things even from childhood. They never seem to struggle to find faith, but rather it all comes as a natural progression. Some meet God in periods of fear, either of life's situations or of death, and others face God when crises of various kinds raise their heads. Some seek out of inquisitiveness or a feeling of helplessness, and still more find God out of boredom or a sense of pointlessness. The reasoned, rational approach to finding God must find its place amongst all these other responses, for it would seem that God uses the whole gamut of human experience and feeling to bring people to himself. If the result is real and lasting faith, then who are we to question the route through which another approaches Christianity? One thing is sure: that we meet representatives of all these groups in prison. In spite of their variance of approach and a propensity of those who come through a realization of a final calling to account, they all have one thing in common – the Holy Spirit himself calls them. For no man will respond to an argument or an appeal to take on faith, however effective they may be, unless God works in his life to show him the truth of the message.

When the followers were out and about in the first century, spreading – or as the original Greek says, 'gossiping' – the Gospel of Jesus, there were those who envied their power over demons and illness. Simon the sorcerer was one of these, and he approached the Christians in an attempt to acquire or buy the power. He saw the reality of the Good News of Jesus and the power of God, but failed to tap into the experience because he was coming via the wrong route. God's power and love are freely given but only to those who seek God in honesty and faith.

Jerry was down on the wing when there were a large group of Christians seeing remarkable answers to prayer.

'I want some of that,' he said to a Christian inmate, 'I want that power,' but of course it was not for the inmates to grant access to the power of God in that way, and the man attracted only by the results of faith was not able to respond to the need to find faith in his own heart.

So those who felt that the team were in some way frightening inmates into the Gospel were missing the point. Firstly, no one came to faith whom God had not touched, and secondly, telling people the truth about their own status before God can hardly be called putting unnecessary fear into people if it's true. No, God was using the inmates' present condition and circumstances to bring them to himself, and those of us who've met the resulting Christians are in no doubt that their response is totally valid.

The problem for many of us outside is, however, that we find it hard to come to terms with final judgement. If we really believe in it surely our sense of urgency for spreading the Gospel will be immense. Somehow we manage to live Christian lives, often steeped in Bible verses or having participated in hour after hour of Christian worship sessions, without grasping the reality of the inevitability of judgement. While on earth we may escape many of the experiences described in this book. We may manage to live by law-abiding principles, either out of fear or of genuine belief in their value, and thereby steer clear of the police, prison and the whole court experience. We may even fail to feel the slightest empathy with those who do undergo the rigours of the law, feeling that they receive only that which they richly deserve.

Nevertheless, one day we will all surely be in their shoes, see the view from where they stand,

and share with them the ignominy of being found out and being called to account for our deeds. At the end of time we will all face the ultimate court experience and the judge will be God himself. Now of course this is picture language, but perhaps the images we acquire from the worldly courtroom are helpful in giving us a 'feel' for the event and a glimpse of the seriousness of the issue. The Bible plainly teaches us that everyone has both done wrong things and failed to do good things. Although we are all often able to escape the results of our sins in this life, this will not always be so.

God has given us life and the world in which to live, and he expects us to live a moral and good life in response. Everyone fails to do so, and the result is that we are cut off from God's love, and will find there is a barrier between him and us when we come to face him at the end of our lives. Everything will then be known, there will be no secrets and no place to hide. We will all have to hear God's verdict on our lives, and unfortunately for every man and woman the result will be the same: 'Guilty' will ring in our ears. There will be no special pleading, no cries of 'He's worse than I am', or allowances for circumstances, because, in some way or other, we have all fallen short of the ideal.

There is of course one huge relief in this horrific scenario, and that is that for some the judgement will not be a fear. Those who have chosen to accept Jesus into their lives and serve him on this earth, instead of themselves, will find that all their guilt and responsibility has been placed on him – the only sinless man the world has ever known. He takes the rap – our place in the dock and our separation from God – and we go free into a new life with him. Amazing? – yes. Too simple? – no – just God's plan to bring us back to himself. No wonder the first Christians called it the Gospel or Good News of Jesus!

So perhaps we can find a tiny patch of room to envy these inmates in our prisons because they understand the seriousness of their condition. The final court may not be such a surprise to them, only to us, who believe in our own good standing. We suffer from an illusion of superiority at our peril, only a true comprehension of our state before God will help us to see what we must do.

Lee knew what he'd done was wrong, and at the end of a service had a fair idea of where he stood before God. A slight, short figure, he looked very young indeed to be inside, although the truth was that he had murdered someone during a fight, and was so high on drugs and alcohol that he had no recall of the events that led him to face such a serious crime.

As the final prayer finished he literally ran to the front and knelt down by the platform. His short blond hair was all that you could see from the back, but he looked up at David with large doleful eyes and pleaded, 'Can God forgive me?' Later he went to the hospital wing and informed the volunteer that, 'My Mummy knows I'm here.'

Lee's life was a total mess by anyone's standards, but he found God that morning, because no problem is too great for the one who made us all. It is a matter of attitude of heart and a willingness to start again that counts.

In contrast to Lee's slight frame, Des was a heavy-set, big bloke who had short hair and tanned skin. He was imprisoned for GBH because he had thrown someone in front of a passing car during a fight. Although on drugs like Lee, he was luckier, because the man he assaulted had not been killed.

Des had asked to see David, but the officers were on their toes that morning and were being protective.

'Not in there, David,' said one officer firmly, 'he's dangerous, that bloke.'

'Well, he has asked to see me,' replied David, anxious to find out what Des needed.

'Well, we'll come with you,' said the officer, obviously concerned for David's safety. 'All three of us,' he continued, beckoning to two fellow officers in the 'bubble' on the wing.

So the four men approached Des' cell, and David spoke through the hatch. 'Des, do you want to see a chaplain?'

The man inside leapt to his feet. 'Yes please,' he replied.

The officer opened the door and the three colleagues watched as David stood in the entrance – these situations were always tricky, and anything involving the safety of the chaplain was important. What happened next was a huge surprise and rather uncommon. The large inmate immediately threw himself at the chaplain's feet, and vast hands gripped David's ankles firmly. Uncontrollable sobbing rose from this obviously penitent man as he cried, 'Can God help me?'

Before responding to this needy inmate, David turned to the somewhat astonished officers and said, 'I think I'll be all right with this one after all, but thanks all the same.'

The officers realized that they could leave, and with a few raised eyebrows left David to it.

Oblivious to the officers' entrance or exit, Des continued to grasp David's ankles in sheer desperation, and although the story has its amusing side it is clear that Des understood his need of God in a way that many others never do. He found faith that day in that cell, and went on to be a real disciple. His problems did not fall away, but he had a new start and a brand new companion in Jesus. His pride certainly hadn't kept him from finding a faith that's sure.

By contrast, Mark had thought about Christian commitment for years and years. A young, bright man, he was posted on the segregation unit nevertheless, because he had had some bother on the wing. His fairly cheerful, if very spotty face confronted David one day and pronounced, 'I've thought about this for years. Lots of my friends and family are Christians and they've prayed for me for ages. Guess I'd like to join them now.'

The apparent ease of this transfer from one side of the fence of belief to the other belies the effect of prayer for him offered by the wealth of Christian contacts he was so privileged to enjoy. Nevertheless his step of faith was real; he had made the move himself, and the jolt of prison could well have been the deciding factor. Quite a contrast to Lee and Des but with the same result – a new Christian beginning his own individual path of faith.

A further example illustrates the range of approach for those who seek to get right with God. During a service, as usual David and the rest of the volunteers prayed for wisdom to know just who needed help that day. Having prayed with two other men, David glimpsed Paul going out of the door back to his cell. The chaplain sprinted the few yards down the chapel, grabbed Paul's arm, and asked, 'You want to accept Jesus this morning, don't you?'

Paul stopped abruptly, and the officer in charge helpfully waved him back into the chapel. Tall and good looking, Paul was dressed all in black, so David knew this was a man on remand as he was not wearing prison clothes. Paul sat for a while with David and, like so many before, gave his life back to God in simple prayer.

Afterwards he looked gratefully at David and said, 'Thank you for finding me out this morning. I really wanted to come forward but I didn't quite make it.'

'That's OK,' replied David, 'you made it in the end, that's all that counts.'

Indeed that is what counts and it illustrates once more how many need to be asked personally to respond to God, because in spite of a real desire to find him, they lack that confidence to ask for help. It is for us, the Christians, to offer that assistance, and if we fail, who knows how many miss a real chance of new life?

David began to end the talks he gives to outside churches with a vivid picture of the end of our lives, because we have grown to be immensely concerned that an urgency for the Gospel be rekindled.

Although it is true that the actual judgement concerning life or death will pass Christians by, because the decisions they make on earth give them the right relationship with God to enter heaven, nevertheless they will be called to account for the stewardship of their time and talents.

'Just imagine,' David would say, 'you go to meet Jesus and he asks, "What have you done with your life?" You will reply, "I attended the church in Wentby for sixty years. I ran the youth group, sat on committees and was their best worship leader ever."

'"Good," Jesus will reply, "I know this; did you learn anything on the way?"

'"Oh yes – I read my Bible daily and studied notes and commentaries all the time. I toyed with New Testament Greek and led many a Bible study."

'"All this is good," Jesus will reply. "So you knew all about me for sixty years?" You will nod your head in muted pride of course, but perhaps then he will ask pointedly, "Did you bring anyone with you?"'

At this point in most meetings there is a deep silence, as everyone begins to take in this questioning of their own response to the commission of Jesus to tell people about him. It will, of course, be a very sad day if at the end of our lives we have failed to bring anyone with us. The spread of Christianity was surely the result of a huge chain reaction, as each new convert passed on the Good News. In the first century the Gospel spread as people moved about the then known world. They took huge risks to bring the Gospel to foreign shores, and eventually even to our own. The life of the Church depends on us all taking up our part in the telling of others, and yet somehow we can escape this task by reassuring ourselves that we are not all evangelists.

Of course we don't all have the same gifts, and there will always be those who excel in this area, but it is for all of us to be witnesses to the Gospel of Jesus. If we leave it all to the few, the Church will fail in its mission. Direct evangelism may be out of vogue, and it is easy to join the bandwagon of laid-back friendship-style programmes, but quite often Christians can be so laid-back about evangelism that they appear almost horizontal in their approach. Naturally our friends should be attracted to God through our lives and faith, but does that really mean that only those with the benefit of a Christian friend can hope to hear God's message of hope to the world? I trust not; indeed, if we truly want to take seriously Jesus' command to spread the Good News to others we will have radically to reappraise our own attitudes to the society in which we live. If we really still believe that everyone will have to face God's judgement one day, then we are at best irresponsible and at worst highly negligent if we fail to tell them now.

The truth does seem to be, however, that we are just a little embarrassed about the concept of final judgement, and would perhaps prefer it to be a little less severe than the Bible writers warn us it will be. However, before we eliminate ideas of judgement from our Christian vocabulary, on the grounds that a loving God will let everyone off in the end, let us check the basis for our decision, because it is doubtful that either Scripture or Christian tradition will provide such evidence. In terms of history, it is only recently that Christians have fought shy of declaring God's judgement on the world and on the individual. Could this be because we now lack the drive of the persecution of ages past, or because we just have an overwhelming desire to be both liked and perceived as very reasonable and rational? Whatever the grounds for our reluctance to accept a concept of judgement, I would challenge the position as wishful thinking. I believe the reality is that we will indeed face judgement at the end of our lives, and that this truth should drive us to spread the news of Jesus to everyone we can.

I also believe we should all be motivated to hear God's 'Well done' in preference to a truly awful awareness that we personally brought no one with us.

One of our chaplaincy team was Stan, a faithful but now retired Salvation Army Officer, who was an immense support to the ministry at Lewes. He had spent a life's work passing on the Good News of Jesus whilst also helping people in many practical ways. Taken to writing poetry, he shared the following poem with us one day, and we feel it to be highly significant to our own ministry, and an inspiration to others to find places where they too can share the good news.

PRISON VISITING

Thoughts on Matthew 25:36, 39, 40

'I needed clothes and you clothed me, I was
sick and you looked after me, I was in prison
and you came to visit me.' 'When did we see
you sick or in prison and go to visit you?' The
King will reply, 'I tell you the truth, whatever
you did for one of the least of these brothers of
mine, you did it for me.'

'I was inside and you visited me.'
Visited you, Lord, how can that be?

I visited lonely and broken men
And sought to renew them in hope again;
I went to the call of a youngish bloke,
And sat and talked while he had a smoke;
I spoke to a man just divorced by his wife
Because he is serving a sentence for 'life';
I entered a cell that was dark and grim
To a man who was reaping the wages of sin;
I went to a cell full of hatred and tension,
And your precious name, I hardly dared
   mention.

And yet, Lord, you say I was visiting you.
I find it quite hard to believe that is true.

'Inasmuch as you did it unto the least –
Of these labelled "scum" and "vicious beast" –

Yes, even these here, the worst of men
I am pleased to call my brethren;
It was even for these that I bore sin's pain
To bring them right back to my Father again;
And though it is hidden and hard to see,
In each one of these there is something of me;
So bring them my love and help them to see
That I died to make them totally free;
I rose that they too my life might share,
And eternal reward begin even in here.'

Dear Lord, in my visiting this is my prayer
That with every man this Good News I might
   share;
That though he may feel he is loved by no other,
Jesus is pleased to call him 'My BROTHER';
And Lord, in each cell, this is my plea:
Each man may see something of Jesus in me!!

Stan Ozanne

This wonderful poem contains the essence of the
Good News about which we have been talking
throughout this book. Jesus died to set everyone
free whatever their past may have been, and to give
them an eternal life that begins here and now. God
himself yearns to relieve us all from hearing that
ultimate verdict of 'guilty' ringing in our ears. He
sent his Son to bear that verdict for us in ways that,
although beyond our comprehension, are totally
valid none the less. His love reaches out to us all
to give free consciences and a new start in life. If
you have never found that love and release yourself, then maybe today is the day of decision and

discovery. Be assured he will not reject you, but has indeed great plans for you in this life and a warm welcome once the time comes to meet him face to face. Hundreds of prisoners have joined the many thousands outside gaol in finding the gospel message to be as true today as it was two thousand years ago. Many of them have been driven by a crisis to see their need, but it is not necessary to have shared their experience of crime in order to find a new life.

At the end of this chapter there follows a simple prayer such as many, many people have prayed down the centuries when they have meant truly to seek God for the first time. The actual words are not important; rather, the desire of mind and heart indicate that something very special is taking place.

The paradox is made clear – those who lose their lives by surrendering to God, discover that they may actually find them in tremendously exciting service to him.

There are countless witnesses to vouch for the trustworthiness of God, and those who pray such a prayer discover themselves part of a vast body of believing people. Of course it takes honesty and real courage to change one's life – many other belief systems seem to make so little moral demand in comparison – but God has made the cross of Christ the point of decision for us all, and his final verdict on us will depend on the responses we have made to his precious Son. As for Jesus, he has clearly promised that those who confess to him in this life will find him by their side both now and in the next life too. It is on this basis that the Christian Gospel is proclaimed throughout the world, to the men and women of this country, and that includes the inmates of any prison.

I trust that the stories in this book have inspired you to see how God is working today in bringing people to him. I also hope it is an encouragement to play a full part in evangelism with renewed commitment and enthusiasm. There is a tendency to demand greater proof of a dramatic kind before we accept former criminals as Christians. Many church members, who may fail to exhibit such sustained and substantial evidence of their own growth in faith, may still require an inmate's conversion to transform him instantly if his first steps of faith are to be accepted. Those of us privileged to work with them, however, rejoice at their sometimes tentative moves towards God, are frequently amazed at the strength of their conversion, and are prepared to wait for God himself to issue his final verdict – on both them and us.

✳

Prayer of Response

Father God,

I realize that your final verdict on me would be that I have both done wrong things and left good things undone. I am truly sorry, and earnestly wish to change my ways. I ask Jesus to take over my life so that I can live a new life now, and live with you in heaven when I die.

Fill me with your Holy Spirit so that I may have the power to make changes in my understanding and behaviour.

Thank you for loving me in Jesus' name. Amen.

If you have prayed this prayer with sincerity and honesty, then God has accepted you whatever you may feel. Do tell a Christian friend or minister of your decision, for they will be able to help you further.

Every Blessing,
Gillian and David Powe

If you wish to respond to anything in this book, or wish to find out further information about supporting prison ministry, we can be contacted at the following address:

> Care of Rev'd D. Powe
> Chaplain
> HMP Belmarsh
> Western Way
> Thamesmead
> SE28 OEB

We want to hear from you. Please send
your comments about this book to us in care
of the address below. Thank you.

ZONDERVAN™

GRAND RAPIDS, MICHIGAN 49530 USA

WWW.ZONDERVAN.COM